06-05

GUIDE
TO A
HEALTHY
CAT

GUIDE TO A HEALTHY CAT

Elaine Wexler-Mitchell, D.V.M.

HOWELL
BOOK
HOUSE

Copyright © 2004 by Elaine Wexler-Mitchell. All rights reserved.
Howell Book House
Published by Wiley Publishing, Inc., Hoboken, New Jersey
Published simultaneously in Canada

For general information about our other products and services, please contact our Customer Care Department within the United States at (800) 762-2974, outside the United States at (317) 572-3993 or fax (317) 572-4002.

Wiley also publishes its books in a variety of electronic formats. Some content that appears in print may not be available in electronic books. For more information about Wiley products, visit our web site at www.wiley.com

Library of Congress Cataloging-in-Publication Data:
Wexler-Mitchell, Elaine.
  Guide to a healthy cat / Elaine Wexler-Mitchell.
      p. cm.
  ISBN 0-7645-4163-3 (alk. paper)
  1. Cats. 2. Cats—Health. I. Title.
  SF442.W455 2003
  636.8'083—dc21

                                                2002014825

Printed in the United States of America

10 9 8 7 6 5 4 3 2 1

All photos by Elaine Wexler-Mitchell

Contents

··

Preface

··

People often ask me why I became a feline-only veterinarian after I started out working on both dogs and cats. I loved working with cats, but had seen how they were often regarded as second-class citizens in comparison to dogs in the veterinary world. I considered my options and I decided to start my own clinic and go feline only so I could focus my time and energy on becoming the best doctor I could possibly be in the practice of feline medicine.

In this book I hope to share my knowledge of cats and their health care with you. Each cat has an individual personality and touches us uniquely. Anyone who has owned a cat knows about their special charm as well as their idiosyncrasies. Are these not the aspects that captivate us as cat owners?

I think that people who do not like cats have, unfortunately, missed out on the experience of these furry creatures. Every day that I spend with cats, I learn something new about how they view the world and I am fascinated by it. By understanding your cat and her health care needs, you will have the tools to enable you to be a fabulous cat owner—that is, if you actually believe you own your cat!

Chapter 1

What Is a Healthy Cat?

More than 73 million pet cats live in households in the United States. What is it about these creatures that has made them America's most popular pet in the last decade? Is it their grace and beauty? Or is it their ability to be somewhat independent and fit into our busy lifestyles? Regardless of the reasons, it is definitely cool to be a cat owner.

You have also decided to become a cat owner—or at least, you'd like to think it was your decision. In reality, it is often the cat who chooses you. Each cat has a unique personality and different behavior patterns, so I hope you will find the perfect fit for your household.

CHARACTERISTICS OF A HEALTHY CAT

Bright eyes, a shiny coat and an alert disposition are all characteristics of a healthy cat. Healthy cats have good appetites, groom themselves well and interact with their owners. There is no one best place to find a healthy cat, so in your search consider local shelters, breeders, neighbors, friends, coworkers and veterinary clinics and hospitals.

The most important factor in choosing a healthy cat is a good personality. You can tell a lot about personality even with kittens. To test a cat's personality, hold her in your arms and see if she is relaxed or tense.

Cradle her upside down in your arms, like a baby, and again, see how she reacts. If you are looking for an affectionate cat, and the one you are testing will not let you hold her for more than a second, you may want to reconsider your choice or plan to do some work on gaining the cat's trust and training her to relax.

Two to seven weeks of age is the period considered to be critical to a kitten's socialization. Kittens who are handled by many people and interact with other cats and animals during this time tend to adjust better socially as adults. Ask about a cat's early experiences when you are considering her for adoption.

The next test is to touch the animal's ears, gently open her mouth and touch her toes. Again, the more the cat is willing to let you handle her, the more likely she is to be trusting of you in general. If you put the cat down and walk away, is she interested in you? Does she follow you? I do think there is chemistry between certain cats and certain people. Is the cat alert, responsive and playful? Test this by throwing a small toy, or even make one from a ball of paper. All these little tests will give you some idea of what the cat's personality is like.

Even with a very healthy kitten, the health care costs for a kitten for the first year are generally higher than they are for an adult cat. Kittens have less well-developed immune systems than adult cats, so they are more susceptible to infections. They also require more routine health care during their first year of life than older cats do. This includes initial vaccines, viral and fecal testing and spaying or neutering.

THE LOWDOWN ON ESSENTIAL CARE

Now that you have your cat and have brought her into your home, you need to make sure you adequately provide for her essential needs. In the wild, cats adapt to their environment by hunting for food, seeking safety by climbing trees and finding shelter against the elements. Confined to our homes, cats need help to live harmoniously in our environment.

If you provide the basics of good food, water and shelter, you will be starting your cat off right. Monitoring the ways in which the cat uses these basic provisions will give you a good idea about the animal's health. Cats are creatures of habit, so any changes in their habits warrant investigation.

Privacy is very important to your cat. Even the most sociable cat needs some time alone. Cats typically like privacy when they groom and when they eliminate. Some cats like privacy when they eat, but others eat more readily when their owners are around.

Cats with more timid personalities should be allowed to hide for at least some part of the day. You can work to make your cat more social, but many felines are scaredy cats by nature and no amount of training will change this trait. People often tell me they think their scaredy cat was abused before they found her, but it is more likely the cat was born that way. Timid cats will learn to trust you and can become incredibly loving companions, but they are not likely to ever warm up to strangers.

Cats who have to acclimate to new cats, dogs or children in a household should be given time alone. It is not fair to expect the existing animal to be happy about and willing to accept newcomers. This is just not the nature of cats. Cats hate change. They prefer things to stay the way they are—the way *they* arranged them! It can take weeks to months for a new cat to accept her new surroundings, or at least to be less fearful.

When a new cat or kitten is brought into a household with children, everyone is excited and everyone wants to hold and play with the animal. Being the constant center of attention is not typically what a cat wants. Parents need to control the handling of the cat and be sure the animal is given an opportunity to rest by herself.

Even the biggest scaredy cat will learn to trust and love you, although she may never warm up to strangers.

Entering a new home is stressful to a cat, and not getting a chance to regroup and relax merely intensifies the stress. Stress has a negative impact on the animal's immune system, so be sure to give the cat a break and help keep her healthy. Make sure the cat has a hiding place where she can go to relax, and make it a rule in your house that when the cat is in her hiding place, she is to be left alone. If you cannot isolate a cat in a quiet room for a break, you might consider placing her back in her carrier for a while. The carrier can offer safety and solitude.

THE SCOOP ON LITTER BOXES

Proper placement of the litter box in your home is essential if you want the cat to use it. Ideally, the cat should feel comfortable, safe and undisturbed when she eliminates. Often, elimination problems arise when a cat is unhappy about the location of her box. Areas where you want the box and where the cat wants the box may not be the same. You will have to give in to your cat's preferences.

Bedrooms, secondary bathrooms and garages are good locations for litter boxes. Many owners want to put litter boxes in laundry rooms. This can work for some cats, but others may be frightened by the noises of the washer and dryer and may choose to eliminate elsewhere.

Starting off on the right track with a good litter box setup will make both you and your cat happy. Litter boxes are available in a variety of sizes and shapes. Your cat will probably be more concerned with the type of litter in the box than she will with the type of box you choose—but some cats can be very picky about the box, too.

There are two main types of litter boxes: open and hooded. Litter boxes are generally made of plastic. Almost all cats are satisfied with an open litter box, but each type has its pros and cons, as outlined in the table on page 5.

In this high-tech era, there are also electronic litter boxes. These are the most expensive types of litter boxes, but they offer convenience because they do not require daily maintenance.

One type, called Litter Maid, is an open box that contains an electronic sensor that detects the cat's presence, automatically rakes the litter after the cat has left the box and deposits the waste materials into a closed plastic receptacle. Owners must dispose of the full receptacles every few days. The box is filled with clumping litter, and both the box and rake need to be cleaned regularly.

OPEN LITTER BOX	
Pros	**Cons**
Easy for the cat to get in and out	Less odor control
Easier for you to scoop	More litter scatter
Takes up less space	Cats can eliminate over the sides
Some cats (especially large ones) feel cramped in a hooded box	Accessible to dogs and babies
	Some cats prefer more privacy

HOODED LITTER BOX	
Pros	**Cons**
More odor control	May be harder for cat to get in and out
Less litter scatter	Less convenient for you to scoop
Prevents access for dogs and babies	Requires more space
Helps contain urine and feces	Some cats (especially large ones) feel cramped
Some cats prefer more privacy	

Another type of electronic box that washes, dries and disinfects plastic litter has been invented. This type of cat toilet, which eliminates any routine maintenance by the owner, is likely to be the litter box of the future.

The height of the sides of the box can vary, and that's another thing you need to consider. Kittens and senior cats may have difficulty jumping into boxes with high sides. The same may be true for injured animals.

Be sure to get a litter box that is big enough to accommodate your cat. The cat should be able to turn around and easily scratch and cover up wastes in her box. You may need to buy a larger litter box as your cat grows.

A cat should have unrestricted access to her litter box. Putting it in a room where the door may be accidentally closed or in a garage without a pet door (or where it gets so cold that she is unlikely to go there) will create problems. The location of the box in the house will also encourage or discourage use. Of course you want to put the litter box in the area that is most convenient for you, but your cat's needs and wishes should be considered first.

A good general rule is to have at least the same number of litter boxes as you do cats in a household. This can pose problems in large, multicat homes. One reason for multiple boxes is to spread out smell and wastes so that they do not become too concentrated too quickly and deter a cat from using the box. Even if you have many boxes, not all cats will use all boxes. But it's still important to have them, because some cats simply will not go where other cats have gone.

Today kitty litter is available in numerous varieties. Some are environmentally friendly and some are easier to clean up. Litters are made from a number of different materials, including clay, pine shavings and pelleted newspaper. You need to determine which factors are important to you when choosing litter and then hope your cat feels the same way. Factors for you to consider are cost, presence of deodorizers, size of packaging, ease of scooping, ease of disposal, biodegradability and litter tracking outside of the box. The factors your cat will consider are size and softness of granules, scent (cats prefer no scent) and cleanliness. When given a choice, most cats prefer clumping litter. The benefits of clumping litter are that urine and feces can be easily removed from the box every day. The texture is similar to outdoor sand or dirt, which is what cats are naturally attracted to. If your cat has a urinary tract problem and you are trying to monitor the amount and the frequency of urination, clumps are easy to evaluate. There is no scientific evidence to prove that clumping litters specifically create any health problems in cats. However, clay, clumping and other litters that produce dust have been shown to increase irritation in the airways of cats affected by respiratory diseases.

Cats like to have a minimum of one inch of litter in their boxes, and most like even more. If the litter level drops and you are not ready to empty the box (for example, if you use clumping litter), simply add more litter.

Litter boxes should be scooped at least once a day. More often is even better. Depending on the type of litter used, the box should be completely emptied, cleaned and refilled every one to two weeks. We like using clean bathrooms, and so do our cats. Plastic liners are frequently used to help make box emptying and cleaning easier, but some cats do not like liners. Again, you'll have to follow your cat's preferences.

Empty boxes should be washed with soap and water or white vinegar and water. Products containing ammonia should not be used to clean litter boxes because urine contains ammonia and cleaning that way will simply intensify the odor.

KEEPING CATS INDOORS KEEPS THEM HEALTHIER

Housing cats exclusively indoors is the best way to keep them safe. The average expected life span of an indoor cat is 13 to 15 years, while outdoor cats may live only five to seven years. Unfortunately, cats are fascinated by the outdoors and some try to sneak out at any opportunity. Some cats like to just bathe outdoors in the sun; others like to hunt and visit neighbors. Once a cat has had a taste of living outdoors, it is harder to keep her inside, but it is possible if you are determined.

Giving cats inside window perches and plenty of interactive playtimes will help keep them stimulated and eliminate the need for them to go outside. If you want to let a cat out, but at the same time protect her, you can build an outdoor enclosure that is securely screened to keep her in and to keep danger out. You might also consider training her to walk on a leash or personally supervising her outdoors for short periods of time.

Dangers cats face when they venture outdoors include cars, wild animals, territorial cats, unfamiliar dogs, unkind neighbors, bad weather, fleas and ticks, more risk of exposure to toxins and disease and getting lost. Where I practice in Southern California, the most common cause of death to outdoor cats is coyote attacks. If you are prepared to

---

SAFE TRAVEL

Cats should always be transported inside a carrier when you travel anywhere with them. Although the cat may cry and scratch in the carrier, it is for her own good as well as yours. You may feel like you have good control of the cat when you are carrying her, but if she's startled, her claws digging into your arms may cause you to release her. There is also danger if you are driving in your car and the cat is not in a carrier. If you slam on the brakes and the cat goes flying, she could end up under your feet or be injured. She might also decide to walk in front of your face or under the brake pedal while you are driving.

take these risks with your cat, then let her go outside. If you are not, then protect your cat by keeping her inside.

If you allow your cat any access at all to the outdoors, it is important to get the cat on a routine where she comes inside from dusk to dawn to limit her exposure to the increased dangers of the night. It is also crucial to place some kind of identification on her such as a collar, tag, microchip, ear tag, tattoo or a combination of these. Nationwide, only 2 percent of the cats picked up by animal control agencies are ever reclaimed by their owners. Without identification these cats are considered strays. Unfortunately, most unclaimed cats face death. If you are concerned about the safety of a collar, breakaway styles are available and work well.

Chapter 2

Kitten Development

....

Kittens develop very quickly and are grown-up cats before you know it. The maturation that occurs during a kitten's first six months of life correlates to the first 15 years of a human's life. From birth to six months, a kitten changes from a newborn to a sexually mature animal. In the past, when I got a new kitten, all I wanted to do was stay home with him all the time. My husband thought I was crazy, but I told him the kitten would be all grown up within a few months and I didn't want to miss his kittenhood. I guess that's what people say about their own children growing up, so it is a natural feeling for all kinds of parents!

Kittens seem to work at two speeds: full power and full stop. They seem to have unending energy, and then they crash and sleep very soundly. Starting off with a new kitten is a lot of fun, but if you are a first-time cat owner, you may have questions about what normal behavior is. Knowing what to expect with regard to kitten development is helpful so you can work on training your kitten properly and be able to intervene if behaviors get out of hand. You have the best chance of molding your kitten into the perfect pet when he is young.

BIRTH TO 1 MONTH

During this period a kitten develops from being totally dependent on his mother for food, warmth and elimination, to being able to handle these things on his own. Newborn kittens can neither see nor hear, but they can smell, and they have touch receptors on their faces that enable them to home in on their mother's body heat.

If you find a newborn orphaned kitten, you will have to perform the duties that the mother cat would have performed. These duties include keeping him warm and safe, feeding him with proper cat milk replacer through a bottle and "pottying" the kitten. Kittens are unable to eliminate on their own until they are about four weeks old, and their mothers stimulate them to eliminate by licking their genitalia. You can replicate this action using a cotton ball or tissue soaked in warm water and gently wiping the kitten's genitalia.

Make sure you use a feline milk replacer, and not any other kind of milk. Although they love the taste of cow's milk, cats are fairly lactose intolerant. They lack the enzyme needed to properly digest the sugar found in cow's milk, so more than a taste or two will usually cause diarrhea.

The mouth is a very important organ for a kitten. A newborn kitten will start using his mouth within an hour of birth, when he starts nursing. Kittens nurse every few hours around the clock for the first couple of weeks of life.

Kittens' ears open around five days of age. They can orient to sounds at about 10 days, but they don't recognize sounds until they are three weeks old. Eyes open between 5 and 14 days after birth, but kittens cannot visually orient until their eyes have been open a few days.

Newborn kittens can feel with both their front and rear limbs. They can walk with uncoordinated motions at two weeks and can visually place their front legs and climb by three weeks.

Immunity is passed to newborns when they receive colostrum, their mother's first milk, during their first 24 hours of life. They are protected from most diseases during their first month if they ingest colostrum, continue to nurse normally and are kept warm and clean by their mothers.

These newborn kittens are only minutes old.

4 TO 6 WEEKS

Most kittens begin to eat some solid food at four weeks of age and can be fully weaned by six weeks. It is normal for kittens to eat dirt or kitty litter during the weaning process, but they learn quickly that these substances don't taste very good. Kittens have all of their baby teeth by six weeks of age. Kittens who go outdoors and are trained by their mothers can learn some rudimentary hunting behavior during this time.

This is a very important period in the socialization process. Kittens who are not exposed to humans and other animals (including other cats) at this stage can have a harder time adjusting to them later on in life. Coordinated social play behavior develops during this time.

The kittens' eyes change from blue to their permanent color, they regulate their own body temperature and start to control their urination and defecation during this time. Protection against disease is still mainly conferred through maternal immunity—the antibodies derived from their mothers.

These three little kittens are seven-week-old littermates.

6 TO 8 WEEKS

This is the earliest time for a kitten to be taken from his mother and littermates and introduced into a new home—although it's best wait until they are *at least* eight weeks old. A kitten of this age should be able to care for his own basic needs. In a new home, a kitten may be scared and lonely at first, but he should be able to adapt.

Maternal immunity wanes, and kittens need to begin their vaccination series to stimulate further protection against certain diseases. Natural exposure to viruses and bacteria causes disease, but it also stimulates antibody production and increases future immunity.

Kittens need the increased protein, vitamin and mineral content of specially formulated kitten foods to support their growth and development. They are able to consume both dry and canned kitten foods.

8 TO 16 WEEKS

During this period kittens adjust to their independence and become stronger and more curious. They grow rapidly and usually gain about one pound per month. They begin to jump, climb and scratch. Owners can make a big impact on their kitten's behavior by training him during this time.

Vaccinations and natural exposure continue to contribute to the kitten's immune system. If not vaccinated, kittens are very susceptible to viruses such as panleukopenia and feline leukemia if they are exposed to other cats who have these diseases. The need for a special kitten diet also continues, and the kitten will be eating more and more.

16 TO 28 WEEKS

From four to seven months of age a kitten loses his baby teeth and gets his permanent adult teeth. Biting and chewing behaviors increase. During this period it is common for kittens to chew on everything in sight, including your hands and feet. They are able to continue eating both dry and canned kitten foods.

The animal's coat fills out and there is more interest in grooming and scratching behaviors. Most kittens do not reach behavioral sexual maturity until after six months of age, but they can be physically mature before then. Kittens allowed outside at this age will roam farther and for longer periods of time.

PUBERTY

Cats go through physical maturation before they are behaviorally ready to reproduce. The time of year has an effect on reproduction, as cats are seasonally polyestrus (during certain seasons of the year, cats can go through their heat cycles multiple times). Veterinarians recommend that cats be spayed or neutered before they begin to exhibit sexual behaviors for many reasons. Some of the important reasons are:

- Neutered cats tend to be calmer and more easygoing.
- Neutered cats stay closer to home (and are more comfortable being indoor-only cats).
- Neutered cats fight less and are less protective of their territory.
- The cycling of sex hormones can trigger some health problems in cats.
- The odor of sexually mature male cats is unbearable.

Male "Coming of Age"

Male kittens start producing low levels of testosterone at about three and a half months of age. They can produce sperm by five months of age, but they are not usually able to copulate before they are 9 to 12 months old. Some behaviors you may see as a kitten begins sexual maturation are gripping the neck of another cat from behind, pelvic thrusting and mounting.

Most male cats have two testicles descended into their scrotums at birth. If the testicles have not reached the scrotum by eight months of age, it is unlikely they ever will. If a testicle is retained (called *monorchid* if one testicle is retained and *cryptorchid* if both are), it should be removed when the animal is neutered to prevent the possible development of tumors. The surgical procedure used with a cryptorchid cat, if the testicle is in the abdominal cavity, is similar to that used when spaying a female cat.

Female "Coming of Age"

Once a female cat begins to have her estrus cycle, she is able to conceive. The estrous cycle is the hormonal cycle that defines female "heat." Cats do not bleed when they are in heat, and the signs of heat in a female cat are all behavioral (see the list below). Most indoor cats will begin to cycle at five to nine months of age.

The kitten's environment plays a role in what age puberty begins, and factors such as exposure to tomcats, cycling females or increasing amounts of light will trigger earlier estrus. Although some cats cycle all year round, most cats in North America cycle between mid-January and late September.

The estrous cycle in a female cat is comprised of four stages: anestrus, proestrus, estrus and metestrus. Estrus is the only time in which a female will allow copulation and can conceive.

Proestrus is the short period one to three days before estrus. A female cat in proestrus may:

- Show a general increase in her activity.
- Roll and rub on objects and people.
- Spray urine.

- Lie low to the ground with her tail to one side and knead with her paws.
- Howl or otherwise vocalize.
- Not yet allow a male to mount her.

The proestrus period enables a female cat to let males know she is available! More information about the other stages of the feline estrous cycle is included in Chapter 11.

6 MONTHS TO 1 YEAR

A cat becomes an adult during this period. Social play decreases and the metabolic rate slows in spayed and neutered animals. The cat must take in fewer calories to avoid obesity, and this is achieved through a switch to adult maintenance diets. These diets have fewer calories and more fiber than diets for younger cats.

The immune system matures and cats have more natural ability to fight infection. This process continues throughout adult life, but wanes during the senior years.

A cat's personality more fully develops and is based on genetics and earlier life experiences. Behaviors become more routine. Cats in multi-cat households assume a position in the social hierarchy of the home.

Chapter 3

Feline Mental Health

Part of the allure of cat ownership is living with a creature who has not truly been domesticated. The process of feline domestication did not take the typical course of selective breeding to produce gentleness or trainability, as occurred with other species. Instead, cat breeding has gone through periods when it has been selective and periods when it has been random, depending on whether cats have fallen in or out of favor.

Cats rely on their natural instincts for hunting, self preservation and elimination. Many of the behaviors cat owners deem undesirable are simply manifestations of natural behaviors. Cats instinctively mark their territory by spraying and scratching, they play roughly with one another, and they pounce on and bite their prey. If you really think about it, many of the ways we demand cats behave are totally contrary to their nature.

I was taught in veterinary school that cats are not social animals, but more recent research has disproved this myth. Cats need individual attention from their owners and are generally better adjusted socially when they are raised with at least one other cat. You are wrong if you think your cat doesn't need you. Although cats can manage staying home alone all day while you are at work, it's really not their preference.

KEYS TO GOOD FELINE MENTAL HEALTH

Environmental enrichment and awareness of your cat's needs are important factors in making her happy in your home. If left outdoors, a cat would spend a large part of her day stalking and eating prey. This activity would provide mental stimulation and challenge. It would also provide exercise and keep the cat in good physical condition.

Cats scratch to communicate visually and by scent, and to keep their nails in shape. Give your cat at least one tall, sturdy scratching post in an easily accessible area. If she is not given appropriate items to scratch and then trained to use them, she will seek out alternative objects in your home.

Indoor cats don't have to work to eat, so boredom and obesity can result. Train cats to perform tricks and reward them with treats. Throw the treats and let your cat chase them. Consider placing small amounts of food in several locations and making your cat roam around to eat.

Create vertical space to keep your cat happy. Cats love to jump up on things and watch the world from a high vantage point. Jumping up keeps cats active, and giving them a high perch gives them an appropriate place to hang out and retreat from other cats, animals and people in a household. If two or more cats must live together in a small home, cat trees and elevated perches give cats more space, create vertical territory, and decrease the stress of sharing a small area.

Cats enjoy climbing and having a high perch for sleeping.

I cannot emphasize enough how important litter box placement and maintenance is to making a cat happy (see Chapter 1 for more on litter boxes). An inappropriate litter box is the number one reason cats eliminate in inappropriate locations. Many feline behaviorists recommend having one box per cat, plus one extra.

Although cats may play less as they age, play is another component of good feline mental health. Many cats will play on their own with toys, but interactive play every day is also very important for your cat's mental health. Play relieves boredom and provides exercise. It provides an outlet for stalking, pouncing and biting behaviors. Don't give up on cats who seem uninterested in playing. Search for fishing pole toys with feathers or laser lights that will stimulate at least a little interest in play.

To keep your cat entertained, set up an outdoor bird feeder that your cat can observe through a window, or install an aquarium. These items will provide a lot of stimulation to a cat who longs to hunt and chase, as well as a couch potato.

SIGNS OF STRESS

Trying to understand how a cat perceives the world is difficult. We do our best to make their lives comfortable, but we do not always properly meet our cat's individual mental needs. Changes in the home environment or with an owner's schedule may seem trivial to us, but they can have a major impact on our feline friends. Cats can manifest their stress through various behaviors.

A trip to the veterinary hospital sends some cats into a frenzy of fearful aggression. Boredom makes some cats engage in destructive chewing and clawing behavior. They often perform these behaviors simply to get negative attention from their busy owners. Some cats overgroom to the point of creating bald patches and sores as a response to stress. This condition is called psychogenic alopecia. Other stressed cats spray urine or eliminate inappropriately around the house.

Pay attention to your cat and look for signs of stress-induced behaviors. Early intervention is the key to preventing unwanted behaviors from continuing, and to making your cat happier.

PROPER HANDLING KEEPS A CAT HAPPY

Holding and carrying a cat properly is important. Of course you do not want to injure the cat, and if the cat feels insecure she may injure you trying to get away. There are various techniques that work well, and you can master them with practice and experience. If you have children, be sure to work with them and teach them how to gently and safely handle the cat. (Cats seem to have extra tolerance around children and are willing to put up with more than they normally would from you.)

The whiskers and tail of a cat are very sensitive to touch. Do not hold or pull a cat's whiskers. A cat's tail is an extension of her spine, and if you pull too hard, you can cause damage to the end of the spinal column where important nerves controlling urination and defecation are found.

When working with a cat, it is important to be gentle but firm. Cats are quite adept at reading human body language. If you are not confident about your ability to pick up or hold a cat, the cat knows it and will take advantage of the situation.

The best way to pick up a cat is to first extend your hand and let the cat sniff it. This gives the cat a chance to know who you are. Next, scratch the cat between the ears and along the cheekbones or chin. Approaching the cat from the side is less threatening than looming over her. Put one hand firmly behind the armpits of the front legs and lift the cat up, then scoop up the hind legs with your other hand from below. Hold the cat gently against your body for additional support. A cat who feels secure is less likely to struggle.

It is acceptable to hold a cat, even an adult, by the scruff of her neck—but please don't try to lift her off the ground this way. This is the hold the mother cat used on her as a kitten. Most cats will naturally relax when held in this manner. A large cat may be difficult to hold well in this way, and you will need to support her hind end.

You can cradle a cat in your arms by scooping her up with one arm at the front of her chest and the other arm behind her tail. This position should also support the hind legs. For more security, you can hold the hind legs in this position with your hands.

Some cats tolerate being carried cradled like a baby. But upside down cradling is a very submissive posture, and many cats will not allow it.

Another way to hold a cat is over your shoulder as if you were burping a baby. In this position, place one hand over the cat's shoulders and the other behind her tail and holding her hind legs. Some cats like to ride on their owner's shoulders, and this is cute when they are kittens, but may not work when they are larger and heavier. The animal's weight and claws can be quite uncomfortable. Be careful if you allow a cat to jump or climb up on you.

If a cat is under something and you want to pull her out, grabbing the scruff and pulling is the safest way—if you cannot entice her out with a treat or a toy. Do not pull on the limbs. Although cats are pretty tough, most humans could accidentally pull one of their legs out of joint.

Each cat has a different tolerance level with regard to being held. Some cats live to be held and carried around. Some will run the other way if they think you are coming to pick them up. Others will accept a little holding, but then scoot away at the first possible opportunity. It's important to respect your cat's preferences and understand that, in general, cats prefer to be cuddled while they are firmly on the ground (or the furniture).

If you have a cat who is scared or injured and you do not feel comfortable picking her up in a conventional manner, you might try throwing a towel or blanket over her head first and then trying to pick her up. When cats cannot see you, they often calm down. For safety reasons, try to transfer the animal to a carrier or box.

WHISKER WONDERS

Whiskers have been called the sixth sense. They are so delicately sensitive that if they move 1/2000th of the width of a human hair, they will send signals to the cat's brain. The anatomical term for whisker is *tactile vibrissae*. These touch sensors are used for stalking, measuring and warning the cat about unseen obstacles. Damaged whiskers lead to misjudgment and fumbling. Whiskers detect wind and deflected air currents, and this information helps the cat locate her prey. In dim light, cats use their whiskers for navigation. If a cat loses her whiskers, she must depend more on sight for getting around and hunting.

ADDING A NEW CAT

Cats are creatures of habit, and they generally would prefer that things stay the way they are. The same holds true when you're introducing a new cat to a household where other pets live. This is a situation when patience is a must. Sometimes all animals involved are amenable to the addition, and other times your former best friend will have nothing to do with you or the new cat.

As difficult as it may be to find the perfect cat for you, it is even more difficult to try to pick out a friend for an existing cat. I always tell people that they should be getting another cat because they want one, not because they think their cat needs a friend. If you get another cat and she does not get along with the original cat, you are still responsible for the new cat.

Cat owners interested in acquiring another cat often ask me whether the sex of the new addition matters. There are no current studies showing that cats have a social preference for living with any particular sex. Many potential cat owners shy away from acquiring a male cat because they are concerned about urine spraying. This is not a common problem in cats who are neutered before they reach puberty. Female cats can spray too, but they rarely do. Both males and females may eliminate outside of the cat box to mark territory or to show their displeasure in certain instances. It is very uncommon for cats to spray or eliminate inappropriately if they live in single or dual cat households, but the risks increase when three or more cats are present.

I think it is easier to bring a kitten into a household with an existing adult cat or cats. In this situation, the territory and dominance of the resident cats are established, and they are not as threatened as they would be if they had to compete with another adult cat. Senior cats may not tolerate a kitten jumping on and bothering them, and they usually keep their distance. It is a good idea to put a young "pest" away in another room, if needed, to give an older cat a break.

Tips for Introducing Cats Successfully

For health reasons, a veterinarian should examine a new cat or kitten before she comes into direct contact with your other cats. She should be tested for feline leukemia, a potentially fatal and contagious feline virus. If she is six months or older, she should be tested for feline immunodeficiency virus (FIV) as well. If the new cat came from a shelter, a large multicat household or a cattery, it would be wise to isolate her from other cats for a minimum of a week to control the spread of any contagious diseases.

Jealousy is a problem to address whenever a new cat joins the household. Dogs and other cats are generally reluctant to share you with somebody else. Give the existing animals lots and lots of attention to ease the transition.

Proper cat introductions reduce conflict and stress. The first time you bring a new cat home, you should confine her in her own room with her own litter box, food and water. This enables the other animals to sniff under the door to begin the introduction. If there is growling or hissing from either side, talk gently and try to calm the animals. Ideally, the initial separation should last a week. The next step is to place the new addition in a carrier in the middle of a common area and allow the other pets to see and sniff her. If all of the animals are calm, let the new addition out of the carrier while you supervise everyone. After a few incident-free, supervised meetings, let the pets to remain in contact and leave the room; be sure to listen for any trouble. If things go well, the successful introduction has been completed.

If you have a dog and are introducing a cat, start with the dog on a leash. Your new cat may have never seen a dog before, and your dog may never have had a cat in his house before, and it is hard to predict how either will react. Most dogs are just curious and may quickly approach a cat, but doing so can scare the cat. Don't leave dogs and cats alone unsupervised until you are sure neither animal will cause problems.

Dogs like to eat cat food and cats like to eat dog food. Everyone always wants what the other guy has. This is not dangerous, but each species has different nutritional needs that must be met. In particular, cats need a lot more protein than is found in dog food, and cannot live on a diet that is predominantly dog food.

Another point to mention is that dogs like to get into litter boxes and eat cat feces, so getting a covered box or placing it in an area less accessible to the dog is recommended. Why does this unappetizing habit occur? Probably because feline diets have higher fat and protein contents, which leads to richer wastes!

There is no standard acclimation period with animals. Until you feel totally comfortable with how all parties are handling the situation, the new addition should be confined when not being supervised. Any resident cats should not be immediately forced to share their food, water or litter box with the new addition. This is another reason for temporary confinement. In a multicat household, competing for food can cause problems such as weight gain and aggression. When the new cat comes out of confinement, each cat should have their own food dish—for life. Asking cats to eat from the same dish, or to eat in close proximity from a side-by-side dish, goes completely against their nature and is just courting trouble.

Litter box hygiene is always important, but even more so when there is more than one cat. The best way to prevent inappropriate elimination and encourage proper litter box use is to have a minimum of one litter box per cat. Although both cats may use both boxes, two boxes become soiled more slowly than one. Scooping every box at least once a day is a necessity to keep things clean.

KITTY'S BEING MEAN!

Cats may bite or scratch humans in their own defense—such as when a child pulls on a cat's tail—but unprovoked aggression is not acceptable. Some cats give warning signs that they are about to blow their fuse by hissing or growling, lashing their tail or twitching their skin, but others just strike out. You need to use caution any time you are handling a cat who has previously shown aggressive tendencies.

Cats are not dogs, so if you see a cat wagging or thumping her tail, don't mistake the behavior for happiness. Cats swish their tails when they are mad. Watch out!

One confusing type of aggression some cats demonstrate is petting-induced aggression. Cats with this behavior will sit contentedly on your lap and act like they are enjoying being petted, then suddenly they will turn and bite. Unfortunately, my hospital cat, Henry, does this. This behavior is seen more commonly in male cats, and the cause is not known. Two theories are:

1. Cats don't know how else to tell you to stop when they are tired of your petting, so they bite.
2. Cats find the petting so pleasurable that they fall into a light sleep, but then startle and feel confined, so they strike out.

You can decrease the chances of being bitten in this situation if you become more aware of the subtle signs the cat may exhibit right before biting, and back off.

Cats can exhibit aggression because they are fearful. I personally am very familiar with this situation because it happens daily in my veterinary clinic. Owners are shocked when their little sweetheart turns into a woman-eating lion during her examination. Speaking in a quiet voice and moving slowly will calm some cats, but others already have their minds made up and are not going to submit to examination quietly. Using protective clothing and gloves helps my staff to protect themselves in these situations. We hate to see our patients get so upset. It's hard on the animal and makes it hard for us to do a thorough job. We prescribe a mild tranquilizer to be administered before the next visit, if possible.

Just like people, some cats will redirect their aggression. Your cat may be stressed or upset by something else, but she takes it out on you or on another cat in the household. For example, your cat might hear or smell another cat outside, feel threatened and respond by biting or hissing at you. Trying to eliminate the source of stress and squirting a cat with water if she attacks are ways to manage the problem.

Aggression may also be caused by illness or neurological disease. If your cat has a sudden behavior change and becomes aggressive, you should have her examined for medical problems.

HOUSESOILING

Housesoiling and inappropriate elimination are two terms used interchangeably to describe urination and/or defecation outside of the litter box on a horizontal surface. They are not the same as spraying, which is directed onto a vertical surface.

Housesoiling is a very frustrating problem for cat owners, because the cat they know and love is ruining their house. An entire book could be written about all the options and treatments for this problem, but the bottom line is that no one can promise a cure. In almost every case the problem can be solved, but it takes a committed owner and early intervention. The longer the behavior has existed, the longer it will take to change. I get frustrated myself when owners bring in a cat they have allowed to eliminate outside of her litter box for years, and then want the problem quickly fixed because they are getting new carpet. I wish it could be that simple!

The keys to eliminating housesoiling are:

- Ruling out any medical problems with the cat
- Early intervention to stop the behavior
- Keeping the litter box immaculately clean
- Making sure the box is in a convenient location
- Providing a litter box for every cat in the home
- Giving the cat a type of litter she likes
- Using drug intervention when behavior modification fails

There are so many factors that can trigger a cat to stop using or only intermittently use her litter box that I use a questionnaire with owners when they bring a housesoiler in for an examination. An owner may not detect problems or stresses that the cat is experiencing, and the situation needs to be evaluated from the cat's perspective.

Many steps may be needed to get inappropriate elimination under control. The very first step, in all cases, is a thorough medical examination, because housesoiling is often a sign of a medical problem. If the cat gets a clean bill of health, proper cleaning of the litter box and environment are always the next steps. Behavior modification is next. If all else fails, drug therapy should be considered.

CLEAN UP RIGHT

Never use products that contain ammonia to clean up urine or feces, especially if a cat eliminates outside of the litter box. Ammonia will actually intensify the odors of the waste products you are trying to eliminate. Simple soap and water may seem to remove the smell, but your cat's sensitive nose can probably still pick up the odor—which encourages her to eliminate in the same place again. Your best bet is to use specially formulated enzymatic pet-odor neutralizers, which are available through your veterinarian, in most pet supply stores and in many supermarkets.

There are a handful of drugs that can be used to try to control inappropriate elimination. Most of them are safe, even with long-term use, but the cat should be monitored regularly for side-effects. In some situations a short course of medication stops the problem. In others the cat may be on medication indefinitely. Most of the antianxiety drugs available take one to two weeks to evaluate their effectiveness. Initially they may make a cat sleepy or dopey, but this effect usually goes away within four to five days.

TURN IT DOWN!

Excessive vocalization can be an annoying feline behavior. Some breeds, such as Siamese, are known for being talkative, and other cats may vocalize excessively and demand constant attention. A move, trauma or some other significant change in the cat's schedule can trigger this behavior. It can occur in older cats who lose their hearing and vision and become disoriented. High blood pressure, pain or neurological disease can also trigger excessive vocalization.

If you have a young, healthy cat, it can help to establish a routine where you give the cat your undivided attention for a few minutes twice a day. This is a good time to involve the animal in interactive play.

If you have an older animal, a veterinarian should examine her to rule out any medical problems that may be triggering the behavior. If no medical problems, such as high blood pressure, are found and the cat's senses of vision and hearing are normal, a senile syndrome called *cognitive dysfunction* should be considered. Medication is available that can improve this condition, although it is not currently approved for use in cats.

If you have tried everything and the cat won't stop howling, tranquilizers or antianxiety medications may be needed to manage the problem.

Chapter 4

Good Grooming

The beauty of a cat comes not only from his graceful movement but also from his haircoat. The coats of cats are usually described as short, medium or long. People like to think shorthaired cats do not shed as much as longhaired cats, but this is not the case. Unless you have a hairless Sphynx cat, all cats shed. The Devon and Cornish Rex breeds have kinky coats that shed less than others, but any animal with hair sheds—even humans!

Healthy cats have good coats and skin. Cats are clean animals, and most cats groom themselves regularly. But every cat needs some help taking care of herself; how much help your furry friend needs will depend on the cat and her coat. Complete grooming of a cat may be as simple as a weekly brushing and regular nail trimming, or it may involve combing, brushing, detangling, shaving, bathing and drying. This sounds like a lot of work, but many cat owners are able to do all that is needed to keep their cat looking good. For those who have trouble, professional grooming services are available.

START WITH THE CLAWS

Trimming the nails is important for your cat's good health. Untrimmed nails can eventually deform a cat's feet, and can even grow back into the pads and become very painful. Regular trimming will also prevent your cat from accidentally scratching you or your furniture, getting snagged in your sweater or hung up on the rug.

Proper technique for toenail trimming is to push on the top of the toe to extend the nail, and then cut off the hooked end with a pet nail trimmer. When you trim a cat's toenails, be careful not to cut the quick. The quick is a bundle of nerves and blood vessels that supply the nail and will look like a pink line or triangle inside a white nail. If you cut the quick, you'll hurt your cat and the toenail will bleed. (If your cat has black nails, just cut off the part of the nail that curls under.)

If you are inexperienced, you might want to start off cutting small amounts of nail and increase over time as you gain confidence with the procedure. You can have a veterinarian or groomer demonstrate the technique for you.

Toenail trimming should be started when your cat is a kitten, so that she becomes used to it. Cats know when you are not confident, so if you are having problems with nail trimming, you may want to stop, regroup and start over a little later. If she senses your anxiety, your cat will take advantage of the situation by squirming, making it even harder for you to trim her nails. You might consider cutting just a few nails at a time or trying to cut the cat's nails while she is napping.

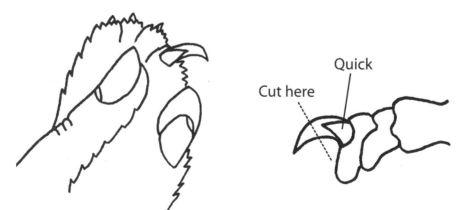

Gently extend the nail by pushing on the top of the toe, then cut beyond the quick.

DOES YOUR CAT HAVE EXTRA TOES?

Polydactyl is a term used to describe an animal with more than the normal number of toes. An average cat has five toes on each front foot and four on each rear foot. A polydactyl cat will have more—usually six but up to eight to ten toes on each front foot and up to seven on each back foot. The condition is caused by a genetic mutation that creates the dominant trait and is totally harmless.

Cats who have extra toes need more nail trimming than average cats, because the extra toenails usually don't get worn down and can grow into their footpads.

SHOULD YOU COMB OR SHOULD YOU BRUSH?

Cat combs and brushes come in numerous sizes, shapes and colors. Most people are familiar with conventional combs and brushes, but mitts, rakes and grooming cloths are also available. What tools you use depends on the length of coat and the tolerance level of the cat. Many cats love to be combed, but others turn into little tigers when the comb comes out. Most cats benefit from being combed or brushed at least once a week. The hair you remove helps decrease shedding and hairballs, and also means less cat hair on your couch and clothes.

It is a good idea to introduce a comb or brush to your kitten within a few days of bringing her home. Start by allowing the animal to sniff (and bite) the tool and see what it is. Gently comb the cat around the neck and back. If

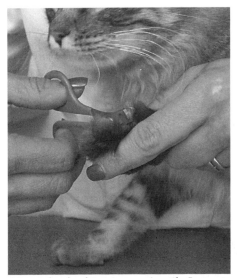

It's not that hard to trim a cat's nails. Just put the cat on a flat surface and get a firm grip.

you are met with hissing and claws, stop and talk calmly to the cat. At first, you may need to hold the cat by the scruff of her neck to keep her still when you comb her. Short, frequent combing sessions will help train her to accept, and even enjoy, grooming. Kittens who do not like being combed may prefer a soft-bristle brush.

Kittens who are trained to allow grooming are more tolerant of grooming as adults. It is much easier to handle a two-pound kitten than an unhappy, 10-pound adult, so it is worth the energy to work on training your cat while she's still young.

If you are having a tough time trying to comb your cat, you might want to enlist the support of a friend or a relative to help hold her. Giving a food treat to the cat after a successful brushing session will positively reinforce the idea of sitting still for grooming. Some cats like to be combed while they are eating. Eating can provide a good distraction to the animal and give you an opportunity to get a few strokes in. (However, some cats like to be left absolutely alone while they eat, and you must respect your cat's preferences.)

The only grooming tool that I think is essential for every cat is a flea comb, and your cat does not have to have fleas in order to benefit. A flea comb has dense, fine teeth. The most user-friendly flea combs have easy-to-hold handles and metal (as opposed to plastic) teeth. A shorthaired cat can be combed from her head to the tip of her tail with a flea comb, but this tool is too fine to use on animals with longer hair.

I routinely use a flea comb on every cat I examine. Its purpose is twofold: to determine if fleas are present, and to check for scabs, scales and dead hair. Owners often look at me in amazement when I comb out a significant amount of hair from their cat, but the fine teeth of the flea comb are excellent at catching stray hairs and getting below the surface hair. If fleas are present, flea dirt and live fleas are caught in the dense teeth of the comb.

Flea combs can be useful for removing small knots in short hair, but the pull is too strong for mats on cats with more hair. If your cat gets food or other substances on her coat, a flea comb can be used to comb the materials out of the hair. The disadvantages of a flea comb are that it can break hairs easily if it is used too vigorously, it can be painful to use on longhaired cats or those with matted fur, and if the fine teeth become bent, they can scratch the cat.

WHAT ABOUT A LONGHAIRED CAT?

For cats with medium to long hair, a medium to coarse metal comb is needed. Many owners like to use a slicker brush (which has short metal bristles), but the problem with this tool is that it can ride on top of the coat and leave hairs matted underneath. Metal rakes are useful for longer coats, especially if there is a lot of dead hair to comb out.

One way to ease the stress of combing a hairy cat is to pick smaller areas to work on, and comb one area a day or every few days. Even cats who are tolerant of combing have limits to the amount of time they are willing to put up with the procedure.

HAIRBALLS

Any cat can have hairballs, but the more hair a cat ingests when she is grooming, the more likely she is to cough up a hairball. That's why frequent brushing is your best defense against hairballs.

Hairballs are normal, and using hairball remedies may decrease their frequency but not eliminate them. The main reason to use hairball remedies is to prevent a hairball from causing an intestinal blockage.

Trichobezoar is the technical term for a hairball. This word is formed from *tricho*, derived from the Greek, meaning "hair," and *bezoar*, which is a concretion of materials formed in the intestines.

Traditional hairball remedies are malt petroleum pastes that come in tubes. Today these pastes are found in different flavors, including tuna, and even come in pump dispensers. These pastes can be very effective, but the petroleum does inhibit the absorption of certain vitamins, so it's important not to give your cat a hairball remedy near her mealtimes.

Psyllium, a type of fiber, is also a useful hairball remedy. It is available in premeasured capsules, in bulk form and as chewable tablets. These products are available from veterinarians and pet supply stores.

Many "hairball formula" foods have been developed for cats in recent years. Most of them contain cellulose, another type of fiber. They work well for some cats, but not all. Hairball treats may contain fiber or have centers filled with lubricants.

MATS AND THEIR PROBLEMS

Even fastidious cats have a hard time keeping all their hairs in place, and mats may form in places that are hard for your cat to reach. Mats are clumps of loose hair that become tangled into the hair that is still growing. They continue to attract more hair and grow larger and larger, until they painfully pull and pinch at your cat's skin.

Regular combing and brushing is the best way to prevent mats. If you're able to comb your pet even a few minutes a day, it can prevent a more time-consuming and painful problem later on. Mats will grow to a more unmanageable size if they are not removed.

It is easy for mats and knots to form on cats with medium to long coats. To prevent matting, concentrate your combing on the areas more likely to mat. These areas are the armpits, abdomen, behind the ears, the tail and under the tail and behind the back legs.

Unfortunately, cats tend to get mats very close to their skin. It is tempting to grab a pair of scissors and cut them out, but this is not the right first step. The best way to remove mats is:

1. Try to comb the mat out with a coarse metal comb by starting at the outer edge of the mat and then working in closer to the skin.

2. If you cannot get a comb through the mat, try to work your fingers through it to separate the hairs.

3. If the cat is in pain from the pulling or if you are not making any progress, work a comb between the skin and the mat.

4. Cut the hair along the comb on the side away from the skin. This will prevent you from cutting the cat's skin.

5. Gently comb out the shorter remaining hairs.

It takes weeks to months for hair to grow back. Often the skin under a mat appears red and inflamed. This is because trapped dirt and moisture have been irritating the skin. It also occurs if some pulling is needed during the process of removing the mat.

Your cat is not going to be happy when you start working on matted areas. Be careful and stop combing if you are at risk of being bitten or scratched, or if your cat indicated that you are hurting her. Get help from a friend or a relative, or turn the job over to an experienced groomer.

Most shorthaired cats who groom themselves regularly don't get mats, but there are exceptions. This most frequently occurs in older animals who do not groom themselves enough and in obese animals who cannot reach many areas on their own. These cats need more routine combing. A persistent owner armed with a flea comb can remove most of the matting that forms on a shorthaired cat.

The matting that forms on shorthaired cats tends to be located along the end of the spine and at the base of the tail. The hair may be greasy, dry and scaly all at the same time. This is because a cat distributes her natural skin oils along the hairs when she grooms herself, and she can't reach these areas where mats form. Don't be surprised if your overweight cat starts biting or licking the air when you start combing these areas. Combing these areas is like tickling the cat in a spot she can't reach, and boy, does that feel good!

Regardless of whether your cat has short or long hair, the least painful and easiest way to remove significant matting is by shaving. Depending on the location of the matting, the shaving may involve one area or the entire body. Shaving can cause some discomfort, but not as much as combing. When cats are severely matted or very intolerant of grooming, it is best to have the animal sedated so that neither the groomer nor the cat gets hurt.

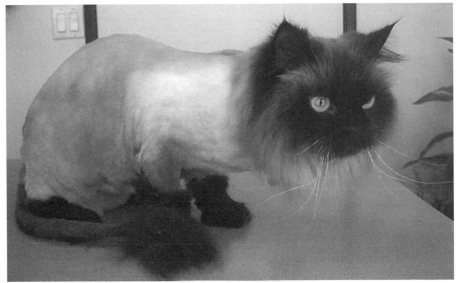

A longhaired cat, like this Himalayan, may benefit from a body shave.

BATH TIME

Surprisingly, some cats like water and will tolerate baths, but for most cats a bath is a hair-raising experience. Owners often ask me how frequently their cat should be bathed. There is no set schedule for bathing a cat, and some cats may never need a bath. Factors to consider when deciding about a bath are:

- Greasiness of the coat
- Presence of fleas
- Dirtiness of the coat
- Smell
- Discoloration

Many cats live to a ripe old age without ever getting a bath, but I think all cats look and smell better after being bathed. Baths can play a role in treating some dermatological conditions and in removing external parasites such as fleas.

It is important to use a proper shampoo on your cat. Most shampoos for human hair do not have the right pH balance for a cat's skin and should not be used. Baby shampoo is acceptable, as are specially formulated pet shampoos. Many of the insecticides found in flea shampoos can be toxic to all cats or specifically to kittens, so be very careful if you want to use a flea shampoo. Make sure it is labeled for use with cats and kittens. With the advent of safe, effective, once-a-month flea preventives, flea shampoos should not be a necessity.

Before starting a bath, you should trim your cat's toenails. This will decrease the potential for injury if the cat gets upset. You should also comb out any mats in the hair, because they will tighten and be harder to remove after they are wet.

Here's how to bathe a cat:

1. Place a towel or mat at the bottom of the tub or sink so the cat does not slide.
2. If possible, use a faucet that has a sprayer attachment.
3. Gently wet the cat's coat with warm water. Hold the cat by her scruff, if necessary.

4. Massage the shampoo into the coat, rubbing away from the head.

5. Use a toothbrush with some lather to clean the cat's face, being careful not to get any soap in the animal's eyes. If shampoo does get in the cat's eyes, rinse with saline solution from a bottle.

6. Let the cat soak for a couple of minutes.

7. Rinse thoroughly with warm water.

8. Squeeze the excess water out of the coat and down the legs and tail.

9. Thoroughly towel-dry the cat.

10. Use a blow dryer on low or medium to dry the coat. Higher settings can cause burning if you are not careful.

11. Comb or brush the hair during the drying process.

If you are fortunate enough to have a cooperative kitty, the process will go well. For cats who are scared or anxious, though, the process can be a disaster if you are not careful. Expect the cat to try to get out of the sink. Consider wearing an apron or old clothes in case you get splashed or have to grab a wet cat. Close the door to the room to help prevent kitty's escape.

GIVE UP?

You may be reading this chapter and thinking, "You've got to be kidding! There is no way I could ever groom my cat." If this is true, or if you have been unsuccessful in your grooming efforts, consider taking your cat to an experienced groomer.

Not all groomers like working with cats, so it is important to find one who does. There are some groomers who have mobile vans and will come to your house, park in your driveway and work on your kitty there. Other groomers work in grooming shops, pet supply stores and veterinary hospitals. There are groomers who have completed courses on pet grooming and have certificates. There are others who have learned by experience.

> **PAMPERING A PERSIAN**
>
> Persians are the most popular type of pedigreed cat. To maintain their beautiful long coats, they need frequent grooming. Most owners are not capable of keeping Persian hair under control themselves. Ask other Persian owners about what is involved and consider selecting a different breed if you don't have the time or money to have the cat regularly groomed by a professional.

How to Pick a Groomer

The best groomer is one who has worked with cats and has access to a veterinarian in case of problems. Medical assistance may be required if the cat is nicked accidentally with sharp grooming tools or if she needs to be sedated so that the groomer can do a proper job. Many cats freak out with strangers or are so badly matted that the grooming process is painful. In these cases sedation is recommended so that neither the animal nor the groomer gets injured.

If you have a cat who you don't feel comfortable grooming on your own, she should be groomed professionally at least every three months. The shorter the interval between grooming sessions, the less matting will occur.

Cat Hairdos

Different breeds of dogs typically have different haircuts, but the same is not true for cats. Most cats do not get haircuts unless they are matted or their coats are difficult to manage. There is really only one haircut for a cat: the body shave. If a cat is shaved, the entire trunk is typically shaved close, like a crew cut. How far down the legs and tail the animal is shaved and how much of the neck or mane hair is removed depends on the cat. If you have never had your cat shaved and you request it, ask to see a sample of what a shaved animal looks like so that you are not shocked with the results.

Don't be surprised if you take a matted cat to a groomer and body shaving is suggested. A shaved cat may not look as good to you as a cat with all her hair, but the pain and discomfort associated with combing out a lot of mats may be extreme. The skin is also very traumatized when there is significant matting, and you could end up with a ragged, patchy coat after combing. Even after shaving, the coat pattern may look irregular where mats were removed, but you've saved your cat from a lot of agony.

Many owners take their cat to a groomer simply for a bath and brush. A groomer may place cats in cages with dryers on the door before finishing with hand drying. Groomers usually have assistants to help them with combing and drying, because four hands are needed to control many cats. Even though cats do not require bathing, clean, fluffed hair does look better. Why get your cat mad at you when you can blame someone else?

Chapter 5

The Best Nutrition for Your Cat

Food has a high ranking on a cat's top 10 list. It ranks higher than affection from you, cravings for catnip and clawing the furniture! Food is a treat some owners use to bribe their cats or get their cat's attention. There is no question that food has psychological importance for both cat and owner. But of course, food's physiological importance came first.

Is there a magic formula by which to feed your cat? Should you feed canned food, dry food, semimoist or a combination? Do you need to be worried about preservatives? Won't your cat get bored if you feed him the same thing every day? Can both young and old cats eat the same food? How much should you feed your cat? All of these questions are important, and the answers aren't always clear.

I am overwhelmed each time I walk through the pet food aisles of a grocery store or pet supply store. The massive variety of products seems to grow daily. The pet food market is a multibillion dollar business, and a lot of companies want a piece of the pie.

PICKING THE RIGHT FOOD

If cats were left outdoors to hunt, mice would be their ideal food, supplying all of their nutritional needs. Other prey a cat would choose are rats, rabbits, birds and insects.

Cats would probably be healthier if they ate a diet of fresh prey, as opposed to commercial foods. And this has prompted some owners to become interested in feeding raw diets to their cats. Most veterinarians do not favor raw diets, however, because to be formulated properly, they are very labor-intensive for an owner. Other problems associated with raw diets include nutritional imbalances, exposure of the human preparing the food and the cat eating the food to bacteria and parasites found in raw meat, acceptability of a raw diet to the cat and odors associated with preparing and feeding the diet.

There are three quality categories of commercial cat foods: premium, sold in the grocery store and generic. I would not recommend generic food because it often does not meet the standards of the Association of American Feed Control Officials (AAFCO). AAFCO is the organization responsible for creating practical nutritional recommendations for pet food. Any food you feed your cat should at least meet these minimum standards, and if it does, it will say so on the label.

There are many brands of cat food that are sold in the grocery store, and almost all meet AAFCO standards. The main differences between these foods and premium diets (which are usually sold in pet supply stores) are the ways in which the nutrition requirements are achieved. Premium diets contain higher quality, more digestible and bioavailable ingredients, which decrease the amount of food the cat needs and the amount of feces kitty produces.

Cats are carnivores, so they need high levels of protein in their diets. Some people call canned food "meat," and it generally contains more protein than dry food, but cheaper canned foods may still have a lot of fillers that are not derived from meat. Most cats like the taste and smell of canned food, but dry foods offer owners more convenience. The cost of canned food is also significantly more than dry. While canned food often has more protein per ounce than dry food, it also contains between 75 and 80 percent water.

Once opened, a can of cat food stays fresh for about two to three days if it's kept covered and refrigerated. Most cats do not like cold food, so warming refrigerated food in the microwave for a few seconds can help increase its odor and palatability. Be sure to stir it to avoid hot spots. Ideally, cats like their food at room temperature.

Recent studies have found that cats with certain health problems, such as lower urinary tract disease and diabetes mellitus, do better on canned diets. For picky eaters, cats who need to gain weight or those who need to consume more water, canned food is also a better choice. Cats who are prone to urinary tract problems may benefit from canned food because its high water content helps produce more dilute urine. If you own a cat with lower urinary tract disease, you should avoid feeding your cat foods with seafood products. These foods contain high levels of minerals such as magnesium, which can contribute to the formation of crystals in the urine.

Feeding a combination of canned and dry food to a healthy cat is a good idea. Cats who eat only canned food tend to build up more plaque and tartar on their teeth than those who also eat some dry food.

People today are more aware of their own nutrition and health, and they want to know about what their pets consume. Most dry cat foods are chemically stabilized and preserved. The safety of these chemicals is constantly being challenged, and pet food manufacturers are constantly defending their safety—backed up by the Food and Drug

DO CATS NEED FOOD ALL DAY?

We tend to think of cats as grazers who eat a few bites of food at a time over the course of a whole day. But free access to food is not necessary for most cats, and grazers can get fat if they consume too many calories. Dry food can be very concentrated, and feeding your cat more than half a cup a day of many brands can cause obesity. Most adult, indoor cats tend to gain weight if their bowls are kept constantly full. When feeding dry food, check the food label and consult with your veterinarian to establish feeding guidelines. Then feed your cat two or more smaller meals a day—some canned, some dry—to control how much she eats. Another option is to feed a little canned food once or twice a day and leave out some dry food during the intervening periods. These methods only work if portions and between-meal treats are measured and controlled.

Administration (FDA). A growing number of companies make "all natural" foods that contain no synthetic ingredients or preservatives. Whether these diets will improve your cat's health and longevity has not been proven. I have seen many cats who have lived into their 20s and have eaten regular, commercial dry foods their entire lives.

If you watch your cat eat, you may see that she does not chew much on the dry food. Some cats eat too much dry food all at once and regurgitate it. Cats who regurgitate need to be fed smaller portions. Mixing in some canned food, or adding some water to the dry food, can also help. Other strategies to decrease regurgitation are feeding a larger sized kibble that must be chewed before its swallowed, and feeding in a shallow bowl that more widely disperses the food. Both of these ideas slow down the pace of eating and decrease regurgitation.

ESSENTIAL DIFFERENCES IN CATS

I have already mentioned that normal cats require a high level of protein in their diets. Proteins are made up of amino acids, and there are nine essential amino acids that all mammals—including humans—require in their diets. Cats also require four other amino acids in their diets: arginine, taurine, methionine and cysteine.

The typical protein sources used in manufacturing cat foods easily supplies adequate levels of arginine. Arginine supplementation is recommended in cases of feline hepatic lipidosis to help support the detoxification of proteins during metabolism.

Taurine deficiency became newsworthy in the late 1980s because a type of heart disease, called dilated cardiomyopathy, was linked to inadequate intake. Pet food manufacturers changed their formulations as a result of this finding, thus virtually eliminating this type of heart disease. Taurine also plays roles in reproduction, neonatal health and vision.

The sulfur-containing amino acids, methionine and cysteine, are needed to synthesize other proteins. Deficiencies of these amino acids are rare.

Two other amino acids become essential in certain situations. Tyrosin is needed for the synthesis of melanin, and a lack of intake or production of tyrosin leads to a reddish discoloration of black coats. Carnitine is thought to be important in weight management and fat metabolism. Supplementation in cases of hepatic lipidosis improves survival.

Vitamin deficiencies are rare in cats who eat commercial diets. Cats require high levels of B vitamins, and B complex supplements are recommended for the diets of sick cats. Unlike other animals, cats cannot synthesize vitamin A or vitamin D, so they must ingest them in their diet. When cats are anorexic or have liver disease, vitamin E and K supplements may also be needed.

Cats, like other mammals, require the essential fatty acid linoleic acid. It is unknown how well cats are able to metabolize and synthesize alpha-linoleic acid, so it, too, should be part of their diets. Animal tissues are good sources for these fatty acids, so deficiencies in meat-based diets are unlikely. Omega-3 and omega-6 fatty acids have received attention for their roles in inflammation, but their optimal ratios are unknown at this time. Fatty acid supplements are used frequently for cats with dermatitis and inflammatory bowel disease.

After seeing all of the needs that must be met to provide good nutrition, it is no wonder commercial diets are so widely used. The diet your cat eats should make him feel and look good, agree with his digestive tract and provide for any special health needs.

VIVA VARIETY

Most veterinary nutritionists believe a cat should be given some variety in foods during her lifetime. Feeding a variety of foods helps make up for any deficiencies that might be present in a single food or diet. Kittens develop eating habits and preferences from watching their mothers. Food preferences develop by the time a kitten is six months old. If they're given a variety of foods as kittens, cats are less likely to be finicky eaters later in life. This makes introducing a therapeutic or new diet (if needed) easier in the future.

Cats do not know that there are unlimited choices available for their feeding pleasure. To prevent your cat from becoming too finicky, limit the flavors and types of food you offer in a single meal. A smorgasbord of different foods is not needed. You can certainly appeal to their preferences, but try to remember who the boss is!

Some cats will starve themselves before they would consider eating food they deem undesirable. Whenever a new diet is offered to a cat, gradually mix it with the previous diet. Over the course of a week or two, increase the percentage of the new food. Cats will more readily accept a slow change, and their digestive tract will be happier, too.

Just like humans, there are some cats who have food allergies and cannot eat certain kinds of proteins. If your cat vomits after eating certain foods, look at the ingredients and try offering her something different. Many cat foods have similar ingredients, so you may need to consult with your veterinarian for help in finding a suitable diet. It can take six to eight weeks for a diet change to significantly decrease vomiting in a cat with food allergies.

FEEDING BY LIFE STAGE

Kittens, adult cats and senior cats all have different nutritional requirements. Kittens should eat kitten food for the first 6 to 12 months of their lives. Kitten or growth formula foods are generally more calorie-dense and have higher levels of vitamins and minerals. Senior cats are usually less active and diets formulated for them contain fewer calories, more fiber and less protein. Adult cats do well on maintenance diets, unless they are pregnant, nursing or have a medical problem that requires them to eat special foods. Once a cat has been spayed or neutered, her metabolic rate slows, so to prevent obesity it is recommended to feed a diet that is less than 20 percent fat.

Many owners are faced with the dilemma of having to feed a kitten and an adult at the same time. The solution to this problem lies in the weight of the adult. If the adult cat is trim, leaving kitten food out is not a problem. If the adult is overweight, the adult maintenance food should be free-fed, and the kitten should be supplemented with kitten food that is fed privately, where the adult can't get at it.

Most special and prescription diets are fine for all adult cats, but may not be suitable for growing kittens or seniors. Discuss these individual feeding issues with your veterinarian so that you can tailor a proper feeding program for your cats.

Dieting for overweight cats is a challenge. Many "light" feline diets are available for overweight cats, but these diets are not equal in quality and some brands have two to three times the number of calories per cup than others.

There are two main diet theories for cats. One is to feed a larger amount of a low-fat, high-fiber diet because it fills them up. The other is to feed more protein and less carbohydrate because it better satisfies cats—the Atkins Diet approach.

To safely put a cat on a weight-loss program, create a diet plan with your veterinarian, stick with it and take the cat back to the doctor for follow-up checks. Food-obsessed cats often will eat low-calorie items such as lettuce, carrot pieces, canned green beans or cantaloupe, which can also help fill them up.

DRINK IT UP

A cat's body, like other small mammals, is 60 percent water. And water is the only beverage a cat needs to drink. Cats normally are not big water drinkers, and they produce very concentrated urine. An average cat will consume about eight ounces of water a day, but the amount of water a cat will drink in a day can vary. Factors that affect water consumption include diet, environmental temperature and activity level. Cats who primarily eat canned foods will not drink as much water as those who eat dry foods. This is because canned foods contain more water than dry foods. When the weather is hot or after thorough grooming, a cat may drink more.

Unlike humans, who know they need to stay hydrated when they are sick, cats do not drink enough when they are sick and they quickly become dehydrated. Cats often need treatment with injectable fluids to restore their hydration when they are ill, because it is difficult to make them drink enough water to keep hydrated.

Water bowls should be cleaned daily, and they should be rinsed and refilled several times a day. You should also monitor your cat's water intake, especially as she matures. If you notice that your cat is drinking more water than usual, this can be a warning sign of diabetes mellitus or problems with her kidneys.

Researchers believe cats taste water in a more complex way than we do, which may explain why many cats like to drink running water.

CAT MILK

As I mentioned in Chapter 2, cats like cow's milk but it is not good for them, because they cannot digest it properly. There is a specially formulated cat milk drink called Cat Sip. This product does not contain lactose, which is the sugar in cow's milk that cats cannot digest. Cats seem to like to drink this as a treat, but your cat certainly doesn't need it.

The sense of taste in cats is probably more sensitive than our own. Some researchers believe that cats like to drink out of running faucets because they prefer fresher tasting water. If you have a cat who demands that you to turn on the faucet, you are not alone. These cats sometimes enjoy a running water fountain; several types are sold at pet supply stores.

In their search for fresher water, some cats develop the unpleasant habit of drinking out of toilet bowls. This is really dangerous if you use the kind of toilet bowl cleaner that automatically dispenses chemicals into your toilet water. Even if you don't, various cleaning products can linger on the bowl, and cats can actually fall in the toilet bowl and have a hard time getting out. To discourage this behavior, close the lids on toilets or keep bathroom doors closed.

Some cats like to drink out of swimming pools. If your cat goes outside it is difficult to prevent this behavior. But don't worry; the amount of chlorine in pool water is generally not dangerous.

If you do not like the taste of your tap water, you may consider sharing your bottled or filtered water with your cat. Bottled water is a profitable industry, and there are companies today who are producing "designer water" for cats. Distilled water may benefit cats who are prone to urinary tract problems and readily form crystals in their urine. Distilling removes the minerals that are normally present in water.

Chapter 6

How Do I Know if My Cat Is Sick?

Our feline friends cannot tell us how they feel, so it is important to have some understanding of the signs that a cat is sick. Cats are generally stoic animals, and often they do not let us know they are sick until the disease has progressed. Observant owners can learn to identify subtle changes in their cat's routine and behavior that may be indicative of illness.

The difficult part of identifying changes is first figuring out what is normal for your cat. Cats do not think or act like a human would in many situations, so many cat activities seem strange to us. An example is coughing up hairballs. If a human spit up hair it would be very abnormal, but for a cat an occasional hairball is quite normal.

This chapter will introduce you to some of the ways you can detect problems in your cat. It will also help you figure out when you should consult a veterinarian.

IS YOUR FELINE ANOREXIC?

Anorexia is a term used to describe a lack of appetite for food. Veterinarians use this term when owners tell them that the cat is not eating or eating very little.

Being finicky and not eating are two different things. Some cats hold out for their favorite foods and this makes them finicky, but anorexic cats do not care what you put in front of them.

If a cat does not eat for 24 hours, you should be concerned. If the lack of appetite lasts more than 48 hours, you should have the cat examined by a veterinarian.

Cats, especially overweight animals, can develop a condition called hepatic lipidosis if they do not eat. Cats with hepatic lipidosis break down their body fat for energy, but the fat overwhelms the liver, injures the normal liver cells and makes the cat sicker. Early intervention with anorexic cats is needed to stop hepatic lipidosis from occurring. Left untreated, hepatic lipidosis can be fatal.

When Your Cat Won't Eat

If your cat is not eating, you need to determine if there is a problem with his diet or if the cat is sick. Some reasons why a healthy cat may not eat include:

- The food is spoiled.
- Ants or other insects are in the food.
- You bought the wrong flavor.
- There is competition at the food bowl.
- People food or treats have affected his appetite.
- The food bowl is in a bad location.
- The cat has been hunting and eating prey or snacking at a neighbor's house.

If none of these reasons is valid, it is likely the cat is sick. Reasons why a sick cat may not eat include:

- The cat is congested and cannot smell the food.
- The cat has a fever, causing a loss of appetite.

- Bad teeth or other dental disease is affecting the cat's ability to eat.
- Liver or other gastrointestinal disease is causing nausea.
- The cat is dehydrated and too weak to eat.

How to Make Your Cat Eat

Sick cats do not eat well, so it is important to encourage them. Offer yummy foods, such as canned cat food, tuna fish, deli meat or meat baby food. Lightly warming the food for a few seconds in a microwave oven can help build a cat's appetite by increasing the food's aroma. Hand-feeding, talking gently and petting the cat can stimulate eating, too. You can hand-feed your cat by offering him some soft food on a spoon or on your finger and encouraging him to lick it off. If a cat seems uninterested in eating, do not leave food sitting out for more than an hour. Pick it up and reintroduce it a few hours later.

When none of these suggestions proves successful, a trip to the veterinarian is warranted. Veterinarians may use prescription appetite stimulants or may even force-feed an anorexic cat. Force-feeding is typically done using a syringe without a needle and squirting some type of strained diet into a cat's mouth. For cats who are difficult or too sick to orally force-feed, feeding tubes can be placed into the esophagus or stomach.

What About Water?

Water intake is extremely important. If a cat (or any animal) cannot keep water down, he should be taken to a veterinarian immediately. This can be a sign of an intestinal obstruction.

A cat who does not eat or drink can become seriously dehydrated within a day. Vomiting and diarrhea can contribute to water loss leading to dehydration. If your cat is not drinking, you can give him some water with a syringe (minus the needle) or an eyedropper, but it is almost impossible to get enough water into a cat this way.

Veterinarians can rehydrate cats by injecting a sterile, balanced electrolyte solution under the animal's skin. This practice is called *subcutaneous administration*. Fluids can also be directly injected into the body through a vein using an intravenous catheter, commonly known as an *IV*. Intravenous treatment requires hospitalization but is necessary for more seriously dehydrated patients.

DOES YOUR CAT HAVE A FEVER?

A warm, dry nose or warm ears does not indicate a fever in a cat. The only way to be certain about the presence of a fever is by actually taking a cat's temperature. The normal body temperature of a cat is higher than that of a human: The normal range is from 100.5°F to 102.5°F.

You may need two people to take a cat's temperature with a rectal thermometer. Here's how to do it properly:

1. Shake down a glass thermometer so that the mercury is below 98°F.
2. Lubricate the tip of the thermometer with petroleum jelly or a water-soluble lubricant.
3. Insert the thermometer into the cat's rectum.
4. Hold the cat standing and as still as possible and leave the thermometer in place for two minutes.
5. Remove the thermometer and read the temperature.

Inexpensive digital thermometers are available at drugstores and can be used rectally in cats. Human ear (tympanic) thermometers are not accurate in cats. Special ear thermometers are available for animals, but they are expensive and are only sold through veterinary distributors.

What Causes a Fever?

In a cat, a fever is generally considered to be a temperature reading above 103°F. Increased body temperature does not always mean the animal is sick, but if the cat has a fever you should try to find out why. An increased body temperature can be due to:

- High environmental temperature
- Stress or excitement, such as putting the cat into a carrier and taking him to the veterinarian
- Intense playing or running
- Bacterial infections
- Viral infections
- Seizures due to increased muscle activity

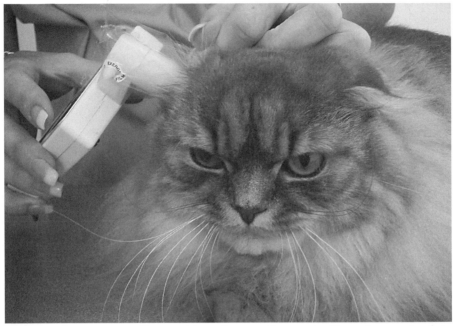

Taking a cat's temperature with a special veterinary ear thermometer. It may be annoying, but it doesn't hurt.

What You Should Do if Your Cat Has a Fever?

If you suspect that your cat has a fever, be sure he is someplace cool. *Do not give any over-the-counter medications made for humans to reduce a cat's fever.* If the cat is alert and acting normal, check his temperature again in an hour. You can hose a cat down with cold water to bring down his temperature, but this rather radical treatment should be reserved for cases when the temperature is above 105°F. You can also apply rubbing alcohol to the cat's footpads to cool him, but if the cat then licks his feet, he will drool a bit.

Whenever a cat has a fever, it is best to have the cat examined by a veterinarian as soon as possible. The doctor will try to determine what triggered the fever and then offer options for treatment. Cold fluids can be injected into a cat to cool him down. If a fever persists for more than 24 hours, more extensive nursing care and diagnostic testing are probably warranted.

```
┌──────────────────    NO ASPIRIN    ──────────────────┐
│                                                       │
│  Never give a cat aspirin, acetaminophen (Tylenol), ibuprofen  │
│  (Advil) or any other anti-inflammatory medication made for    │
│  humans. Cats lack the enzymes needed to metabolize these drugs, │
│  and they can be life threatening. If your cat accidentally ingests one │
│  of these drugs, seek veterinary care immediately.             │
│                                                       │
└───────────────────────────────────────────────────────┘
```

WHAT TO DO WHEN YOUR CAT IS ACTING FUNNY

We've come back to the issue of deciding what is normal behavior for a cat. Each cat is an individual with unique habits and preferences. Owners of adult cats have a good idea of what is normal for their cat when it comes to eating, drinking, playing and sleeping; but for a new kitten owner, these behaviors may not yet be established. Cats are creatures of habit, so if your normally "bouncing off the walls" kitten couldn't care less when you come home from work, he is likely not feeling well. In general, cats who are sick become quieter than usual and keep to themselves or even hide. They seem as if they do not want to be bothered with regular daily activities.

Irritability

Sometimes when cats are not feeling well they become irritable. Signs of irritability include:

- Hissing or growling
- Striking out with a paw or claws
- Biting
- Moving away from you when normally they would not
- Less tolerance for other people and/or animals in the house

If your cat becomes more irritable, try to determine if he is not feeling well and wants to be left alone or if the behavior change does not have an apparent trigger. In either case, you will likely need to have the cat examined by a veterinarian to see if a more specific cause for his irritability can be found. A veterinarian can treat any underlying medical problems and work with you to solve behavioral problems.

Failure to Respond

Cats are usually very alert and tuned in to the activities around them. If your cat suddenly becomes disinterested or unresponsive, this is not normal. As cats age, their activity level is reduced, but if vision and/or hearing are not impaired, cats will still react to things around them.

Diseases that affect the nervous system are not that common in cats, but they do occur. Any sick cat with behavior changes should have his nervous system assessed by a veterinarian. Diseases that affect other organ systems or electrolyte imbalances can also cause behavior changes.

TYPICAL SIGNS OF ILLNESS

There are many clinical signs a sick cat can exhibit. One isolated episode of any of the common clinical signs does not indicate a sick cat. Signs that last more than a day or that progress indicate problems that are unlikely to be resolved without treatment.

Every cat owner has a comfort level with evaluating the signs that their cat shows, but whenever there is uncertainty, consult with your veterinarian.

COMMON CLINICAL SIGNS OF ILLNESS IN CATS

Anorexia	Head shaking
Bad breath	Itching
Bleeding	Jaundice
Bloating	Limping
Bloody urine	Nasal discharge or congestion
Conjunctivitis	Redness (of skin, eyes, face)
Constipation	Seizures
Coughing	Sneezing
Diarrhea	Straining
Drinking more than normal	Swelling
Excessive licking	Vomiting
Fever	Weight loss
Gas	Worms

IF THESE SIGNS LAST MORE THAN 24 HOURS, TAKE YOUR CAT TO THE VET
Anorexia
Bloody Urine
Coughing
Diarrhea
Fever
Squinting
Vomiting
Weight-bearing lameness

Cats are very protective and defensive by nature, so they hide their illnesses well. Often cats do not let us know that they are sick until a condition is quite advanced.

WHEN TO GO TO THE EMERGENCY ROOM

There are a few clinical signs that warrant immediate attention. These include:

- Difficulty breathing
- Inability to urinate
- Uncontrolled bleeding
- Jaundice
- Inability to stand
- Seizures
- Vomiting blood

Signs such as these can be indicative of life-threatening problems. If you think your cat may have sustained a severe trauma such as being attacked by a larger animal, getting hit by a car or falling from a roof, get the cat to a veterinarian as soon as possible, even if he seems to be OK.

Even if your regular veterinarian closes his hospital at night and on holidays, he should be able to provide you with a source of after-hours emergency care. Veterinary clinics have an answering service or message machine that can give you a phone number for emergencies or refer you to an emergency clinic. Emergency veterinary clinics can also be found in the Yellow Pages.

The cost of emergency services is higher than services provided during regular business hours. Emergency veterinary clinics provide aggressive diagnostics and treatments. Be sure to discuss any recommendations with the doctor and try to understand what is being done and how necessary it is, so that you will not be surprised when you see your bill. You need to feel comfortable with your animal's treatment.

CHECKING OUT YOUR MEDICINE CABINET

Cats are very sensitive to medications, but they can be safely treated with a few products for humans. It is important to read labels and check ingredients before treating a cat. Call your veterinarian's office before giving your cat any medications. If the animal is not responding to your care within 24 hours, don't wait to get help.

Cleaning Cuts

Any small wound or abrasion can be safely cleaned with hydrogen peroxide. This solution can fizz and bubble when it comes in contact with blood, but it does not sting the way rubbing alcohol does.

Another disinfectant that you may keep around the home is a Betadine solution. This type of solution has an iodine color and can cause staining, so be careful where you apply it.

Ointments and Creams

After a wound, puncture or abrasion is cleaned, it is safe to use a triple antibiotic ointment. One common product is Neosporin, which can be safely used topically twice daily.

Hydrocortisone cream or ointment can be applied to a minor rash that is itchy to a cat. This drug is useful to treat itching and inflammation if there is no infection, but if bacteria or fungus are present, it can make an infection worse.

Cats like to keep themselves clean. If you apply any topical cream or ointment to a cat's skin, expect the animal to lick it. Using topical products sometimes draws a cat's attention to an irritated area and the skin can become more irritated if the cat licks it too much. Sometimes cats don't know when to stop.

Cleaning Around the Eyes

Many cats, especially Persians, have some discharge from the eyes, which forms in the corners of the eyes and can be hard to remove. It is best just to use warm water on a cotton ball around the eyes and nose. A saline solution made for people with contact lenses can also be used to clean the eyes and nose. It is safe to use a mild boric acid solution around the eyes and nasal folds.

Kitty Has an Upset Stomach

If you have a cat who is vomiting but is still able to hold down water and small bits of food, you can try treating him with Pepcid AC. A cat can take one-quarter to one-half of a 10-mg tablet once a day. If you think the vomiting is due to a hairball and you do not have any type of hairball remedy, try putting half a teaspoon of white petroleum jelly on the cat's nose. Cats hate to have a dirty nose and will lick it clean, thereby ingesting some lubricant.

Some types of diarrhea will respond to treatment with Kaopectate or Pepto-Bismol. Both of these formulas currently contain bismuth subsalicylate, which must be used cautiously in cats. A five-pound cat can take one teaspoon (5 ml) of these medications twice a day for two or three days.

One other drug for humans that can be safely used for cats for a short period is Imodium A-D. This drug should only be given in small amounts; the dose is one-eighth of a teaspoon for a 10-pound cat, three times a day, for no more than two days.

Again, it is always best to call your veterinarian before giving your cat any type of medication.

Kitty Is Constipated

It is normal for a cat to have a bowel movement at least once a day. Cats who pass less frequent, dry stools need help. You can use a hairball remedy for mild constipation, because it acts as a lubricating laxative.

Cats can become constipated due to diet, dehydration or just by grooming themselves and ingesting too much hair. If you think that your cat is constipated, you can buy a premeasured veterinary psyllium

```
━━━━━━━━━━━ ▪  WATCH YOUR BOY  ▪ ━━━━━━━━━━
```

There is a subtle posture difference when a cat urinates or defecates. If you observe your male cat straining to eliminate and you
are not sure he is constipated, you should consult with a veterinarian immediately. Male cats can get life-threatening urinary blockages, and straining to urinate may be the only sign they show.

product or you can get plain Metamucil and give your cat one to three
teaspoons a day. One tablespoon of canned pumpkin two to three times
a day also works as a laxative.

Kitty Gets Carsick

Whether it is stress or motion sickness, some cats vomit when they travel in a car. You can give a cat half a 25-mg tablet of Dramamine 30 minutes before travel to calm his stomach. This drug is an antihistamine, so
your pet may get sleepy. Removing your cat's food and water for a few
hours before travel also decreases the likelihood of vomiting during a
car ride.

Kitty Was Stung by a Bee

It is unusual for a cat to have an anaphylactic reaction to an insect bite
or sting, but it is normal for redness and swelling to occur at the site.
(An anaphylactic reaction is a severe and potentially fatal allergic reaction that can occur within seconds of contact to an allergen.)

Benadryl can be given to cats to help prevent the localized allergic
reaction that results from a sting. You can give half a 25-mg tablet to a
cat or 12.5 mg of the liquid. Be sure the medication you are using is
diphenhydramine only, because many antihistamine preparations also
contain acetaminophen, which can be life-threatening to a cat.

Chlor-Trimeton, the brand name for chlorpheniramine, can be used
for cats. It comes as a 4-mg tablet and a cat can take half a tablet, twice a
day. This antihistamine can be used for an allergic reaction or for itchy skin.

Encounters With Oil

Cats who go outside often crawl into spots they shouldn't. One of the
possible results is that they can become covered in oil or grease from

the underside of a car. These products will make the cat sick if he licks much of them off himself. Regular cooking oil is also too much for a cat to groom away himself.

A safe way to remove grease or oils from a cat's coat is to bathe the animal in Dawn dishwashing liquid. It is normally not recommended to use any type of detergent on a cat, but this one is safe because it does not contain phosphates, which are dangerous to cats.

A SPOONFUL OF SUGAR HELPS THE MEDICINE GO DOWN

One of the challenges of feline medicine is getting medications into our patients. As most cat owners know, their loving kitty can turn into a wild animal when it comes to taking medicine. There are some tips that can make medicating easier.

The most important aspect of getting medicine into a cat is the confidence of the owner. This may sound strange, but believe it or not, your cat knows when you are intimidated and will take full advantage of the situation. A positive attitude about getting the medicine into the cat's mouth is necessary for success. If you start the process with doubts, you will likely fail.

There Must Be an Easier Way

When I dispense medication to a client, if there are alternatives, I will ask if they prefer liquid or tablets. If a client is unable to give their cat the medication I prescribe, the cat may not get well, so I need to try to make medicating the cat as easy as possible for the owner. If an owner has not medicated the cat before, a doctor or staff member will give the cat the first dose and demonstrate the procedure.

MEDICATION TIPS

Varying the medicating routine can help. If you give medicine at the same time each day and go through the same preliminary steps to prepare it, your cat may get smart and be out of sight when it's time to give it to him.

Giving a treat as a reward after medicating can serve as positive reinforcement to the cat.

To administer liquids, insert the dropper into the corner of the cat's mouth and squirt slowly.

Medicating a cat is easier if you put the animal up on a table or a countertop. By doing so, you are taking the cat off his turf and giving yourself an advantage. The harder you try to hold a cat down to medicate him, the more he will resist, so minimal restraint is best. Wrapping a cat in a towel like a baby is necessary in some cases.

Liquid Medication

Liquid medications can be dosed with either an eyedropper or a syringe without a needle. How quickly you will be able to squirt the medicine into the cat's mouth depends on the volume that is administered. Small volumes, up to 0.5 ml, can usually be given in one squirt. Larger volumes may need to be split into three or more squirts, to give your cat a chance to swallow. You do not need to pry a cat's mouth open to give liquids. Simply insert the tip of the dropper into the corner of the mouth, lift the cat's chin and squirt slowly.

Owners frequently ask if they can mix the liquid medication into the cat's food. I generally do not recommend this, because cats have a great sense of smell. When they detect a foreign substance in their food, they will not eat. Many of the liquid antibiotic drops are fruity and have sweet tastes and smells. They are not the perfect complement to a tuna dinner.

Tablets and Capsules

Tablets or capsules can sometimes be crushed and successfully mixed into food, but learning how to directly pill a cat is better. When I teach owners to give pills, I ask whether they are right- or left-handed and then demonstrate with the same hand they will use. For example, I tell right-handed people to put the cat on a table parallel to their body with the cat's head pointing toward their right side. The cat's head needs to be grasped with the left hand around the cheekbones, and then tilted

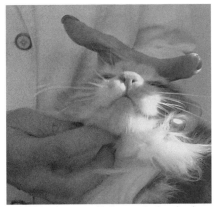

To administer a pill, first grab the cheekbones . . .

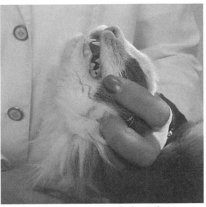

. . . point the nose toward the ceiling . . .

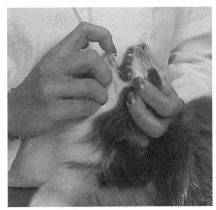

. . . open the lower jaw . . .

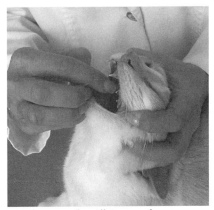

. . . then pop the pill in over the tongue.

so that the cat's nose is pointing toward the ceiling. When done cor-
rectly, the cat's mouth will automatically open, and the more coordinated right index finger can pop the pill over the back of the cat's
tongue while the middle finger holds the lower jaw down. In this situation, you are not opening the cat's mouth with your hands; you are
using leverage to position the mouth open. (A left-handed person
should turn the cat the other way and reverse the hand positions.)

Research has shown that if a pill or capsule is not followed with a
swallow of water, it can remain in the esophagus for hours. Certain pills,
such as the antibiotic doxycycline, cause severe irritation to the esophagus if they get stuck. If your veterinarian does not give you one, ask
for a small syringe to squirt water into your cat's mouth after pilling.

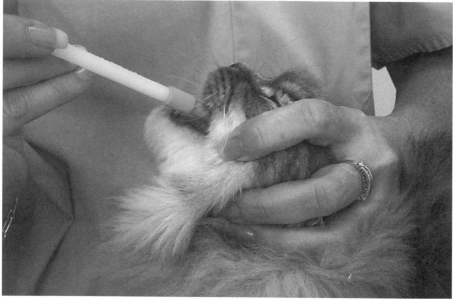

A pill gun can help you give your cat his medication.

Many cats will gag and foam after being medicated. This can be due to the bad taste of the medication, not swallowing initially or stress. Foaming is only rarely due to an allergic reaction to the medication, so do not panic if your cat begins to drool.

Plastic pill guns are available if putting your finger into the cat's mouth is dangerous or unsuccessful. Ask your veterinarian for one of these tools if you think you need it. Coating a pill with butter is another option. It will make the pill taste better and slide more easily down the throat. Some cats will lick up pills that are coated in hairball lubricant, because they like the taste of the lubricant so much.

Doesn't It Come Another Way?

More and more veterinarians are using compounding pharmacies. These pharmacies will take medications and reformulate them into liquids that cats prefer or into capsule sizes that are easier to administer. Some compounding pharmacies create medicated chews that are flavored treats containing medication. I must confess that one of my own cats is extremely difficult to medicate, and this form has been the answer. If you are having difficulty giving your cat a medication, find out if it can be reformulated.

DON'T GUESS

Never administer any kind of medication to your cat without first consulting your veterinarian. Do not assume a remedy that has been recommended in the past for a particular symptom will again be appropriate if the same or a similar symptom appears. Many medical conditions resemble one another, but their treatments may be very different. Don't guess at what treatment is right for your cat.

Using a compounding pharmacy can add to the cost of the medication, but it's worth it if you are then able to get the medicine into your cat.

Another form of medication becoming more widely used is transdermal. The medication is made into a cream that is applied to a hairless area, such as the inside of the ears. The biggest problems with transdermal medications are that they are not uniformly absorbed through the skin, there is no easy way to measure whether they are reaching therapeutic levels in the blood and it is not known if they are biochemically changed when they are absorbed. At this time, routine use of transdermal medications is cautioned except in cases where a response can be measured, such as lowering thyroid hormone levels in the blood of cats treated with transdermal methimazole.

A final option for the difficult-to-medicate patient is taking him to a boarding facility where trained staff administer the medication properly. However, sick cats seem to do better at home, where the stress levels are lower than at a boarding facility. So if you can medicate your cat yourself at home, it's worth the effort.

Chapter 7

How to Choose a Veterinarian

· ·

Most veterinarians have earned a four-year undergraduate degree and then attended veterinary school for four more years to earn their doctorates. All veterinarians receive similar basic training in veterinary school, and after graduation pick the type of practice and job they want. Veterinarians are well-educated professionals, and each has their own personality and level of experience.

If you have other pets or have had other pets in the recent past, you may have already developed a good relationship with a veterinarian. If you don't already have a vet, is a good idea to familiarize yourself with a veterinary clinic so that you can get your new cat checked out right away. If you have a positive experience, this clinic will be a resource for questions or problems that may occur later on.

SELECTION BASICS

If you live in a metropolitan area and look in the Yellow Pages, you will see listings for numerous veterinarians. How can you choose the perfect one? There are many factors to consider, and each of them will have a different value to you.

Location

We all have busy lives, so we often choose to work with businesses that are conveniently located for us. Each individual is willing to drive a certain distance to buy something or to receive a service, and this distance can vary depending on the situation. The same is true for obtaining veterinary care.

Depending on where you live, real estate costs and the availability of good locations will determine where veterinary practices are found. I think location is a valid reason to choose a veterinary clinic, because you are more likely to use services that are easier to obtain. You might want to consider investigating veterinary clinics that are close to your home or work, or are located along the way.

Face Value

The way a veterinary facility looks is a reflection on the philosophy of the clinic owner. A neat, clean facility requires more maintenance and care, which shows that the clinic is kept to a certain standard. You may infer that the doctors will want to take extra care and effort to treat your cat, because they care about appearances.

Consider visiting a veterinary clinic and touring the facility before bringing your cat there. If a doctor is proud of the clinic and how it is run, this should not be a problem, but it is best to call ahead so that you don't show up in the middle of an emergency.

A bigger facility is not always a better facility. The size of the facility is not as important as what it contains. A basic veterinary clinic has a reception area, exam rooms, a treatment area, a ward for cages, a surgery room, an isolation area, a pharmacy and the veterinarian's office.

First impressions are always important, but they need to be put in perspective. If you enter a veterinary hospital and there is a strong urine smell, it could be because a tomcat was just in as a patient (which is not a problem), or it could be due to urine-soiled floors and dirty litter boxes (which definitely *are* problems). Dirty counters and floors don't look good, and they may make you question the cleanliness of the areas where your cat will be treated. Do remember, though, that it is hard to control hair and debris in the middle of a hectic day at a veterinary clinic.

Is This a Full-Service Clinic?

Most veterinary clinics offer a variety of services, including:

- Behavior consults
- Boarding
- Dentistry
- Flea control
- Grooming
- In-house laboratory
- Medical care
- Nutritional counseling
- Pharmacy
- Surgery
- X rays

Some clinics also offer ultrasound, endoscopy and laser surgery. During the course of your cat's lifetime, there is a good chance she will need most of these types of services at one time or another. Having a competent full-service facility makes your life a little easier. If you use multiple services, the staff and doctors will become familiar with you and your cat and will be able to serve you better.

Depending on the size of the facility and the staff, services such as boarding and grooming may be available. Before boarding your cat, I recommend checking out the boarding area. Cages vary in composition and size, and you will want to have a good idea of the accommodations offered. If the cages are small in a boarding facility, find out if there is any opportunity for a cat to get out and stretch. The cleanliness and ventilation of the boarding area are more important than the size of the cage.

What About Referrals?

When choosing a veterinary clinic, it is a good idea to ask friends and neighbors who have cats for recommendations. You can consult with your state or local veterinary association, and you can even search for veterinarians who have a special interest in cats by browsing the web site of the American Association of Feline Practitioners (www.aafponline.org).

A veterinary clinic's reputation is very important, and conscientious doctors want to be respected in the community. If someone tells you to avoid a clinic, find out specifically why and evaluate the validity of the reason. It is always best to make the final judgment yourself.

FEELING COMFORTABLE

All of the factors I have just discussed are important when choosing a veterinary facility, but I think the most important factors are the customer service and communication offered to clients by the veterinarian and clinic staff. These less tangible qualities require extra effort and care.

Effective Communication

A client must be able to have effective communication with the clinic staff and veterinarian. Clear lines of communication will ensure that your cat receives the care you want, and that best service and treatment options available can be recommended.

Many people call around before deciding to use a veterinary clinic, and a decision to use a facility may be based solely on their conversation with a receptionist. If the receptionist is knowledgeable and friendly, you may feel comfortable going there without knowing anything about the veterinarian. This is a good example of how much a first impression can influence you. If you want to know about the doctor and the staff and get more information, just ask. A good veterinary receptionist spends time listening and talking to clients.

Was This a Good Experience?

During your first visit with the veterinarian, you can evaluate your experience by answering the following questions:

- Did the doctor handle your cat kindly and compassionately?
- Did you find the doctor easy to communicate with?
- Did the doctor have a professional appearance?
- Did the doctor listen to you?

- Did you understand your cat's diagnosis and the recommended solutions?
- If medication was prescribed, did the doctor or staff show you how to administer it properly?
- Did the doctor spend enough time with you and answer all your questions?

A good veterinary clinic will have a competent support staff comprised of receptionists, technicians and assistants. These staff members will be able to answer most of your questions or find out the answer if they are not sure. The veterinarian may not always be available to answer your questions outside of a scheduled visit, so it is worth asking a staff member. You might be able to get help right away.

The most highly trained staff member at a clinic, aside from the doctor, is the licensed animal health technician. These technicians have been educated in this specialty, have passed a certification exam and are legally able to perform many procedures. Their knowledge and training in animal care are comparable to those of registered nurses.

Does Price Matter?

Each veterinary clinic will have different prices for the services they offer. Veterinarians set their prices based on many factors, including facility, staff, level of expertise and continuing education, location, anesthesia and products used, and competition.

Some clinics try to bring you in the door by quoting a low price over the phone but then tack on extra costs for ancillary services that they require. It is important to try to compare costs for the exact same services, using the same drugs and techniques, if you are shopping around by phone and trying to decide which clinic has the best prices.

Do You Get What You Pay For?

I may be biased, but I do believe a good veterinarian is a professional who has to charge a fair price to be able to offer you high-quality services. If you want to have a procedure performed on your cat, you need to decide if price or quality is the most important issue. When low prices are charged, something has to be sacrificed. When fair prices are charged, you should be getting the best care. Note that veterinarians will often try to work out a payment plan for expensive, nonroutine procedures.

GET IT IN WRITING

If you are dropping a cat off for a procedure, or if a veterinarian recommends multiple treatments or procedures, ask for a written price quote if you're not offered one. This will protect both you and the veterinarian by ensuring that you both have the same expectations.

At a vaccine clinic, you might wait in line while a veterinarian goes down the row and injects animals without looking at them. Of course, getting a vaccine in this manner is relatively inexpensive, because no expertise or care is provided and there are no costs for maintaining a veterinary hospital. However, your questions won't be answered, and you could even be inadvertently hurting an animal who is not in good health. Taking your cat to a vaccine clinic may also stress her more than a regular veterinary visit, because she is not protected in a room by herself without other animals around. In this type of situation, you are getting what you pay for—not much.

Your Cat Is Unique

As I will describe in Chapter 8, the annual physical exam and consultation you have with a veterinarian will greatly benefit your cat's health and improve her longevity. These visits are certainly more important than a rigid vaccination schedule. There is great value to the information your veterinarian can provide when assessing your cat individually. Aside from the physical exam, you have a chance to discuss your cat's behavior and nutrition. There is also value in the doctor's observations of trends in your cat's weight, body condition and general health.

Many clinics offer wellness plans for cats. These plans are tailored for certain life stages. Wellness plans can provide a package of services at a discounted price rather than paying for each service separately. The plans are good deals if your cat can benefit from the included services but not if there are unnecessary add-ons. If you choose a wellness plan from a good veterinarian, you might be able to detect problems with your kitty as they arise and begin treatment at an earlier and more beneficial stage.

Veterinary Specialists

Although all veterinarians graduate from veterinary school with the same degree, some decide that they want to become more highly trained in a particular discipline and attain board certification. Currently there are 36 specialties in which a veterinarian can become board certified. About 11.5 percent of the approximately 65,000 veterinarians in the United States are board certified.

What Is a Feline Practice?

Veterinarians have the option of working on one or many species. Regular small-animal and mixed-animal practices are able to capably handle feline patients, but with the increasing popularity of cats as pets, many veterinarians are dedicating their practices strictly to felines. Any veterinarian can become a feline practitioner simply by treating only cats, so if you want to differentiate among veterinarians, you may want to check other credentials.

If you are interested in a feline-only practice, it's a good idea to contact the veterinarian and investigate what makes that practice special. A veterinarian can affiliate with three different organizations related to feline medicine. They are:

- American Association of Feline Practitioners (AAFP)
- Fellow Membership of the AAFP
- American Board of Veterinary Practitioners (ABVP)

Any veterinarian can affiliate with the AAFP and receive current information on feline care through their newsletters and conferences. The Fellow Membership is a subgroup within the AAFP comprised of veterinarians who have completed certain amounts of continuing education and have belonged to the AAFP for three or more years. Fellows are given the opportunity for even higher levels of continuing education in feline care and are involved with research grants and feline practice guidelines.

If a veterinarian truly wants to call herself a "feline practice specialist," the only way to achieve this status is by becoming board certified through the ABVP. Becoming board certified requires a lot of work and dedication, and I think it shows the optimal commitment to feline medicine.

HOW DO YOU FIND A BOARD-CERTIFIED SPECIALIST?

Board-certified specialists usually list themselves as such in their Yellow Pages listing. Your regular veterinarian can refer you to one if you ask. If these options are unsuccessful, you can contact the AVMA at www.avma.org/careforanimals/animatedjourneys/aboutvets/vetspecialists.asp or call (846) 925-8070. Local veterinary associations also have listings of specialists in their areas.

To become board certified in feline (or in canine and feline practice) through the ABVP, a veterinarian must have been in practice at least six years, completed a certain amount of continuing education, obtained letters of recommendation, written publishable case reports and passed a certification exam.

What if Your Cat Has a Special Problem?

Your regular veterinarian may not have the facilities or the experience to handle certain diseases your cat may face. In these situations, they may refer you to a board-certified specialist. Or you may decide yourself that your cat needs a second opinion, and it is always best to get one from a specialist. Some board-certified specialists have their own private practices, some work in groups and others work at veterinary teaching hospitals.

Some of the board-certified specialists who are frequently consulted are internists, surgeons, neurologists, ophthalmologists, dermatologists, cardiologists and oncologists. If you live in a metropolitan area, it is very likely one or more of each of these veterinary specialists is available in the surrounding area.

Emergency Providers

There are veterinarians who offer emergency services themselves and others who refer clients to emergency clinics that are only open after hours and on weekends and holidays. Some emergency facilities employ veterinarians who are board certified in emergency medicine and critical care. Make sure you know where the local emergency clinic is now; trying to find out later, when your cat is having an emergency, can be harrowing.

In a true emergency, if possible, take your cat to a facility that has a veterinarian and staff already on the premises and ready to help. The cost of emergency services is usually significantly higher than those received during regular business hours, but the same is true in human medicine.

Even though you may not be thinking clearly in an emergency, try to understand the diagnosis and the treatment options available. Question the veterinarian if you are unsure and be clear on your choices before making decisions.

Holistic Veterinarians

Aside from offering typical Western medicine, there are some veterinarians who practice holistic care. I will be the first to admit that traditional medicine and the tools that are currently available cannot cure all health problems. Because of this, some veterinarians are turning to alternative medicine.

Types of alternative veterinary care include:

- Acupuncture
- Chiropractic
- Dietary supplements
- Herbal remedies
- Homeopathy
- Nontraditional diets

If you seek alternative care, find out how the veterinarian has gained their knowledge. There are organizations comprised of veterinarians interested in holistic care, and some do have certification programs. You can learn more about them on the web site www.altvetmed.com. Many of the treatments may be effective, but there are not many conclusive scientific studies supporting their efficacy.

Chapter 8

Annual Health Care

Although cats are said to have nine lives, they only have one, and you can help that one along. In the wild cats do a good job of taking care of themselves, but housecats live much longer than their wild cousins.

The quality and length of a cat's life can be extended by routine health care. By making sure your cat receives regular veterinary examinations, needed vaccines, dental care and parasite control, you can offer your cat the best preventive health care.

DID YOUR CAT PASS HIS PHYSICAL?

Cat owners often ask me what they can do to provide the best possible care for their pet. I tell them two things: keep him indoors and be sure a veterinarian examines him at least once a year. Good owners can be very observant about their cats and notice important changes, but a veterinarian can objectively evaluate the animal regularly. It is difficult for owners to assess subtle changes, such as weight loss that occurs gradually over a period of time, but a veterinarian can consult records and monitor trends.

What's Involved in an Annual Exam?

A veterinarian should examine a cat annually, from the tip of his nose to the end of his tail. Each doctor may have their own routine when conducting a full physical exam, but the best exams are thorough exams. A full physical exam should include:

- Measurement of body weight
- Measurement of body temperature
- Evaluation of the eyes, ears and nose
- Opening the mouth and assessing the teeth and gums
- Palpation of external lymph nodes
- Evaluation of the coat and skin
- Evaluation of muscle tone and body condition
- Listening to the heart and lungs with a stethoscope
- Examination of the legs, paws and claws
- Palpation of the abdomen
- Examination of the rectum and genitalia
- Examination of the tail

Depending on the individual cat and how cooperative he is and the skill of the veterinarian, this examination can take anywhere from 2 to 10 minutes. In most situations, a veterinarian can conduct the exam without help, but when the patient is wiggly, scared or aggressive, more hands are needed.

When cats are hot or frightened, they are only able to sweat from their feet, because the footpads are the only body parts that contain moisture-secreting sweat glands. If you notice damp footprints on your veterinarian's exam table, you will know why.

Does It Hurt?

A routine physical exam is not painful to your cat. If the cat squawks and squirms, he is probably just resisting restraint rather than showing discomfort. Animals who have not been fully examined before by a veterinarian are generally less cooperative than those who previously have been examined, but some cats are so frightened that they act worse at each successive veterinary visit.

**A TRANQUILIZER
MAY HELP**

If you have a cat who acts up when taken to a veterinary clinic, you should consider medicating him beforehand with a mild tranquilizer. It is not good for the cat to be stressed, and it is more difficult—if not impossible—for the veterinarian to do a good job with an uncooperative patient. Let your vet know if you have tranquilized your cat. Also be sure to warn veterinary staff before they handle your cat if he has a history of fractious behavior.

Let the professional veterinary staff handle your cat during any veterinary visit. Many animals become scared and defensive when they are outside their own homes and become fractious. Owners are often bitten or scratched by their own cats when they try to help hold the animal during an exam. Experienced animal assistants and veterinarians are trained to manage these situations. The best way you can assist is by talking to your pet in a calm, reassuring voice.

At the end of a physical exam the veterinarian should discuss any abnormal findings and assess the general health of the cat. If you do not understand what the doctor has told you, be sure to ask questions. I like it when clients ask me questions, because then I know that they are paying attention to what I have told them.

I also like it when clients come to the physical exam appointment armed with questions. A veterinarian and her staff should be a resource for information on all aspects of caring for your cat, including nutrition and behavior. Write down any questions you have on these issues and bring them along to discuss during your cat's annual physical exam. This prevents you from going home and wishing you had asked the doctor something about your cat that you forgot during the appointment.

VIRAL TESTING

Testing for the feline leukemia (FeLV) and feline immunodeficiency (FIV) viruses may be part of an annual exam. Your cat's status regarding these two viruses should be known. There is an in-clinic screening test for these viruses, and it only takes a few drops of blood and 10 minutes to get results. If the result is positive, blood is sent to a laboratory for a confirming test. There are false positive results, especially for FeLV, so no decisions should be made about a cat until a second test proves or disproves the first result.

Cats most at risk for these viruses are strays, pet cats who go outdoors and cats who live in households with FeLV– or FIV–positive cats, since fighting and direct contact are the main routes of transmission. Although vaccination helps protect cats, those with a high risk for exposure should be regularly tested.

WHAT ABOUT VACCINES?

Vaccines are an important aspect of preventive health care. However, many people wrongly believe that vaccines are more important than the hands-on exam by the doctor. Low-cost vaccine clinics have flourished on this premise, and as a consequence many cats do not receive adequate health care.

For years, owners have mistakenly believed that vaccinating their cat every year was the best they could do in terms of health care, but this is not the case. Studies show that vaccinating cats annually may not be necessary. Some cats have adverse reactions to vaccines and are better off without annual boosters. Vaccinations are a complex subject and will be discussed in Chapter 9.

A CHESHIRE CAT SMILE

In a perfect world, cats would brush their teeth every day just like we do. The reality is that cats cannot brush their own teeth, and many owners are not willing, too busy or don't know how to brush their cat's teeth. Like humans, cats develop dental disease as plaque and tartar build up on their teeth. This can progress to gingivitis, which is inflammation of the gums.

As dental disease progresses, it can cause bacteria to enter the cat's bloodstream and affect other parts of the body. Some experts attribute the frequent occurrence of kidney disease in senior cats to long-term exposure to bacteria in the blood. Dental abscesses and infected jawbones may also be a result of dental disease.

Brushing Your Cat's Teeth

You can brush your cat's teeth, and there are many different products to use on cats. If you are able to brush your cat's teeth at least once a week, it will deter plaque and tartar buildup and therefore decrease dental disease. Here are some tips to follow for brushing your cat's teeth:

- Start brushing your cat's teeth at a young age to get the cat used to it.
- Use a small bristled pet toothbrush or fingerbrush without toothpaste during your first attempts.
- Try to rub the cat's teeth at the gum line two or three times a side, both upper and lower teeth.
- Add a pet toothpaste to the brush if you are meeting with success.

Do not use toothpaste made for humans on cats. Toothpaste for humans is not meant to be swallowed. Pet toothpaste can be swallowed and will not cause problems when ingested. Oral rinses or wiping with enzymatic pads are alternative methods of home dental care.

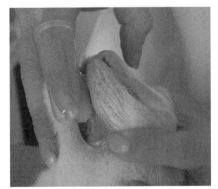

You can clean your cat's teeth with a fingerbrush.

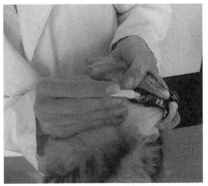

Or you can use a pet toothbrush.

Other Ways to Keep Teeth Clean

Dry foods tend to cause less plaque buildup than canned foods, so feeding some dry food can help the teeth. Feline diets that are formulated to prevent plaque buildup are available and can be fed as a maintenance diet or as a treat. Specific dental treats are also available, but none of these products will knock the existing plaque off the teeth.

Do You Need to Take Your Cat to a Dentist?

Your regular veterinarian should be able to provide routine dental examinations and care. Some veterinarians are able to perform restorations and root canals. Some can even perform orthodontics! If veterinarians choose to pursue it, they can be board-certified in dentistry.

During your cat's annual physical exam, his teeth and gums should be examined and evaluated. Your veterinarian should let you know the condition of your cat's teeth and if dentistry is needed. Each cat builds up plaque at a different rate, but almost all cats need to have their teeth professionally cleaned by the time they are four years old. How frequently the animal will need the procedure repeated varies, but many cats need their teeth cleaned every year. Cats with bad gums may even need cleaning every six months.

If your veterinarian tells you your cat needs "a dental," she is usually talking about cleaning, polishing, treating with fluoride and removing any infected, eroded or broken teeth. These procedures are performed with the cat under general anesthesia, but as an outpatient; the cat comes to the clinic in the morning and goes home at the end of the day. Your cat's teeth are cleaned the same way yours are, but unfortunately, cats are not willing to open up and say "ahhh."

When dentistry is performed properly, many precautions are taken. You should discuss any fears that you have regarding the procedure with your veterinarian. Age is not a valid reason to decline a dental procedure for your cat. Bad teeth and infection are harder on the cat's body than dentistry and anesthesia.

Even if your cat is eating well, it doesn't mean his teeth don't hurt. Owners frequently tell me how fabulously their cat is doing post-dentistry. They say they did not realize how uncomfortable their cat was until after the procedure was performed.

Pulling Teeth

When significant damage to a tooth has occurred, your veterinarian will likely recommend that it be extracted. Unlike in humans, it is very difficult to save a cat's damaged tooth with any type of filling material. Extractions can be performed during the same anesthesia used for the dental cleaning. A combination of hand tools and a power drill may be used to properly extract a tooth.

Cats do not have the same cosmetic need for teeth that we do, but their teeth do play a role in picking up food and holding it in their mouths. Owners naturally are very concerned about their cat's ability to eat if several teeth need to be removed, but believe it or not, even cats without teeth can eat dry food once their gums have healed. They can make a mess because food drops out of their mouths, but they are happy.

PARASITE CONTROL

There are two types of parasites: internal parasites, such as gastrointestinal worms, and external parasites, such as fleas. It is common for kittens and cats who go outdoors to have parasites, but adult indoor-only cats have little exposure to these bothersome creatures.

Intestinal Parasites

It is recommended that all kittens have their feces checked for worms. During a fecal examination, the sample is examined for worm eggs and protozoal parasites. The common intestinal parasites are:

Roundworms
Coccidia
Giardia
Tapeworms
Hookworms
Whipworms

Eggs for roundworms, hookworms and whipworms can be found by examining feces under a microscope. It is not common to see tapeworm eggs; you are more likely to see the worm segments. The segments look like rice when they are fresh (you'll see these crawling around under your cat's tail) and then like sesame seeds when they dry out (you'll see these in places where your cat has been sitting).

Over-the-counter de-worming medications are available that can be effective against some types of worms, but rarely are they effective against tapeworms. If you choose to use a non-prescription de-worming medication, read the label carefully to make sure you are treating for the right worm and giving the appropriate dose. If you don't know what type of worms your cat has, a visit to the veterinarian is advised.

Coccidia and giardia are protozoal parasites—one-celled organisms that can be seen under a microscope. Both are common parasites, but giardia is more difficult to find in a fecal examination.

All gastrointestinal parasites can cause diarrhea, but this symptom will not always be present. It is possible for your cat to have worms without you knowing it. During a routine physical exam, a veterinarian should look under the cat's tail to check for tapeworm segments. A fecal exam should be performed on all kittens, and during an adult cat's annual visit, it is a good idea to have a fecal sample checked.

Veterinarians can diagnose and treat intestinal parasites with medicine that's specific for the type of parasite your cat has. Some parasites can be eliminated with one treatment, but others need successive days of treatment or repeated treatment two weeks later. Parasites are not present in every fecal sample, so if your veterinarian recommends repeating a fecal check, she has a good reason.

Worms are not deadly to a cat, but they make absorption of nutrients less efficient and they can cause diarrhea. Small kittens with large numbers of worms are affected the most, and their growth and condition can be impaired. Protozoal parasites are more dangerous than

PARASITES UNITED

Fleas and tapeworms are two parasites that have a connection. Cats get tapeworms by ingesting fleas that are carrying tapeworm larvae. Cats who hunt can pick up tapeworms from eating rodents and rabbits carrying the parasites. Humans cannot get tapeworms from their cats; a human would have to either eat a flea to get the same tapeworms or ingest tapeworm eggs from the environment or in raw meat.

worms if uncontrolled, because they can cause dehydration and more severe diarrhea.

Cats do not carry pinworms. If you have a child with pinworms, do not blame your cat; they came from another source. Humans, though, can become infected with feline hookworms or roundworms.

Flee, Fleas!

Aside from causing discomfort to your cat, fleas can cause:

- Allergic dermatitis
- Anemia
- Tapeworms
- Discomfort to you and other pets

Cats are very sensitive to many chemicals, so any time you use an over-the-counter flea product, be sure to read the label and be careful. *Never use flea control products labeled for use with dogs.* They can be deadly to your cat. One common canine flea control chemical, called permethrin, causes tremors, seizures and shock in cats. It is best to get professional advice regarding flea control, and your veterinarian and her staff are a great resource.

In the 1990s, there were great advances in products that are effective against fleas. Some of the safest and most effective products are only available through veterinarians. Types of flea control products include:

- Flea combs
- Oral or injectable preparations or collars with insect growth regulators
- Spot-on adulticides
- Shampoos
- Dips
- Sprays
- Foams
- Powders
- Collars
- Interior home treatments
- Yard sprays

Program, Advantage, Revolution and Frontline are among the new products that have revolutionized flea control. Program is administered orally or by injection. The other three products are spot-ons, which means you place them on the back of the cat's neck. Although expensive and available generally through veterinarians, they are very safe, effective and work for up to a month. These products have made shampoos, dips, sprays, powders, collars and foams obsolete. Flea experts recommend using an insect growth regulator, such as Program, and an adult flea killer, such as Advantage or Frontline, in combination to prevent the emergence of resistant fleas.

Cats who stay indoors generally have fewer problems with fleas than cats who go outside. It is more difficult to control fleas if you have several pets. These factors are all important in deciding which flea control products to use. The flea has historically developed resistance to all products developed to eradicate it, so it will be interesting to see what happens with the newer products available. Will fleas continue to beat the system?

Fleas like to live in warm, moist environments. They can live inside all year round, and in warmer climates they can survive outside all year. The best way to monitor a cat for fleas is to comb him regularly with a flea comb. The comb will catch fleas in its teeth and also trap flea dirt (little black spots that are actually digested blood). If you find signs of fleas, continue to comb and try to pick them all off, or you can use the comb as a gauge of your success with other products.

Other Parasites That Can Make Your Cat Itch

Cats can be infested with other external parasites, including mange, mites and lice. Luckily, these feline-specific parasites are not usually contagious to humans. More information on these parasites is included in Chapter 15. Your veterinarian can make recommendations on ridding your cat of these parasites.

Chapter 9

Tell Me About Vaccines

When you get a vaccine reminder card in the mail from your veterinarian, you probably think it looks like a game of Scrabble. What are FRCP, FeLV and FIP? Many owners don't ask about what these letters stand for, and just tell the veterinarian to go ahead and give the cat all the shots she needs. I don't think this is a good idea.

As a cat owner, it is useful to have some basic knowledge about the diseases you protect your cat from with vaccines. You may be surprised to find out that vaccines are not as protective as you have been led to believe, and that annual vaccines may not be in your cat's best interest. The purpose of vaccinating is to "teach" the cat's immune system to fight specific infectious agents. Does the system need to be reminded every year?

HOW DO VACCINES WORK?

Antibodies obtained from their mothers protect newborn kittens from many diseases. This maternal immunity decreases between 8 and 12 weeks of age, and the kitten then needs other protection. The purpose of vaccinating is to "teach" the kitten's immune system to fight specific infectious agents. In almost all cases, vaccinating at 8 and then again at 12 weeks of age is adequate. Vaccination at these times provides protective immunity to the disease agents in the vaccine. This immunity protects against most symptoms connected with the disease agents but may not fully prevent infection. It can take up to 14 days after the vaccination for full immune function to develop. It is not known for sure how long the protective immunity lasts after that.

Annual vaccinations for cats have long been veterinary standard practice, and owners have been taught to vaccinate their pets each year. However, in the 1990s the veterinary profession began to question the need for annual vaccinations. This comes in light of new information regarding the duration of immunity derived from vaccines, and adverse vaccine reactions, including tumors, that may be associated with sites of vaccination.

The vaccine manufacturers have recommended annual re-vaccination based on studying the duration of immunity for a few weeks to months. They have not been required by the USDA to determine longer durations of immunity, except in the case of the rabies vaccine. Although rules have changed for establishing minimums, maximum duration of immunity studies are not required, so we do not know exactly how long a vaccine will protect a cat.

HOW DISEASES ARE SPREAD

Infectious agents are viruses, bacteria and fungi—microorganisms capable of causing disease. Infectious agent exposure can occur by many routes. Each agent has its own way of passing between cats. Airborne infections are more likely to affect cats housed in boarding facilities, catteries or shelters. Diseases that are spread by direct cat-to-cat exposure are more likely in cats who go outdoors, where uncontrolled contact between cats can occur.

Introducing a new cat into your home also has the potential to introduce infectious agents. This is especially true if the cat has come from a cattery or shelter. To try to prevent problems, isolate a new addition to the household for at least one week and have her examined by a veterinarian before introducing her to your other cats.

WHAT YOU SHOULD KNOW ABOUT VACCINATING YOUR CAT

In the mid 1990s the American Association of Feline Practitioners (AAFP) took a bold step and created an advisory panel on feline vaccines. They first published feline vaccination guidelines in January 1998 and then revised them in 2000. These recommendations base vaccine administration on a cat's individual risk factors, history and age. They question the necessity of vaccinating every cat every year for every disease.

The following information highlights some of the vaccination guideline recommendations. Your veterinarian may or may not be familiar with these specific guidelines, but discussing your individual cat's vaccination needs is important.

The AAFP Feline Vaccination Guidelines state, "The objective of feline vaccination protocols should be to vaccinate more cats in the population, vaccinate individuals less frequently, and only for the diseases for which there is a risk of exposure and disease." Assessing an individual cat's risk of infection is a cornerstone in developing a vaccine protocol. The three items that need to be evaluated are the cat, the cat's environment and the infectious agents the cat may be exposed to.

Evaluating Risk

When making a decision about vaccination, risk factors to consider are:

- Age of the cat
- Number of cats in the household
- Exposure to outdoor or free-roaming cats
- Whether the cat will be at a boarding facility
- Where the cat lives (cattery, shelter or private home)
- Whether the cat is shown or routinely goes out for other types of activities

Because they have immature immune systems, young kittens are more susceptible to disease than adult cats. Initially, kittens are protected by antibodies they receive through their mother's milk. The first milk a queen produces is called *colostrum*, and it is rich in protective antibodies. These antibodies provide maternal immunity and are absorbed into a kitten's system during her first 24 hours of life. Maternal immunity wears off by 12 weeks of age, and kittens must then develop antibodies on their own. Antibodies are developed after vaccination or after exposure to infectious diseases.

The number of cats in the home and the chance of exposure to other cats also play major roles in assessing risk. The chance of exposure to infectious agents in a household with one or two cats is significantly less than in a larger multicat household. Cats who go outdoors and come in contact with free-roaming or other indoor/outdoor cats face a higher risk of disease exposure.

Cats who are housed in boarding facilities, catteries, or shelters have a greater opportunity of being exposed to infectious agents. This is due to stress, crowding, and simply the number of cats in the facility. Cats who regularly go out to shows or on visits also are at greater risk. That's because cats who come from different environments can bring different infectious agents with them.

It can take up to 14 days post-vaccination for the full immune response to develop. So if you vaccinate your cat for the first time today, she will not have protective immunity until at least 14 days after the initial vaccine series has been completed.

The decision to vaccinate against a particular infectious disease agent should be based on reviewing the patient's risk assessment. Currently, vaccines exist to protect against 11 different infectious diseases in cats, and several manufacturers produce vaccines. The infectious diseases are:

- Rhinotracheitis virus (feline herpes)
- Calici virus
- Panleukopenia virus
- Chlamydia (pneumonitis)
- Feline leukemia virus
- Rabies virus
- Feline infectious peritonitis virus
- Bordetella
- Ringworm fungus
- Feline immunodeficiency virus
- Giardia

CORE VACCINES

The AAFP guidelines have created two categories of vaccines: core and non-core. A core vaccine is recommended for all cats. This recommendation is based on several factors, including severity of the disease, potential risk to humans, prevalence of the disease, and safety and efficacy of the vaccine. A non-core vaccine may be appropriate in certain situations, but is not recommended for all cats.

The four vaccines that have been deemed "core" are the ones that fight feline panleukopenia virus, feline rhinotracheitis virus (feline herpes), feline calici virus and rabies virus.

Feline Rhinotracheitis, Calici and Panleukopenia

This vaccine is most commonly known as the FRCP or three-way vaccine. The general recommendations for this core vaccine are:

1. Vaccinate kittens at their initial veterinary visit (at six to eight weeks)
2. Vaccinate again every 3 to 4 weeks until the kitten is over 12 weeks of age
3. Give a booster one year later
4. Booster every three years, unless the cat has a higher risk of exposure such as boarding or traveling to cat shows

Feline panleukopenia (FPV, also sometimes called feline infectious enteritis) is usually fatal to affected cats. It attacks white blood cells. The virus is shed in feces and transmitted through fecal-oral contact. Panleukopenia virus can contaminate cages, bowls and litter boxes and be spread through poor hygiene. Most vaccines available against this disease stimulate complete protective immunity. Clinical signs associated with panleukopenia can include fever, anorexia (loss of appetite), vomiting and diarrhea. Death can be rapid due to severe dehydration and electrolyte imbalances. The most characteristic finding is an extremely low white blood cell count when a complete blood count is run.

According to the AAFP report, there is some research to indicate that immunity is sustained for at least seven years after vaccination. However, the research is not definitive and the report recommends a three-year interval for now.

Feline herpesvirus and feline calicivirus are estimated to cause up to 90 percent of upper respiratory disease in cats. These diseases are rarely fatal but are extremely prevalent. Transmission occurs through sneezing and is spread through the air, by direct contact and by touching contaminated objects. The most common signs are sneezing, anorexia and conjunctivitis (inflammation of the tissues around the eyeball).

Feline herpes virus (FHV-1) does not cause disease in humans. (Humans can be affected with Herpes simplex, which causes fever blisters, and Herpes zoster, which is responsible for chicken pox and shingles.) Cats can develop chronic herpes virus infections that cause long-term, intermittent bouts of sneezing and conjunctivitis. Feline calici virus (FCV) infection can also cause limping or severe gum disease.

Currently the most common form of vaccination is injectable, but the FRCP vaccine is also available as a topical vaccine. Topical vaccines may be administered intranasal (in the nose) or intraocular (in the eye). The benefits of topical vaccinations are that they stimulate more rapid protection and there is no chance of developing an injection site tumor. This type of vaccine can be useful in boarding, cattery, and shelter situations when quicker and more frequent upper respiratory disease protection is needed. The disadvantages of topical vaccination are that they can trigger mild sneezing, coughing and conjunctivitis.

Vaccination against herpes and calici viruses does not prevent infection but does reduce the severity of the associated clinical signs. In addition, the calici virus vaccines that are currently available probably do not protect against all forms of the virus.

Rabies

Rabies is among the core vaccines because of the potential for a rabid cat to bite and infect a human and because the disease is lethal to cats. Rabies is transmitted primarily through bite wounds, and the virus is present in the saliva of infected animals. Clinical signs associated with rabies infection are behavioral changes, pupil dilation changing to constriction, drooling and stumbling. Normally friendly and affectionate animals can suddenly and unexpectedly turn aggressive and agitated when infected with rabies, and normally aloof cats can become very friendly. Infected animals can die within four days of developing clinical signs. Once clinical signs develop, there is no effective treatment for rabies.

The incubation period of the virus—the time from bite wound to clinical signs—varies. Rabies is introduced into a cat's body by a bite, spreads up nerves to enter the central nervous system, then spreads to other body tissues. For some reason, the virus likes to go to the salivary glands.

A few species of animals are more likely to carry rabies than others. Always use caution if you come in contact with bats, skunks or raccoons (especially during the day, since these are normally nocturnal animals), because they are common carriers. These animals can carry rabies but not develop clinical signs.

The rabies vaccine can be administered to kittens over 12 weeks of age, one year later and then every three years, according to the AAFP recommendations. However, the frequency of vaccination may be governed by state and local laws. Certain states require cats to be vaccinated against rabies, while others do not. Each locale may also have different rules regarding quarantine of animals who bite humans. Healthy, nonvaccinated animals who bite humans may be under observational quarantine for 10 or more days.

NON-CORE VACCINES

The decision to vaccinate with one or more of the non-core vaccines should be based on the previously discussed risk factors. Non-core vaccines are not necessary for all animals. They should be considered for those cats who have a risk of exposure to the particular disease. You should discuss the pros and cons of vaccination with your veterinarian.

Chlamydia

Chlamydia felis is a bacterial infection that causes upper respiratory disease in cats. Transmission is through direct cat-to-cat contact. The most common clinical sign is severe conjunctivitis. Vaccination does not prevent infection with chlamydia, but it can lessen the associated clinical signs.

Don't be alarmed when you hear about feline chlamydiosis caused by *Chlamydia felis*. This is not the same agent that causes venereal disease in humans—that bacteria is *Chlamydia trachomatis*.

The prevalence of *Chlamydia felis* in the United States is considered to be low. Some veterinarians believe vaccines for chlamydiosis produce a relatively high adverse reaction rate. Chlamydia is commonly the fourth component of a four-way booster vaccine (FRCPC—Feline rhinotracheitis, calici, panleukopenia and chlamydia), so be sure to ask your veterinarian what she is giving your cat.

The AAFP report says that because this upper respiratory disease is not severe and most cats can be treated, and because the adverse events associated with the use of the vaccine are relatively high, its routine use is not recommended. At this time, the duration of immunity conferred by the vaccine is unknown, and annual vaccination is recommended only for those animals who are at risk.

Feline Leukemia Virus

Feline leukemia virus (FeLV) is a potentially fatal virus of cats. It is passed by direct cat-to-cat contact or by a queen to her kittens. Testing and identifying FeLV-positive cats is essential to controlling infection. Clinical signs associated with FeLV are nonspecific and can range from anemia to immunosuppression to tumor formation. FeLV can cause latent infections, which hide quietly in the cat but may cause clinical signs months to years later.

Vaccination is recommended for cats who test negative for FeLV but live in environments where it is possible for them to be exposed to the virus. Some veterinarians recommend that all kittens receive initial vaccinations to FeLV because their exposure risk may not yet be defined. For example, even though you do not want your kitten to go outside, things might change and the animal could end up going out at some point in the future. You would want her to be protected in this situation. However, FeLV vaccine is not recommended for cats who have little or no risk of being exposed to other infected cats.

The vaccination schedule for FeLV is as follows:

1. Vaccinate at nine weeks of age or older.
2. Repeat vaccine four weeks later.
3. If the cat remains in a high-risk environment, continue vaccinating annually.

Cats at risk for exposure to FeLV include cats who go outdoors, stray cats, feral cats, open multicat households (new cats are often brought into the home), FeLV-positive households and households with unknown FeLV status. Vaccination confers fair to good immunity in some cats, but this varies among vaccine manufacturers. The current vaccines do not induce protection against the disease in all cats, so preventing exposure to infected cats is still the best way to prevent FeLV. FeLV vaccines have been associated with adverse reactions. They are administered in the left rear leg muscle.

Feline Infectious Peritonitis

Feline infectious peritonitis (FIP) is a fatal virus of cats. The mode of transmission is not definitively known, but the current theory is that it is passed through oral or nasal contact with feces infected with feline enteric corona virus (FECV), a common virus, which then mutates in certain individuals to become FIP. A mutation is a change in the virus's genetic code. Transmission may also occur from a queen to her kittens.

Circumstances that may influence whether or not FECV mutates to FIP are:

- Age of cat (most susceptible cats are less than one year old)
- Breed of cat
- Genetics
- General health
- Immune status
- Environmental stresses

On its own, FECV is not a life-threatening virus, but it can cause diarrhea and is contagious among cats. In some catteries and multicat households, every cat will have an antibody titer (which indicates exposure) to a feline corona virus. This corona virus titer test does not differentiate between FECV and FIP, so it is not a reliable screening test. This, in turn, makes assessing protection from vaccination difficult. The efficacy of the FIP vaccine has been controversial, because some studies show that it offers some protection against the disease and others fail to demonstrate significant protection. The AAFP report states that since the vaccine has not yet been proven to be beneficial, it is not recommended. Fortunately, the incidence of FIP in pet households is low.

The AAFP panel was unable to come to a consensus regarding what constitutes an "at-risk" cat. One at-risk category would be cats in households where FIP has previously been diagnosed, and vaccination in that situation could protect cats who have not already been exposed.

This vaccine is administered initially in two doses, three to four weeks apart in cats over 16 weeks, and then boosters are given annually. FIP vaccine is only available in an intranasal form.

Bordetella

Bordetella bronchiseptica is a bacterium that is better known for causing kennel cough in dogs. It has been cultured from cats with upper respiratory infections and also in cases of pneumonia. Within the veterinary community there is debate as to the necessity for this vaccine, because

Bordetella does not seem to cause disease in many pet cats. The highest incidences of Bordetella are in purebred catteries and in animal shelters. Pet cats do not appear to be at a high risk for infection.

In addition, the AAFP report states that the efficacy of this vaccine has not been independently evaluated, and how often to revaccinate has not yet been determined. Routine vaccination is not recommended, but it is reasonable to consider vaccinating cats in environments where the infection is present. Discuss this vaccine with your veterinarian.

Ringworm

A vaccine for *Microsporum canis*, one of the fungi that causes ringworm (also known as dermatophytosis) is available. *M. canis* can affect both cats and humans, but generally infections are limited to skin rashes. Although ringworm is a somewhat common infection, most veterinarians feel that the vaccine is not needed as a preventive. In addition, the AAFP report states that vaccination has not been demonstrated to prevent infection or to eliminate the disease-causing organisms from infected cats.

A complete ringworm treatment program aimed at preventing and eliminating the fungus can involve oral and topical treatment of the cat and household premise treatment. The vaccine is probably most useful as an addition to this program, when infections linger despite aggressive measures.

While the vaccine may decrease the visible lesions on the cat's skin caused by the fungus, it does not necessarily make a cat less contagious to others. The duration of immunity conferred by the vaccine is questionable as well.

Feline Immunodeficiency Virus

This virus suppresses a cat's immune system and makes him more susceptible to infections. Feline immunodeficiency virus (FIV) is most often transmitted between cats through biting. Stray, intact male cats who fight are the most common carriers. Casual, nonaggressive contact is unlikely to spread infection. There is no cure for the virus, and most infected cats live for years without showing any clinical signs. When cats do become sick, it is due to the secondary infections their immune systems can no longer fight off.

A vaccine to protect against FIV became available in the fall of 2002, but unfortunately it is not an ideal vaccine and at this time it is not recommended for routine use. Vaccinated cats will test positive on routine screening tests for FIV, thus making it impossible to distinguish cats who have been vaccinated from cats who are actually sick. Also, the vaccine does not protect against all of the common strains of FIV, so its efficacy is questionable.

If you have a cat who is at high risk for exposure to FIV, discuss the vaccine with your veterinarian. High-risk pet cats are those who come in contact with outdoor, free-roaming cats.

Giardia

The vaccine against giardia, a protozoan parasite, was developed for use with dogs but has also been used with cats. The efficacy of the vaccine in cats is unknown. Giardia is most often passed via contaminated water, but cats can also become infected by ingesting infective cysts in the environment during grooming. This vaccine is not recommended routinely. However, infected cats who were vaccinated had less severe signs of the disease and were contagious for shorter periods of time, so vaccination could be considered as adjunct therapy for resistant infections that are not responding to drug therapy.

KITTY NEEDS SHOTS

What does all this mean? Well, your cat does need shots, and what shots she needs should be based on a thorough risk assessment that you and your veterinarian do together. One year after the initial vaccine series has been completed, the cat should receive booster vaccines. Vaccination in subsequent years should be based on the cat's risk of exposure and individual lifestyle.

My vaccine recommendations for kittens are:

- Feline rhinotracheitis, calici, panleukopenia (FRCP) at 8 and 12 weeks
- Feline leukemia (FeLV) at 10 and 14 weeks
- Rabies if required by law, or if the cat goes outside at 12 to 16 weeks

My vaccine recommendations for adult cats are:

- FRCP annually to every three years
- FeLV annually if the cat has a risk of exposure to outside cats
- Rabies every three years if required by law, or if the cat goes outside

ADVERSE RESPONSES TO VACCINES

The AAFP has standardized vaccine administration sites to help identify causes of local adverse reactions, and to aid in the treatment of vaccine-associated sarcomas. Abbreviated, FRCP vaccines should be administered over the right shoulder, FeLV in the left rear, and rabies in the right rear; all should be administered as far down the leg as practical. If a veterinarian has given different vaccines in different sites, then it's clear which vaccine caused the problem.

Adverse responses to vaccination do occur. Common reactions that go away on their own include pain or swelling at the injection site. If any type of lump, bump or swelling occurs in an area where you think a cat may have been vaccinated, you should have it examined by your veterinarian. It is not uncommon for a temporary reaction to occur, but if it lasts for more than a month, it should be evaluated by cytology (a microscopic examination of cells to determine the cause of a disease) and/or biopsy (removing tissue for microscopic examination and diagnosis). You should consult with your veterinarian if any type of reaction occurs after your cat receives a vaccination.

Allergic reactions can occur in some cats after they have been vaccinated. These reactions can range from mild to severe anaphylaxis (potentially fatal allergic reaction). If your cat has previously had any type of allergic reaction, you should alert your veterinarian and discuss possible preventive measures. These could include splitting up multiple vaccines so the cat has just one vaccine at a time, medicating with an antihistamine and/or a corticosteroid before the cat gets the vaccine, or even discontinuing certain vaccines.

If your cat has an allergic reaction or vomiting and lethargy after vaccination, discuss splitting up the combination vaccines into individual vaccines that are given at different times. The AAFP report discourages the use of polyvalent vaccines (a single shot that contains the vaccine of more than one illness), other than combinations of FPV, FHV-1 and FCV, because using combination vaccines may force doctors to administer vaccines that a cat does not need. In addition, as the number of agents in a single vaccine increases, so does the possibility of adverse vaccine reactions. Your veterinarian may even be able to split up the FPV, FHV-1 and FCV vaccines into single doses that your cat can receive at different times if she is particularly sensitive. These vaccines must be ordered specially, but they are available.

Another possibility is discontinuing vaccination altogether. The purpose of vaccines is to help protect your cat, not make her sick.

Have Vaccines Been Linked to Cancer?

An increasing incidence of a type of tumor called fibrosarcoma has been noted in locations on the body where vaccines are routinely administered to cats. Research is being conducted and a national veterinary task force exists to determine the relationship between vaccines and fibrosarcomas. The incidence of vaccine site fibrosarcomas is estimated at one to three out of every 10,000 vaccines administered, which is an extremely low number.

The general consensus in the veterinary community is that the risk of disease from not vaccinating is much higher than the risks associated with vaccinating, but a rethinking of how, when, where and why we vaccinate cats has resulted. This is an extremely controversial issue for veterinarians, and not all veterinarians are in agreement over which vaccine protocols should be followed.

The information obtained so far from past and current research has failed to pinpoint a specific cause of fibrosarcomas in cats. Initially it was thought that aluminum adjuvants (chemicals added to a vaccine to enhance its effectiveness), were responsible for tumors, and many cases seemed to be linked to adjuvanted FeLV and rabies vaccines. Further study showed that this is not necessarily true and that many types of vaccines and other injectable products resulted in tumors in some cats. Even vaccines that use newer recombinant DNA technology, touted as unlikely to produce tumors, have been linked to tumors.

At this time the consensus is that the genetics of the individual cat may be the most important factor in whether a cat develops vaccine-associated sarcoma. Certain cats may carry genes that predispose them to form tumors at sites of inflammation. Vaccines and other drugs create various levels of inflammation where they are injected. Research is ongoing, and should eventually find the answer.

Chapter 10

Common Surgical Procedures

There are a few elective surgeries that you will consider during the first year of your cat's life. These are routine procedures that are performed at a veterinary clinic. Any surgical procedure involves some risks and anesthesia, but experienced veterinarians and modern drugs decrease the potential for problems.

Many cat owners look for deals on the price for these procedures, and prices can vary greatly. Keep in mind that to use good anesthesia and other drugs, monitor the patient adequately and perform the procedure in a sterile and painstaking manner does involve expense. When prices are low, corners need to be cut somewhere.

TELL ME ABOUT DECLAWING

In veterinary medicine, declawing cats is a controversial issue. Declawing is a surgical procedure that permanently removes the last joint of each toe, including the claw. Scratching is a normal cat behavior, and some people feel that it is cruel and inhumane to remove a cat's body parts just because it makes the owner's life easier.

Many owners routinely have kittens declawed to prevent problems later, when the cat may use prized household possessions as scratching posts. Not every cat engages in destructive scratching though, and most cats can be trained to scratch in an appropriate spot.

In Britain it is illegal to declaw a cat. The British have stricter laws than Americans do regulating cosmetic and surgical procedures being performed on animals.

What's Involved in Declawing?

When a cat is declawed, the last joint on each toe is amputated. Many people think declawing involves cutting the nail very short or just removing the nail the way we might have a toenail removed, but it actually requires removal of bones. That means the cat's paw pads must be cut open, the joints severed and the pads reclosed. There are a few different surgical techniques to do this, and each veterinarian has his or her preference.

Most of the time, only the front claws are removed during a declaw procedure, but in some situations owners ask that all four feet be done. No matter which surgical technique is used, there is some pain involved with declawing. If an owner wants to declaw a cat, I urge them to do so at a young age (between 8 and 16 weeks). The pain associated with the procedure is much less in smaller, younger animals.

Injectable and/or inhalant anesthesia is required for the surgery. The recovery period varies and depends on the size and age of the cat. It also depends on the use of pain relievers and the occurrence of any complications.

Some veterinary clinics use a laser, rather than a scalpel blade, to declaw cats. Lasers cut and cauterize tissue at the same time, so healing may be faster. Laser procedures are significantly more expensive because of the cost of the equipment used. There are other variations in techniques. Some veterinarians stitch up the toes after the bones are removed, some apply sterile surgical glue and others just bandage the foot.

After a cat has had declaw surgery, the paws may be wrapped, and the animal may be hospitalized for one or two nights. Using shredded or pelleted newspaper litter for the first few days after surgery helps to keep small particles (from clay or clumping litter) out of the surgery sites.

Veterinarians can use pain-relieving drugs to help with discomfort after surgery. Oral pain relievers can be prescribed, but the application of a patch that continuously releases small amounts of a painkiller is becoming more and more popular. Ask your veterinarian about post-operative pain relief if you declaw your cat.

Is Declawing Cruel?

There are different opinions regarding declawing. I personally think it is a painful procedure, and before declawing your cat, you should try to train him to use a scratching post. If a cat is being destructive or injuring you with his claws, and you have bought the cat a suitable scratching post (tall enough, sturdy enough, of a suitable material) and placed it in a spot where your cat likes to scratch, and a serious attempt at training is not successful, and you are going to keep the cat inside, declawing may be a valid alternative. It should not be done routinely without a sincere attempt to first train the cat to redirect his natural instincts.

Many humane groups and the Cat Fancier's Association condemn declawing, but it is a personal choice for each cat owner. Some breeders and cat rescue groups will require you to sign a contract stating that you will not declaw any cat you buy or adopt from them.

During the recovery period it is common for cats to be hesitant to jump, and they may hold their paws up in the air when sitting. These signs indicate the cat is in pain. Owners are frequently concerned after the surgery when their cats show these signs, but they need to understand that it takes time for healing and calluses to form around the newly exposed bones and nerve endings.

Declawing Alternatives

The most basic alternatives to declaw surgery are trimming a cat's nails every few weeks and training the animal to use a scratching post.

Vinyl nail caps, called Soft Paws, are available. They cover the cat's normal nail with a smooth cap, thus preventing nails from causing damage, and last about a month. Many veterinarians carry this product and will apply the caps for you. Take-home kits are available if you want to apply them yourself.

Digital flexor tenectomy is an alternative surgical procedure, but not one that I favor because I don't think there are enough benefits. Instead of amputating the bone in the toe, a small piece of the tendon that controls claw movement is removed. It prevents the cat from pro-truding or retracting her claws, and it is a less painful procedure since no bone is removed. When this procedure is performed, the cat's toe-nails still need to be trimmed regularly because the animal cannot con-trol them and the nails will not wear down.

Side Effects of Declawing

It is rare for physical complications to arise from declawing, but it is always a possibility. Infections are not common, and they do respond favorably to antibiotic treatment. Swelling of the paws can occur and is controlled with bandaging. If a veterinarian uses careless surgical tech-niques, a toenail or part of a nail can regrow. Noticeable regrowth may not be apparent for years following surgery, but presents as swollen toes with areas that drain fluid, or have pieces of nail sticking out.

Studies show that declawed cats do not bite any more than clawed cats. Declawing does not directly change a cat's behavior, either. Declawed cats can still climb (but not as well), but their ability to defend themselves is curtailed, so they should not be allowed outside unsupervised.

PREVENT A PATERNITY SUIT

Part of being a responsible owner is sterilizing your cat, whether the cat is male or female. Men who own cats are sometimes empathetic about their male cat and do not want to castrate him, but this is ridiculous. Cats have sex to reproduce, not because they derive any pleasure from it.

Neutered cats live happier, healthier lives and make much better pets than intact animals. If you have ever smelled the urine of a tomcat, you will understand why you would not want one in your home. Once tom-cat urine soils something, the odor cannot be removed. It is even hard to deal with the smell of tomcat urine after a litter box has been emptied!

HIGHER RISK

Two deadly viruses, feline leukemia virus and feline immunodefi-ciency virus, are much more common in intact male cats. This is because the viruses are passed by direct contact, especially through biting—and biting and fighting occur most often between two male cats. Neutering can help prevent the spread of these diseases.

What Is Neutering?

When a male cat is neutered, both testicles are surgically removed. In doing so, the main testosterone-producing organs are taken out of the body. Testosterone is responsible for:

- The terrible odor of tomcat urine
- Wide facial jowls
- Thicker skin
- Increased territoriality
- Marking territory by spraying
- Aggressive tendencies, including fighting between male cats
- The tendency to roam farther from home
- Stud tail, a greasy spot at the base of the tail

All of these problems are eliminated or at least decreased by neutering. A male can no longer produce sperm without testosterone, so he is infertile, as well. And the cat has no chance of developing testicular cancer and a much lower chance of developing prostate problems.

Will Neutering Change Your Cat's Personality?

Neutering does not change any of the good aspects of a cat's personality. It can take the aggressive edge off an animal, but an affectionate male will love you (perhaps even more) after being neutered. The evening after surgery your cat could still be feeling the effects of anesthesia and may act differently, but that wears off on its own by the next day.

The beneficial effects of neutering are not seen immediately, and if you neuter a kitten who has not reached puberty, you will not see any changes. Neutering a young animal prevents behavioral and odor problems. If you neuter a cat who has reached puberty, it will take a few weeks for behaviors and odors to change as the testosterone level declines.

Owners sometimes ask me whether their cat could have a vasectomy instead of castration. Although one of the purposes of neutering is to prevent reproduction, the main reasons are to decrease the undesirable behaviors associated with testosterone. If a cat had a vasectomy, testosterone would still be present and so would the associated undesirable behaviors.

When Should You Neuter?

The general recommendation for neutering a cat is at six months of age. This is before an average cat reaches puberty. Many humane groups and breeders will neuter kittens, if they have two testicles in their scrotums, at eight weeks of age, to ensure that the cats never mate. This early-age neutering is considered safe, and it does not cause problems later on in life.

Most veterinarians neuter cats as an outpatient procedure: The animal will come in the morning, have surgery and then go home the same evening. Neutering is a surgical procedure usually performed under injectable anesthesia and does not require stitches. There is little aftercare, and a post-surgical visit is not needed.

Cats With Only One Testicle

All male cats have two testicles, so if they are not in the scrotum, they are somewhere else. During normal development, the testicles move from inside the abdominal cavity to outside into the scrotum. When this does not occur, the testicles are considered retained. Most male kittens are born with testicles in their scrotums. If testicles are still retained at eight months of age, it is unlikely they are going to descend.

Cryptorchid is the term used to describe a cat with only one testicle present in the scrotum. The term *monorchid* may also be used. If a male cat has neither testicle in the scrotum, he is called a *bilateral cryptorchid*.

Retained testicles still produce testosterone, but cryptorchid cats are less fertile than normal cats. Because testosterone is present, these animals should definitely be neutered. Cryptorchidism is heritable, and animals with this trait should not be bred.

The surgical procedure for a cryptorchid cat is similar to a spay (described in the next section). The retained testicle is either going to be in the abdominal cavity or somewhere along the path through which it would normally descend, such as the inguinal canal. This procedure costs more than an uncomplicated neuter, because the surgery needed to find the testicle takes longer and is more complex.

PREVENT UNWANTED PREGNANCY

Cats are very efficient at reproducing, and once a female feline has reached puberty, she is sexually mature and can reproduce. Female cats usually reach puberty around six months of age, but during the spring mating season and in multicat households, puberty occasionally comes earlier.

Female cats exhibit some bizarre behaviors when they go into heat. Most cats get very friendly, rub up against you and other animals in the family and stick their rear ends up in the air. During a heat cycle they may howl and writhe on the floor, even looking as if they are in pain. Cats do not bleed when they are in heat. At my veterinary clinic we frequently get calls from new cat owners who are in a panic after observing these behaviors in their cat.

Cats are seasonally polyestrus. Their heat season generally runs from February to September, and females can have a heat cycle every two weeks during this time unless they are bred or stimulated to ovulate. This explains how cats can produce a new litter of kittens every few months.

What Is Spaying?

The technical term for a spay is *ovariohysterectomy*, which means surgical removal of the uterus and ovaries. Most veterinarians perform ovariohysterectomy surgery with the cat as an outpatient. Although this is a routine procedure, people often do not realize that an abdominal surgery is being performed. The cat is placed under general anesthesia, usually with some type of gas anesthetic, and an abdominal incision is made. The ovaries and the uterus are removed, and the surgery site is closed with stitches. The stitches may be absorbable or you may have to return to have them removed in 10 days, depending on the preference of the doctor.

When to Spay

If possible, you want to spay a cat before she goes through even one heat cycle. This can be achieved by spaying at six months of age. As with male kittens, early-age sterilization is possible as young as eight weeks of age. There are no benefits to having a cat experience a heat cycle, and certainly there is no benefit for a cat to have a litter of kittens. These are myths.

Meanwhile, there are benefits to spaying a cat before her first heat cycle. Female cats who have experienced one or more heat cycles are more likely to develop malignant breast cancer than spayed cats. Spaying before six months also spares her (and you!) the difficult experience of a heat cycle. In addition to the behavioral changes I've already mentioned, cats in heat may groom excessively, experience loss of appetite, and may also urinate outside the litter box.

The Benefits of Spaying

Aside from stopping annoying heat cycles, spaying will prevent your cat from contributing to pet overpopulation. Each year tens of thousands of cats are put to death in the United States because no one wants them.

Intact female cats are at risk for pyometra—a life-threatening uterine infection. An infection like this cannot occur if there is no uterus.

Spayed female cats are less likely to roam in search of a mate, and they are less likely to be aggressive. As with male cats, sterilizing will not change any of the positive aspects of the animal's personality.

There are always some slight risks involved with surgery and general anesthesia, but for a young, healthy cat they are negligible. If complications were to occur, they would most likely be due to an underlying health or congenital problem or poor surgical techniques. This is another reason why you should think about factors other than cost when choosing a doctor to perform the surgery.

An ovariohysterectomy is an irreversible procedure, so once a cat is spayed she will never be able to reproduce. Some cat owners want to experience the birth of kittens, especially if they also have children. Instead, I think they should visit their local animal shelter and see what happens after the miracle of birth when homes are not found for the kittens.

On occasion, the owner of a purebred kitten tells me that he wants the cat to have kittens so that he can recoup what he spent to buy the cat. I think this is a terrible reason to breed a cat. Responsible breeders sell purebred kittens as pets because they are not up to show quality. They want you to sign a contract that you will not breed the animal. You should buy a pet purebred cat because you want a cat of that breed, not because you want to make money. If any complications arise during the pregnancy and measures such as a caesarian section are needed, the litter will end up costing you a lot of money.

HERNIAS IN CATS

Some kittens are born with hernias, which are holes in a muscle that should normally be solid. These defects are usually not very serious and can be corrected with a simple surgical procedure.

The most common type of hernia is an *umbilical hernia*. It occurs when the kitten's belly button does not close properly after birth. The hole that is left is usually quite small and it appears as an out-pocketing at the middle of the belly, covered by skin. If you touch it, it feels soft. You can even reduce the hernia temporarily by gently pushing the abdominal fat back into the small hole in the body wall with your finger.

Umbilical hernias are not an emergency, and they can be repaired when the animal is sterilized. Repairing an umbilical hernia involves putting a few stitches in the abdominal wall and the skin. A spay incision can usually be extended to include and then close an umbilical hernia. In a male cat, a hernia repair will be at a different site than the castration surgery. If your cat has an umbilical hernia, ask your veterinarian about repairing it at the time of sterilization.

Another type, called an *inguinal hernia*, appears as an out-pocketing in the groin region. Abdominal fat or organs can push out of this hole in the abdominal wall. Inguinal hernias can be a congenital defect (one a cat is born with) or they can occur as a result of a physical trauma. Inguinal hernias are usually not emergencies, but because they can enlarge, they should be repaired.

Two other hernias are occasionally found in cats. These are *diaphragmatic* and *pericardial-diaphragmatic hernias*. These types of hernias occur in the chest cavity and are diagnosed with an X ray. You might suspect one of these in an animal who is having some difficulty breathing. Breathing is affected because abdominal organs that would normally be held back by an intact diaphragm (the muscular band separating the chest and abdominal cavities) are able to move into the chest cavity and compress the lungs.

Diaphragmatic hernias are most often due to trauma. The muscle tears away from the body wall. This injury needs to be surgically repaired. Diaphragmatic hernias should be repaired as soon as it is safely possible.

The risk with any hernia is that if it gets larger, organs can get trapped in abnormal locations and be damaged. It is rare for an umbilical hernia to get larger, and if surgery is not performed, it could simply close by developing scar tissue with a bubble of fat protruding, or it could stay open throughout a cat's life and continue to feel like a soft out-pocketing. The risk with a diaphragmatic hernia is severe impairment of breathing.

Pericardial-diaphragmatic hernias are congenital defects. In this condition, the diaphragm is connected to the pericardium, which is the sack surrounding the heart. This malady sounds serious and looks terrible on an X ray, but the surgical repair can be more dangerous than living with the defect.

A pericardial-diaphragmatic hernia should be left alone unless it affects the animal's ability to breathe or compromises digestive functions. Some kittens born with this defect never show signs, because their bodies slowly compensate as they grow.

Chapter 11

Pregnancy and Queening

Cats are very efficient at reproducing and are able to have several litters a year with multiple kittens in each. Most cats go through puberty at an early age—somewhere between five and nine months. Females can be fertile for about seven years, while males may be able to reproduce for 11 years or more.

The large numbers of feral cats (cats who have returned to a wild existence) demonstrate that in an uncontrolled environment, cats will keep reproducing. Today's methods of sterilization are surgical and thus are not easily applied to the vast numbers of feral cats. Researchers are working on new methods of feline contraception, including oral medications and even vaccines. These methods will help stop kitty overpopulation in the future.

THE ESTROUS CYCLE

Most females reach puberty around six months of age and cycle every two weeks until they are bred or induced to ovulate. The cycle begins with proestrus, which lasts one to three days. This is the stage when female cats start showing they are ready to mate, but they will not yet allow males to mount them. Restlessness, increased vocalization, facial rubbing and rolling are the not-so-subtle female signals.

Estrus is the period of sexual receptivity that follows. The behaviors that began in proestrus become more apparent, plus the female will now permit copulation. If there are no tomcats and therefore no mating, estrus lasts about 10 to 14 days, then the cat gets a break for 2 to 3 weeks, then estrus returns. Repeated estrus can be annoying for owners, because there is nothing that can be done to calm the cat's behaviors. It is also stressful for the cat, who cannot control her urges to find a mate. Cats have been known to lose their appetite and sleep poorly during estrus.

When a female cat is in estrus, she does not bleed like a dog; rather, she has changes in behavior. The changes can include:

- Increased vocalization
- Rolling on the ground and crying
- Lying on her belly with her rear end pushed up in the air
- Acting more affectionate
- Attempting to escape the house and get outside
- Urinating outside the litter box, often on vertical surfaces

Metestrus occurs the day after estrus ends. During this time females aggressively reject male approaches. Pregnancy follows if fertilization occurred during mating.

Anestrus is the quiet part of the estrous cycle. It occurs between periods of estrus and during the late fall, when the seasonally polyestrus cat does not cycle.

THE ACT

Male cats have the ability to be continually sexually active once they have reached puberty. Females, however, are only sexually active when they go through their heat cycles.

Female cats will only accept a male mounting them and copulating when they are in heat (estrus). If a female is not in heat, she will not stand still for a male. If she is in heat, she will allow a male to mount her, then, after intromission occurs, she will bite and strike at him to leave her alone.

Female cats are *induced ovulators*, which means the act of copulation stimulates them to release their eggs. They can ovulate more than one egg during each breeding and can be quite unparticular about their partners, allowing several males to mount them during estrus. This makes it possible for different males to sire different kittens in the same litter. A female may allow four or more breedings (with the same or different males) to occur during a few days of a heat cycle. Intact tomcats are ready to do their duty at all times, but they are not the decision makers. They may attempt to mount females who are not in heat, but they will be rebuffed. As a dominant behavior, some male cats even try to mount other male cats.

An average healthy male is usually fertile. Problems with male reproduction may be caused by:

- Lack of libido
- Low sperm counts
- Hair caught around the penis
- Cryptorchidism
- Lack of coordination

If someone is trying to breed a male cat, they will most likely put him with an experienced female for the first attempt. Often when two kitty virgins are put together, neither knows what to do and the male can get frustrated and lose interest if he is not successful.

Most professional cat breeders keep one or two intact males in their catteries with four or more females. Keeping a tomcat can be a smelly experience, and because one male can breed with several queens (unspayed female cats), fewer males are needed to have a good breeding program.

The entire mating process of cats can last a few short minutes and can be repeated several times within a day. Cats do not care who their partners are, and the female could care less about the male after he has done his duty.

If you have ever observed cats mating, you've likely noticed that it is a rough activity. The tom will mount the female and bite her on the back of the neck. After intromission, the queen will scream, turn around and bite the male until he releases her.

WHEN YOUR CAT IS PREGNANT

If she's in heat and given the opportunity to be with an intact male, chances are a female cat will get pregnant. The average cat's gestation period is 63 to 65 days. There are many physical changes a female cat will experience during a pregnancy.

The tom takes no role in raising his kittens, and some toms are even aggressive toward kittens. On the other hand, a queen will be very protective of her babies.

You may remember Scarlet, the mother cat who made headlines in 1996. Scarlet entered a burning building five times to save her five kittens, although she was severely burned in the process. A mother cat will also protect her kittens from you. If you are caring for a feral queen, be careful of how much you handle her kittens, because she may reject them. She may also become aggressive with you if you try to handle them in her presence.

Signs of Pregnancy

An inexperienced cat owner may be unaware of the signs of heat. Some cats put on more of a show than others. If you have a cat who has come in and out of heat and suddenly seems to stop cycling, she's probably pregnant.

Cats do not need much special care to maintain a pregnancy. They seem to do fine on their own. Other than allowing a queen to eat what she wants and protecting her from illness and parasites, you can leave the rest to her.

Because cats are only pregnant for about nine weeks, things happen fairly quickly. The progression of signs is:

1. Increased appetite and weight gain
2. "Pinking up" of the nipples within two weeks of being bred
3. More rounded appearance of the abdomen
4. Engorgement of the mammary glands

A veterinarian can palpate a female cat's abdomen and confirm a pregnancy three to four weeks into gestation. The fetuses develop bones at about 54 days, so an X ray at this time can tell how many kittens will be born. An average litter contains three to five kittens, but in reality, litter size can vary a lot. X rays do not damage the fetuses, and they can be useful if you want to know what to expect. Ultrasound is useful for confirming pregnancy as early as two to three weeks, but it is not reliable for determining the number of fetuses.

Can You Terminate Your Cat's Pregnancy?

Purebred cat breeders know when their females are cycling and try to plan their pregnancies. Ideally, they mate cats who are not too closely related and try to produce offspring who are healthy and have certain characteristic traits. Owners of pet cats may want their female to have a litter, and they have the right to do so—although again, I suggest that they visit their local animal shelter first and see what happens when there are too many kittens and not enough good homes.

Sometimes time just gets away from a cat owner, and his cat is in heat and pregnant before he's had a chance to have the animal sterilized. What are the options?

Ovariohysterectomy

Pregnant cats can be safely spayed, but most veterinarians do not like performing the surgery when a cat is close to full term. If you know your cat is in heat and that she got outside, she can be spayed before significant fetal development has occurred.

If you are already noticing that the cat's belly is distended and she looks pregnant, chances are the cat is at least six weeks pregnant. The risks of spaying a pregnant cat are slightly higher than performing the surgery on cat who isn't pregnant, due largely to blood loss and increased surgery time. However, if you do not want kittens, spaying at this time should be considered.

Medical Intervention

Currently there are no safe and reliable medications that will terminate a feline pregnancy, and if your queen is bred by an undesirable male, you are out of luck. Drugs are available that will cause the pregnancy to abort, but they can also harm the queen. For the safety of the queen, let her have the kittens if you are set on breeding her again; otherwise, spay her.

Kitty Birth Control

Veterinarians do not prescribe birth control medications for cats because of the risks they carry. There is one drug, however, that is occasionally used by breeders to suppress a female's heat cycle. Called megesterol acetate, it is a synthetic hormone.

Because most hormones have multiple functions, there are possible side effects to any hormone treatment. Cats who receive even small doses of megesterol acetate run the risks of:

- Developing diabetes mellitus
- Developing pyometra, a uterine infection

- Mammary gland enlargement
- Developing mammary cysts
- Mammary cancer
- Decreased fertility

THE BIRTH OF KITTENS

You can expect that a queen will soon be delivering when she shows interest in creating a nest for the kittens to be born. You can express milk from her mammary glands a day or two before she delivers.

You can monitor a queen's rectal temperature twice daily if you are not sure when she will deliver. Twenty-four hours before delivery, the body temperature of most queens drops to about 99°F.

What Happens During Labor?

The length of a queen's labor depends on whether she has had kittens before and how many kittens she is having. The period from the start of contractions to the end of labor can be minutes, hours or even a day if several breedings were responsible for the litter.

You may observe a mucus plug being passed when a cat begins labor. Contractions will follow and kittens will be born. The queen will lick and remove the sac from the kitten; if she does not, the kitten can suffocate and you need to intervene. The queen will then bite off the umbilical cord that connects the kitten to the placenta.

When kittens are born, they weigh only a few ounces and are extremely fragile. They are very dependent upon their mother for survival because their eyes are closed, their ears are not completely developed and they can only crawl.

The queen may continue her labor and produce more kittens. She will continue to lick and clean the kittens that have been born and gently nudge them toward her nipples so that they can begin nursing. Kittens are able to nurse within an hour of being born.

Kittens receive their initial immunity to disease by absorbing antibodies present in their mother's colostrum. Kittens are only able to absorb the antibodies in colostrum during their first 24 hours of life. It is therefore very important for kittens to nurse from their mothers as soon after birth as possible.

The queen may eat the placentas, and as unappetizing as this looks, it is very normal. She may have a vaginal discharge for up to two weeks

RESPONDING TO A DIFFICULT LABOR

Just like humans, cats can experience problems with delivery. *Dystocia* is the term used to describe difficulty during the birthing process. A cat who has a prolonged, nonproductive labor, has gone 67 days without going into labor or has a kitten stuck and protruding from the vulva would be considered in dystocia. A weak or sick queen, a kitten turned backwards in the birth canal, a kitten who is too large to pass through the birth canal and a dead kitten in the uterus holding the others back are all causes of dystocia.

If a queen is having contractions for an hour without producing any kittens, seek veterinary help. A veterinarian will take an X ray to see where the kittens are and to see if there are any abnormalities. He will also check the queen's blood to see if she is having any problems, such as low calcium or low blood sugar, which would prevent her from having normal contractions. If ultrasound is available, this test can check for fetal heartbeats and distress.

A doctor may induce the queen's labor with drugs or even consider performing a cacsarian section, depending on the situation. If there are no apparent problems, the first step is to induce labor. If induction is not successful, a caesarian section is necessary. When surgery is performed, there is increased risk that the kittens will not survive.

after giving birth. The discharge might look like blood or might even be green and mucoid, but it should not look like pus. If it looks like pus, consult your veterinarian.

If you have a queen who likes to roam, try to confine her in a room with her kittens so that they aren't neglected. Also be careful about flea control. If a queen has fleas, they can jump to the kittens and cause life-threatening anemia.

Examining Newborns

Unfortunately, kittens can be stillborn. If a kitten is not crying and wiggling after the placenta has been rcmovcd, pick her up and try to see if she is alive. You can *gently* shakc her upside down to try to clear any mucus from hcr mouth and throat. Touch the chest to check for a heartbeat. Check for jaw and muscle tone by opening the mouth and moving the limbs, and if all feels limp, the kitten is probably not alive.

Within a few hours after the kittens are born, you should look them over for any apparent birth defects or you can take them to your veterinarian for an assessment. Things to check:

1. Open the mouth and look for a hole in the roof of the mouth. This is called a cleft palate.
2. Check to see that there are four legs and a tail.
3. Check the umbilical area and make sure a hole is not present at the abdominal wall.
4. Check under the tail and see if there is a rectum and a set of genitalia.

Kittens who are unhealthy at birth generally do not survive. Queens may abandon or cannibalize kittens who are not healthy.

RAISING AN ORPHAN

Mother nature knows best, and kittens who are cared for by their mothers have a better chance of survival than orphan kittens who are raised by humans. If you find kittens who have been abandoned by their mother or have kittens who are not being cared for by their mother, be prepared for a lot of work and possible disappointment. But if all goes well, there are few more rewarding experiences than raising an orphan kitten into a healthy cat.

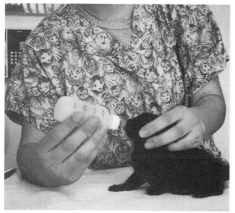

A special bottle with kitten milk replacer is used to feed an orphan kitten.

Feed Me

Newborn kittens need to eat every two to three hours. They have very small stomachs and require small amounts of food regularly. Do not give cow's milk to a kitten, because it will cause diarrhea and dehydration. You need to use a commercial kitten milk replacer. There are several brands available through veterinarians and pet supply stores. There are also pet nursing bottles with small nipples. Kitten milk needs to be fed warmed, but not hot—just like the milk you would give to a human baby.

Potty Me

Kittens do not have control over their urination and defecation until they are about four weeks old. From birth until that time, their mother normally stimulates them to eliminate by licking their genitalia. Of course, you don't have to go this far; you can simulate this action by using a warm, damp washcloth or cotton ball, turning the kitten over, and gently rubbing the genitalia until urine and feces pass. This should be done after each feeding.

Keep Me Safe and Warm

Kittens do not have any body fat to keep themselves insulated. They usually pile on top of each other next to their mom and share her heat. If you have an orphan, you need to keep her warm using a hot water bottle or a heating pad set on low; both should be covered with a towel. Make sure the kitten has a way to crawl off the heating pad or bottle if she becomes too hot. Except when you are handling her, a newborn kitten should be confined in a small box with a towel in an area free from drafts. Because newborns cannot see, it is essential to know where they are at all times to keep them out of trouble.

Orphans are weaned in the same manner as kittens raised by their mothers. They can be introduced to a gruel of meat baby food at four weeks of age. Litter box introductions are also recommended at this time.

Behavior problems are common in orphaned kittens because they miss out on being trained by another cat. Orphans tend to bite more, be less tolerant of restraint and play roughly. They would not get away with these actions if their mother, siblings or other cats were around. Other cats teach manners and appropriate responses by biting back, reprimanding with their paws and demonstrating by example. Exposing orphans to humans and other cats at a young age helps. Don't allow an orphan kitten to bite you or play with you in an aggressive manner. It only reinforces bad behavior.

Chapter 12

How to Care for a Senior Cat

Cats do not live forever, although we'd like them to. When you have shared your home with a cat for many years, he becomes an integral member of the family, and you develop strong emotional attachments. Cats provide undemanding and unending love. They are always there for you.

You can prevent many problems that could shorten your cat's life by following the suggestions about care that are offered in this book. Cats are very good at disguising their problems, so as they age, you need to be even more attuned to changes in their everyday activities and behaviors. Early detection of problems is the key to improving your cat's longevity and quality of life.

HOW LONG WILL MY CAT LIVE?

There are many formulas for calculating a cat's age in relation to human age. An old standby is that seven cat years are equal to one human year. Actually, in her first few years a cat does a lot more growing up than that. So the first few years of a cat's life are equivalent to more than

112

seven human years, and the later years are equivalent to fewer. The table on page 114 compares the age of a cat with that of a human.

Owners want to know what the life expectancy is for their cat, and in general I tell them it is between 13 and 15 years, especially if the cat stays indoors. However, we have many 19- and 20-year-old patients, and our oldest is 24! If a cat goes outside, her life expectancy is shortened because of the increased risks outdoor cats face. She is exposed to more diseases and dangers, such as poisons and cars.

There are many different opinions on when a cat is "old." There is no consensus on the age at which a cat becomes a senior, but a Panel Report on Feline Senior Care published in 1999 by the AAFP recommends beginning a senior preventative health care program by 7 to 11 years of age. By 12 years almost all cats start experiencing the effects of aging.

There are certain diseases and conditions that occur in cats due to degenerative processes. Each cell in an animal's body is programmed to last a certain amount of time, and this programming is different for each individual animal. Some animals look and act old at 10 years, while others are fit and spry at 15 years. Certain organs seem to age at a faster rate than others, and this is perhaps why certain health problems are more common in older cats.

SENIOR HEALTH CARE PROGRAM

Cats need the most veterinary and owner care when they are kittens and when they are seniors. Middle-aged cats are usually healthy and take pretty good care of themselves and can get by with once-a-year visits to the vet for their physical exams.

SENIOR CARE PROTOCOLS

The Panel Report on Feline Senior Care published by the AAFP recommends health care protocols based on a cat's age and clinical signs. For cats 7 to 11 years and up, twice a year physical examinations and annual diagnostics are recommended. Other issues that are addressed in the report are behavioral changes, pain relief, anesthesia concerns, nutrition, dentistry and coping with the death of a pet. An awareness of all of these issues is essential to providing optimal care to senior cats.

CAT YEARS	HUMAN YEARS	CAT YEARS	HUMAN YEARS
1	16	11	58
2	21	12	62
3	26	13	66
4	30	14	70
5	34	15	74
6	38	16	78
7	42	17	82
8	46	18	86
9	50	19	90
10	54	20	94

Regular veterinary examinations will objectively note small, gradual changes, which can add up to significant changes over a period of time. Even if you've lived with your cat for years, you may not notice subtle changes that occur in her conformation and health as she ages.

A preventative health care program for healthy animals may include a complete history and physical exam and some diagnostic testing, including a CBC, blood chemistries, viral testing, urinalysis and measuring blood pressure. I think it's beneficial to start a program like this around nine years of age.

By establishing baseline values on body condition and organ function, you can detect changes as the animal ages. If a cat has an illness, she should be monitored at least every six months.

WHAT MAY CAUSE YOUR KITTY'S DEMISE?

Although you may not like to think about it, it's a good idea to be familiar with the kinds of problems a senior cat can develop. As with any disease, early identification and treatment can help slow the progress of the disease and prevent related maladies. There are six diseases that are particularly common in senior cats:

1. Hyperthyroidism
2. Chronic renal failure
3. Hypertension
4. Cancer
5. Diabetes mellitus
6. Inflammatory bowel disease (IBD)

Liver disease, heart disease, neurological diseases and lung disease are also found in senior cats, but their frequency is greater in geriatric humans than in cats.

Hyperthyroidism

Hyperthyroidism is very common in senior cats and is usually the result of a benign growth on one or both of a cat's thyroid glands, which are located in the neck. The thyroid glands produce hormones that affect general metabolism and organ function, and overactive glands make excessive levels of hormones.

Hyperthyroid cats produce too much of the thyroid hormones. They can have ravenous appetites but still lose weight. They may have rapid heart rates, arrhythmia (irregular heartbeat), vomiting and diarrhea. This disorder is diagnosed by a blood test, and treatment is aimed at suppressing the gland medically or removing the overactive tissue by surgery or radiation. Chapter 18 contains much more information about hyperthyroidism in cats.

Chronic Renal Failure

Chronic renal failure is a degenerative process that slowly impairs the important functions of the kidneys, which filter the blood and produce urine. They are also responsible for water and electrolyte balance in the body. Kidney function is measured through urinalysis and blood testing, but these tests don't even start to indicate problems until more than 50 percent of all kidney function has been lost.

Cats with chronic renal failure typically drink a lot, urinate a lot and lose weight. As kidney disease progresses, the cat becomes thin, dehydrated and develops a terrible odor from the mouth.

Treatment of chronic renal failure is aimed at maintaining an animal's hydration and electrolyte balance as well as controlling some secondary problems that are associated with kidney failure (these can include anemia, dental disease and weight loss).

SOUNDS SIMILAR, BUT . . .

Don't confuse hyperthyroidism with hypothyroidism, in which the thyroid glands produce too few hormones. Hypothyroidism is rare in cats. Symptoms include lethargy, weight gain and a dull coat.

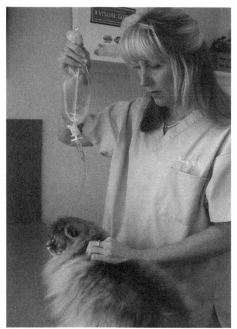

Owners are often able to administer subcutaneous fluids at home to treat kidney disease and dehydration. A needle is placed under the skin between the shoulder blades, and sterile fluid is given.

You can help prevent kidney disease by feeding your senior cat a good diet that does not over-acidify the urine and providing plenty of clean, fresh water.

The kidneys are organs that do not regenerate, so once they are damaged, disease will progress. By intervening with diet, fluids and other treatment, the process can be slowed but not cured. It is hard to know how quickly problems will progress, so monitoring changes in blood urea nitrogen (BUN) and creatinine will give a veterinarian an idea of the stage of degeneration. BUN and creatinine are products that are present at higher levels in the blood when cats have kidney disease. However, as I've already mentioned, abnormally high values of these products are not even detectable until more than 50 percent of kidney function has been lost.

If it is detected in the early stages, kidney disease can be managed, possibly for years. Management requires active owner participation and care, including fluid supplementation.

Chapter 20 contains more information about renal problems in cats.

Hypertension

High blood pressure (hypertension) does occur in cats. Most often it is secondary to hyperthyroidism or chronic renal failure. Testing a cat's blood pressure can be tricky, because cats are generally stressed when they go to a veterinary clinic and stress increases blood pressure. Hypertension can be addressed by controlling the primary disease that caused it, and by using oral medications.

Chapter 16 contains more information about hypertension in cats.

Cancer

Cats are living longer now than they ever have, and this has increased the incidence of cancer. Cancer is new tissue produced by the unregulated growth of cells. The cause of most cancers in cats is not known—just as it is not known in humans. Some types of cancer progress rapidly, while others are slow to spread. Some types are external and can be observed by owners, and others are detected when a veterinarian is palpating an animal during a physical examination.

There are veterinary oncologists who specialize in animal cancer treatment, and each year leaps and bounds are made in cancer treatment. Many of the same types of drugs and therapies used for humans are available for cats. And new, gene-based therapies are being studied as possible treatments for pets even before they are being studied for humans, as cancer care centers for both people and animals team up to find the best ways to fight this terrible disease. The prognosis is different for each type of cancer and for each individual cat. The treatments available for cancer include:

- Chemotherapy
- Surgery
- Radiation
- Cryotherapy (freezing the cancer cells)
- Immunotherapy

The goal of treating cancer in animals is to prolong life while maintaining a good quality of life. It is not simply to keep an animal alive. If an animal is having problems handling the treatment, it is changed or discontinued. Veterinarians do not want the treatment to be worse than the disease.

UNDERSTANDING THE LINGO

Neoplasia is another term used to describe cancer. *Neo* means new, and *plasia* means abnormal growth. There are two types of neoplasia: benign, which means nonaggressive and unlikely to spread and cause problems; and malignant, which means aggressive and likely to spread (metastasize) to other organs.

Cancer will cause a variety of clinical signs, depending on where the cancer is. Most cats with cancer will have weight loss, elevated white blood cell counts and anemia. The blood tests available today are not geared to specifically detect cancer. Testing for cancer markers in the blood of cats is not as advanced as it is in humans, but expect the technology to be available in the future.

Diabetes Mellitus

A cat with diabetes mellitus is unable to properly use glucose, which is the major source of energy for the body. The cat will eat food and produce glucose in the blood, but that glucose will not be transported into cells for nourishment, so even though the cat is eating, her body starves.

The clinical signs associated with diabetes are similar to those of chronic renal disease. Diabetic cats have voracious appetites, and they typically drink a lot of water, urinate a lot and lose weight.

The condition arises when the islet cells of the pancreas are unable to produce enough insulin to metabolize the glucose. Insulin is the hormone that allows glucose to enter cells in the body. Most diabetic cats need to be given insulin injections twice a day. Chapter 18 contains more information about diabetes in cats.

Inflammatory Bowel Disease

Inflammatory bowel disease (IBD) is a problem that affects the lining of the stomach and/or intestines. Cats with IBD typically have vomiting and/or diarrhea that does not respond to conventional remedies. To definitively diagnose IBD, biopsies of the stomach and intestine are needed. Biopsies can be obtained using an endoscope (a tube with tiny instruments at the end that is passed down the cat's digestive tract—under anesthesia, of course) or through exploratory surgery.

Treatment for IBD involves reducing inflammation, controlling infection and, usually, long-term medication. The prognosis for cats with IBD is good, but IBD can progress in some animals to a type of cancer called intestinal lymphosarcoma. Chapter 14 contains more information about IBD in cats.

Liver Disease

The liver is a vital organ responsible for digestion, vitamin and mineral storage, metabolic processes and removing wastes from the bloodstream. If it is not too severely damaged by disease, the liver can regenerate.

In a geriatric cat, the liver can become inflamed, infected or cancerous and stop functioning normally. Signs of liver disease include jaundice (yellowing that is especially visible in the eyes), vomiting, weight loss and anemia.

Blood tests and palpation of the liver provide clues, but most liver disease can only be diagnosed by a liver biopsy. Biopsies can be obtained through exploratory surgery or with a needle guided by ultrasound. Chapter 14 contains more information about liver disease in cats.

Heart Disease

Cats do not develop arteriosclerosis—clogged arteries that impair blood flow to the heart and lead to heart attacks in humans. Instead, most feline heart disease occurs in young and middle-aged cats. When a geriatric cat experiences heart failure, it is usually in connection with another illness.

As mentioned earlier, a common disease in older cats is hyperthyroidism, and when this condition is not controlled, heart failure can occur. The heart muscle simply wears out after being overstimulated for a period of time. When the heart fails, the rhythm of the heartbeat is affected, fluid can pool in the chest and circulation can be impaired.

Signs of heart disease include weakness, panting, open-mouth breathing and coughing. Diagnostic tools available to evaluate heart disease include X rays, ECG (electrocardiography) and ultrasound (echocardiography). Chapter 16 contains more information about heart disease in cats.

Neurological Disease

Seizures are periods of abnormal electrical activity in the brain. If an older cat has a seizure, possible causes may be hypertension, metabolic imbalances or cancer. When routine diagnostic testing does not pinpoint a cause, other tests are available.

To evaluate the neurological system of a cat, tests may include a cerebral spinal fluid tap (CSF), magnetic resonance imaging (MRI) and computer-assisted tomography (CAT scan). Chapter 19 contains more information about neurological disease in cats.

Cognitive dysfunction is another neurological disorder occasionally seen in senior cats. It is characterized by disorientation and confusion, disturbances of the sleep-wake cycle, reduced social interaction and loss of housetraining. These signs must be present in the absence of hormonal or metabolic imbalances, medical diseases and other neurological problems to make the diagnosis. The diagnosis is tentative

DO CATS HAVE STROKES?

Strokes are not very common in cats, so when neurological signs are present, other diagnoses need to be considered. A stroke occurs when oxygen flow to the brain is impaired and brain cells are damaged. A stroke could affect an animal's ability to walk, eat and eliminate, so if improvement in clinical signs is not seen within a few days, the prognosis is poor.

without a brain scan and cerebrospinal fluid (CSF) analysis—a laboratory test that examines a sample of the fluid surrounding the brain and spinal cord. The drug selegiline (l–deprenyl) is used to treat cognitive dysfunction, because it can increase dopamine levels in the brain (dopamine is a chemical transmitter that carries nerve signals across the spaces between nerve cells).

Lung Disease

Cats who have had life-long asthma or long-standing infections can develop scarring in their lungs. As they age, the scarring can progress and cause respiratory collapse. Cats can die suddenly from respiratory collapse. If an animal's lungs are unable to inflate properly, oxygen cannot enter the blood and the animal can suffocate.

Fluid also prevents the lungs from expanding, and certain disease processes can cause fluid to build up in the lungs (pulmonary edema) or within the chest cavity (pleural effusion). Both of these are potentially life–threatening conditions.

Cats who are having problems breathing will often sit upright, cough, breath with their mouths open and clearly appear to be in distress. They need immediate veterinary help. X rays of the chest cavity and removing a small amount of fluid or lung tissue with a needle for examination (called needle aspiration) can help diagnose the cause of lung disease. Chapter 13 contains more information about lung disease in cats.

KEEPING YOUR OLD FRIEND COMFORTABLE

As different parts of the body wear out, it may be difficult for a cat to maintain her regular activities. If you have an older cat, you want to be sure to make things as easy as possible for your old friend.

It is common for vision and hearing to be impaired as a normal part of the aging process, although it is unusual for a cat to go completely blind solely due to aging. If vision is compromised, the animal can usually see better in daylight than at night. She will do better if important items such as food bowls and the litter box are always kept in the same areas where she can easily find them.

Although it is best to keep all cats indoors, it is extremely important to do so if your cat is deaf. Complete deafness occurs occasionally in older cats. You should not let a deaf cat outside alone, because she will not hear noises that would normally alert her to danger, such as the sound of approaching cars.

The Importance of Water

Because kidney disease is so common in older cats, maintaining good hydration can make a big difference in how an older cat feels. At my clinic, we teach many owners how to give their cats fluid injections under the skin at home to help maintain or improve their pet's hydration. This process is called *subcutaneous administration* of fluids. (The word subcutaneous is derived from *sub*, meaning below, and *cutaneous*, meaning related to the skin. Instead of going directly into a vein, fluids injected in this manner are absorbed by the blood vessels under the skin.)

It is difficult to make a cat drink under the best of circumstances, but it is even harder when the animal is dehydrated and weak. Depending on the cat and the owner, giving subcutaneous fluid injections can be easy. If this is something you would be willing to try, you should discuss the procedure with your veterinarian.

Senior Nutrition

Because they are not building muscle and are less active than younger cats, senior cats need less protein and fewer calories. As a cat ages, the digestive and absorptive processes of the gastrointestinal system can become less efficient. Many companies produce "senior" or "geriatric" diets formulated for these situations. However, an active, healthy senior cat does not automatically need to be eating a senior diet. Discuss your cat's condition with your veterinarian before you switch her diet.

Dental disease is common in older cats and can affect how much and what a cat will eat. Dental health should be assessed at each veterinary visit, and the diet changed to accommodate the cat's dental function.

Softer foods that require little or no chewing may help an older cat. For a cat with a poor appetite, dense foods that provide a lot of nutrition in a small quantity can be appropriate. It is always important for a senior cat to eat and at least maintain her body weight.

Arthritis

It is inevitable that joints will develop at least some mild arthritic changes over time. Arthritis, or degenerative joint disease (DJD), can cause pain and restrict a cat's movement. If a cat cannot get around well, she may not be able to perform her normal functions.

Arthritic cats who spend time outdoors are in danger because they cannot run and jump as well as they might need to in a dangerous situation. When joints hurt, it is more difficult to jump down from places the cat has jumped up on. It is a good idea to start keeping an older, achy cat indoors for her own protection.

The location and type of litter box might need to be changed for an arthritic cat. You want to make it as easy as possible for the cat to get in and out. Consider uncovering a hooded box or getting a box with lower sides if the cat is having a hard time using it.

The placement of food and water bowls should also be considered. If a cat cannot move her head and neck well, elevating the bowl could make a big difference in her ability to comfortably eat and drink. See Chapter 17 for more information about arthritis.

Kitty Comforts

Older cats can lose body fat and muscle. They can become less insulated against cold temperatures and can develop calluses and "bed sores" when bony parts rub against hard surfaces cats lie on. Be sure your cat has something soft and warm to lie on, such as a towel, throw rug or kitty blanket that will keep her more comfortable.

Bugs and Pests

As horrible as it sounds, insects like to take advantage of weak animals. Older cats may not be able to move away or scratch when insects bother them. Insects want to get a meal as easily as possible, so if an animal is not shooing them off, they are going to stay and eat.

Check your older animal for fleas and use flea control when needed. (Always make sure the product you are using is appropriate for older cats.) If the cat goes outside, monitor the areas she sleeps in and make sure ants are not bothering her. Also check to make sure that flies are not bothering an outdoor cat. Flies can lay their eggs on animals who don't move away, and the eggs will hatch into maggots about 12 hours later.

KNOWING WHEN TO LET GO

Each owner will have different feelings about how far they are willing to go financially and emotionally with the treatment of their cat. There is no right or wrong when it comes to treating a geriatric cat with a life-threatening illness. For some owners, a year or two more of life is worth it; others are ready to say goodbye when the news is bad.

I always tell owners that there is never a "perfect" time to make a decision about a cat's life. It is uncommon for a cat to die comfortably and quietly in her sleep, and in most situations, an owner is faced with a decision about euthanasia.

The phrase "quality of life" is used a lot, but people don't always know what it means. My interpretation is that if an animal is able to eat, drink, eliminate and get around reasonably well and does not seem to be in constant pain, then her quality of life is probably pretty good. When these basic functions cannot be performed, then quality of life is in question.

Unfortunately, in many older cats, one part of their body is not working at all, but otherwise they're in good health. Under these circumstances, making a decision is difficult. We cannot truly assess how much pain an animal is in with most diseases, so we use their clinical signs as a guide.

Euthanasia

When an animal is "put to sleep," she is given an overdose of an injectable barbiturate anesthetic. If the injection is given intravenously, the animal dies within 20 seconds. Everything in the cat's body slows to a stop, including the heart, so the process is painless.

Cats do not close their eyes when they die. After death some cats empty their bladders or have muscle twitches. This is all normal.

Each of us has different feelings about death and what it means. A few things to consider about euthanasia:

- Do you want to be present when your cat is given the injection?
- Do you want any special arrangements made for the body?
- If there are young children in the family, how will you explain it to them?
- Will you need help coping with the loss of your pet?

As much as you do not want to have to plan for your cat's death, it is often hard to think clearly when the time comes. It is best to be prepared so that you do not have to make hasty decisions later.

Are You Crazy to Be This Upset?

I am upset any time I have to put a cat to sleep. Certainly, it is the worst part of the job of being a veterinarian. I am able to derive comfort from the fact that I know I am able to end an animal's pain and suffering through euthanasia. Anyone who has ever been close to a pet knows how much it hurts emotionally when a pet dies, but people who have not had pets often do not understand.

I think it is normal to want to cry when a pet you have loved and shared your home with dies. I personally feel sadder about putting a cat to sleep when the owners are not upset. I think it is vital to let your emotions out, whether you are a man or a woman. Why should you have to keep them bottled up? Those of us in the veterinary profession do understand how painful it is to make a decision about a pet's life.

All family members, even those who may have previously claimed not to care about the cat, will feel some sort of loss with the animal's death. It is good to talk about it when possible. If there are children in the family, let them know that you are sad too, but that all living creatures will die at some time.

If you live alone, you should tell others about the loss of your pet so that friends and relatives can help you and be supportive of your feelings. Although no one else you know may have felt the same way about the pet as you did, other support options are available. These include:

- Local pet loss support groups
- Pet loss support hotlines available by phone
- Web sites dedicated to pet loss

See Appendix C for pet loss grief counseling hot lines.

Should You Get a New Pet?

Each person should go through a grieving period, but the length of time will vary. A new cat will never replace an old one, but each animal should find her own place in your heart. I personally think owners who feel a void in their life from the loss of a pet should consider getting a new pet, because they obviously have a lot of love that another pet would benefit from.

You may or may not want to get the same color, sex or breed of cat. The decision is up to you, but remember the new cat is not a replacement—she is an entirely new family member. You must also remember that if you get a kitten, her behaviors and your responsibility to the animal will be different from those you have been accustomed to.

Chapter 13

The Respiratory System

Breathing is a bodily function that healthy, normal animals usually do not think too much about. The process is controlled automatically by the brain and nervous system.

The respiratory system of an animal has a lower and an upper part. The nose and throat make up the upper respiratory tract and the trachea and lungs make up the lower respiratory tract. Both parts must be functioning for a cat to breathe normally.

Animals exchange oxygen and carbon dioxide by breathing. Oxygen is essential to maintaining life and body functions, so if an animal becomes starved of oxygen, it will die. Some of the diseases that affect the respiratory tract of cats are life threatening, but others are more of a nuisance and discomfort for the animal. This chapter will introduce you to some of the most common disorders of the feline respiratory system.

A cat's respiratory anatomy is very similar to ours. Although our noses are shaped differently, and theirs are hairier, the functions are the same. Air enters into the body through the nostrils (or, less often, the mouth). Mucus and small hairs cover the lining of the nasal passages and trap small particles and bacteria in the air. The air is warmed and moisturized as it passes through the nasal cavity and into the lower airways.

SNEEZING

Cats cannot blow their noses, and unfortunately because of this they sneeze out a lot of junk. This sounds gross, and it is. Sneezing is a nonspecific sign that occurs when the nasal passages become stimulated by secretions or an irritant.

There is no "cure" for sneezing because there are so many different causes. Possible causes of sneezing include:

- Viral infections
- Bacterial infections
- Fungal infections
- Allergies
- Irritants
- Foreign objects

Antihistamines, decongestants and nasal sprays for humans are usually not very useful for sneezing cats. If you have a sneezing cat, the best thing to do is have her examined by a veterinarian, so that a cause can be determined and a specific treatment suggested.

Although examining your cat's nasal discharge is not a pleasant task, the color and consistency hold clues. In general, if the discharge is clear and watery, it is nothing to worry about. If the discharge is green, yellow or bloody, medical care is required. Cats can get bloody noses from dry air and irritation, just like we do, but a bloody nose can also be a sign of severe infection or even a nasal tumor.

Allergies

Although most cats with allergies have itchy skin, some do sneeze. Cats can be allergic to just about anything in the world, including pollen, house dust and even kitty litter. Allergies usually produce a clear discharge when the animal sneezes. Allergies can be managed, but they can't be cured.

It can be quite difficult to determine specifically which allergen is causing the cat to sneeze. Although it is impossible to test a cat for all possible allergens, your vet can test for some common ones. If specific allergens are identified, you can either remove them from the environment or try to desensitize the animal with allergy shots.

Irritants

Smoke, cleaning products and even a cat's own hair can irritate the nasal passages and cause sneezing. To determine if an irritant is causing the sneezing, it must be removed from the environment and then the sneezing must cease.

Cigarette smoke can be very irritating to cats, and cats are susceptible to all of the problems of secondhand smoke that humans are. These include sneezing, bronchitis and even lung cancer. If you smoke, try to keep the smoke away from your cat.

Foreign Bodies

Cats are like small children; they are subject to accidents, and objects can become lodged in their noses. The most common object to get stuck in a cat's nose is a blade of grass. If you have a cat who sneezes 8 to 10 times in a row, it might be due to a foreign object stuck in her nose.

It can be difficult for a veterinarian to find something in a cat's nose without sedating the animal. Most cats are not thrilled with the idea of having a scope put up their nostril or keeping their mouth open while a veterinarian probes the back of the mouth. In some cases a special fiber optic scope is needed to look into the rear nasal passages. This is called *rhinoscopy*.

How You Can Help Alleviate Sneezing

Wiping a cat's nose and keeping it free of discharge will help improve the animal's comfort. If the cat sounds congested, you may try putting her in a steamy bathroom or in a small room with a vaporizer to help open up the airways. Seek veterinary advice if the sneezing persists or if the cat is showing signs of discomfort.

CATS DO CATCH COLDS

Upper respiratory infections are common in cats, and they can be caused by viral, bacterial or fungal infections. These kitty colds can range from mild to severe, with kittens being the most susceptible to infection. Cats are routinely vaccinated against some of the agents that cause upper respiratory infections. However, vaccines only decrease the severity of the clinical signs and do not completely prevent infection.

Upper respiratory infections can last a few days to weeks, so it important to monitor your cat's clinical signs and work with a veterinarian if you are not seeing any improvement. These colds can be very annoying and frustrating infections to deal with.

Stress and crowding are two factors that increase the risk of an upper respiratory infection. It is very common for a cat who has been adopted from a shelter or foster home to start off healthy, only to develop a cold shortly after her arrival in her new home. The animal was likely exposed to a microorganism that caused the infection before she was adopted, but the stress of being in a new home weakened her immune system and triggered the infection.

Viral Infections

Viruses are the most common cause of kitty colds. The good news about viruses is that they go away on their own over time, but the bad news is that it can take a long time and there is not any specific treatment or cure. The clinical signs typical of a viral upper respiratory infection are sneezing, runny nose, runny eyes, mild lethargy, decreased appetite and fever.

A veterinarian may treat a cat with a viral upper respiratory infection with fluids, antibiotics, ophthalmic medication, pediatric nasal sprays, antihistamines, immunostimulants or with nothing at all. Treatment depends on the clinical signs exhibited by the cat.

Two immunostimulants used by many veterinarians are l-lysine, an amino acid supplement that has shown antiviral effects, and alpha interferon, a genetically engineered human product that has effects against viral RNA, DNA and cellular proteins.

Most veterinarians will base their diagnosis of a viral upper respiratory infection on their interpretation of the animal's clinical signs. Definitively diagnosing viral upper respiratory infections is difficult

KEEP EATING!

Sick cats must eat and drink. Cats with upper respiratory infections will often have decreased appetites because they cannot smell. If your cat is not eating, try offering her smellier canned cat food, baby food or tuna. You can also try heating food in the microwave oven for a few seconds to increase its aroma. If the cat will not eat on her own, she will need to be hand-fed or even force-fed.

because the lab tests that isolate viruses are expensive, can take weeks for results and may only be 50 percent accurate. Don't get too frustrated if your veterinarian cannot make a positive call on the cause of infection. Continue to pursue treatment options if you think your cat is uncomfortable.

> ## CAN MY CAT CATCH MY COLD?
>
> Cats get upper respiratory viruses and people get upper respiratory viruses, but we do not pass them back and forth. Cold viruses are host-specific. That means the kinds of viruses that attack cats do not attack people, and vice versa.

Feline rhinotracheitis is a very common cause of upper respiratory infection, and because it is a herpes virus, it can cause recurrent disease. Cats infected with rhinotracheitis can have colds and conjunctivitis off and on as kittens, but they tend to grow out of it by the time they are two years old.-

Bacterial Infections

Bacterial upper respiratory infections can occur on their own or as secondary infections along with viruses. The clinical signs associated with bacterial infections are:

- Fever
- Enlarged lymph nodes
- Yellow to green discharge from the nose and/or eyes
- Sneezing
- Coughing
- Decrease in or loss of appetite
- Lethargy
- Dehydration

Treatment is aimed at killing the bacteria and supporting the cat. Treatment can include antibiotics, fluids, ophthalmic medications, antihistamines, pediatric nasal sprays, immunostimulants and hand feeding. Bacterial cultures are not routinely run on cats that develop *acute* upper respiratory infections, but they may be performed if the infection does not resolve, worsens or becomes chronic.

ACUTE OR CHRONIC?

The terms *acute* and *chronic* are used to describe diseases. Acute means a disease comes on suddenly and eventually goes away. A chronic disease is one that lasts for a long time or that does not completely go away.

Culturing the specific bacteria that are causing an upper respiratory infection is difficult, because the nose is also the home of many normal bacteria that can contaminate a culture. To get a more reliable culture specimen the cat should be sedated, sterile saline flushed into a nostril, and a sample collected from the back of the nasal passages.

Fungal Infections

Fungal upper respiratory infections occur occasionally, with *Cryptococcus neoformans* being the most common fungus. Cats with compromised immune systems, such as those infected with FeLV or FIV, are most at risk for developing fungal upper respiratory infections. This fungus can be found in bird droppings and, as unlikely as it seems, it can affect cats who live indoors.

Fungal upper respiratory infections are usually slowly progressive and do not improve with antibiotic treatment. As fungal infections progress they can cause growths in the nostrils and bulging of the sinuses. Fungal upper respiratory infections may be diagnosed by examining a smear of nasal discharge microscopically, by performing a blood test for *Cryptococcus* or other fungi common in your area, or by a biopsy or needle aspirate of a nasal growth. Antifungal drugs are effective against fungus, but the treatment may last months and the drugs are quite expensive.

If the Cold Doesn't Go Away

If treatment by your veterinarian is not helping, more aggressive care and hospitalization may be needed. Other diagnostic tests should be done that will look for other diseases that can mimic upper respiratory infections, including:

- Complete blood count and blood chemistries
- FeLV and FIV tests
- Microscopic evaluation of nasal discharge

- Bacterial culture
- Fungal blood titer and/or culture
- Skull X rays
- Rhinoscopy (examination of the back of the nasal passages with a fiberoptic scope)
- Nasal biopsy
- Tracheal or bronchial wash
- Bronchoscopy

Other possible diagnoses are nasopharyngeal polyps (growths that block the back of the throat), inflammatory conditions, sinus infections and neoplasia (abnormal tissue growths). These other diseases will not respond to conventional upper respiratory infection treatments.

COULD YOUR CAT HAVE ASTHMA?

Cats do get asthma. Asthma is a form of bronchitis—an inflammation of the large airways in the lungs called the *bronchi*. In asthma attacks, the muscles surrounding the airways constrict and the internal lining of the airways swell. This combination blocks adequate oxygen from passing through and creates respiratory difficulty.

Allergies or irritants can cause asthma, and since asthma affects the lungs, it is a lower respiratory disease with serious implications. Diseases that affect the lower respiratory tract are potentially more dangerous because the lungs can be permanently damaged.

Signs of Asthma

The clinical signs associated with asthma include:

- Coughing
- Gagging
- Increased respiration rate
- Open-mouth breathing
- Wheezing
- Lethargy
- Difficulty breathing and distress

The number and severity of the clinical signs is usually in proportion to the severity of the asthma. Asthma can progress to a life-threatening situation. It can only be diagnosed definitively by an X ray. A complete blood count could also be a helpful test, because some cats with asthma have higher levels of a specific type of white blood cell called an *eosinophil*.

Treating Asthma

There are various drugs veterinarians prescribe to treat asthma, including cortisone, antihistamines, bronchodilators, antibiotics, oxygen and even some asthma drugs made for humans. Most of the time the cause of asthma is not found, but it is often linked to allergies. A condition linked to allergies is managed rather than cured, and the cat can have recurrent problems.

Do not treat your cat for asthma unless she has had a chest X ray. The clinical signs that are typical of asthma can also be present with heart disease or when fluid is present in the chest cavity, and these serious conditions require very different treatments.

Observant owners can tune in to their cats and detect asthma, when it recurs, at an early stage. The early clinical signs are a nonproductive (no phlegm comes up) cough or gag. Some cats need to be on long-term medication to control their problems, and medication can be injectable, oral and/or delivered by an inhaler.

Inhalers are being more widely used to treat cats with chronic asthma. Special chambers with one-way valves and a mask are used to deliver the medication into the cat's airways, because, as you can imagine, it is impossible to make a cat breathe in when an inhaler is depressed. Human inhalers containing cortisone are used first, and if the response is inadequate, inhalers with bronchodilators are added. Benefits of inhaler treatment are that medication is immediately delivered directly to the location of the problem—the lining of the airways—and side effects of long-term cortisone use are eliminated, since medication is not entering the bloodstream.

IT'S NOT ALWAYS HAIRBALLS

When cats cough and gag, owners can be quick to blame the problem on hairballs. Although initially an asthmatic cat may appear to be coughing up a hairball, nothing will come up and the problem will progress. Do not ignore this important clinical sign of asthma.

An inhaler will be attached to this chamber and mask to deliver asthma medication directly to the cat's airways.

Allergy testing and hyposensitization (giving allergy shots) helps some cats with asthma. Eliminating inhaled irritants in the cat's environment, such as cigarette smoke, dusty cat litter and construction dust, helps, too.

Some cats can have lifelong asthma that causes permanent damage to the lungs through scarring. Scarring prevents the lung tissue from expanding normally, and as it progresses can lead to respiratory collapse. Managing the inflammation, by effectively treating asthma, helps prevent scarring.

PNEUMONIA

Pneumonia is an infection in the lungs. Viruses, bacteria and fungi can all cause pneumonia. Pneumonia is most common in young cats and is infrequent in adults. It is a serious condition, because if it progresses, it can lead to severe congestion within the lungs and respiratory collapse.

Young cats can get pneumonia by choking and aspirating fluid into their lungs. This might occur when a bottle-fed kitten does not suck normally and the milk is swallowed improperly. Pneumonia can then ensue. A cat might also get pneumonia when she has another disease that has weakened her immune system and allowed infection to travel down into the lower respiratory tract.

A third cause of pneumonia could be parasites. There is, for example, a species of worm known as *Aelurostrongylus abstrusus*, which like to live in the lungs and cause infections. These worms can be carried by the birds, frogs or rodents that cats eat when they hunt. Sometimes gastrointestinal worms migrate in an abnormal manner and become lodged in the lungs. In addition, a protozoal parasite, *Toxoplasma gondii,* can occasionally cause pneumonia in cats.

Pneumonia can only be definitively diagnosed by a chest X ray. Additional tests are needed to pinpoint the cause of infection.

Because a lower respiratory tract infection poses much graver risks than an upper respiratory infection, aggressive therapy is needed. A cat with pneumonia usually requires hospitalization, intravenous antibiotics, fluids, diuretics, bronchodilators, oxygen and nebulization. Nebulization is a process in which saline and antibiotics are mixed and turned into very small particles that are made into a mist. This mist can enter the lower airways when an animal breathes in.

The prognosis for a cat with pneumonia is uncertain. If the infection responds to treatment and the lung is not permanently damaged, recovery is possible. The longer the lung stays congested, the harder it is to treat.

Chapter 14

The Gastrointestinal System

· ·

If your cat is anything like either of my cats, eating is an important part of each day. Taking in and processing food sustains life for a cat, so disorders of the gastrointestinal (GI) tract can have serious implications. The gastrointestinal system includes many organs and extends from the mouth, to the esophagus, to the stomach, to the small intestine, to the large intestine and finally to the rectum. Along the way the liver and the pancreas get into the act.

There are many diseases that can affect the GI tract. In this chapter, I will describe some of the diseases and some common signs of GI problems. Diet, stress, infectious agents, parasites and age all play a role in GI health.

IT ALL STARTS IN THE MOUTH

Digestion begins in the mouth with food being taken in by the lips, chewed by the teeth, mixed with saliva and pushed into the esophagus by the tongue. I don't know if cats ever have good breath, but cats with

135

disease in their mouths have noticeably bad breath. Bad breath can be an indicator of dental disease, gum disease or problems with the tongue.

Even if you perform routine dental care on your cat, dental disease can occur. A veterinarian should perform a dental exam on your cat at least once a year and evaluate the teeth, tongue and gums. Just as some people have bad teeth, some cats naturally have bad teeth. Others develop bad teeth because of diet and lack of care. Teeth can break, crack, develop erosions, abscess and fall out on their own. Owners are sometimes shocked when I show them that their cat is missing teeth. They cannot believe how well their cat is eating. Decreased appetite or problems eating are not always present in oral disease, and cats with significant infection or inflammation in their mouths may eat normally.

Infections from the mouth can get into the blood and spread to other organ systems, so regardless of age, cats with dental disease must be treated. Before performing any dental procedures, a cat's general health and metabolic state should be assessed and stabilized.

Gum Disease

The signs of gingivitis or gum disease are red or swollen gums, gums growing up and over teeth, drooling, bad breath and inflammation at the corners of the mouth, making the mouth difficult to open.

Similar to other disease processes, the longer gum disease persists, the harder it is to control or cure. Early intervention against gum disease is very helpful. When significant gum disease is present, causes to consider are:

- Feline Leukemia Virus (FeLV)
- Feline Immunodeficiency Virus (FIV)
- Tooth infection
- Inflammatory condition
- Neoplasia

A cat with bad gums should be tested for FeLV and FIV. If these tests are negative, the teeth should be cleaned and any affected teeth repaired or removed. A gum biopsy and treatment with antibiotics may be necessary if there is significant gingivitis. The biopsy results can then guide any further treatment.

There is a group of inflammatory conditions of unknown origin that can cause severe dental disease and oral inflammation. An example is called lymphocytic-plasmacytic stomatitis. Treatment of this condition can include cortisone, antibiotics, immunostimulants and full-mouth dental extractions. Some veterinarians treat this condition with lasers. Inflammatory conditions tend to be chronic and very painful if not adequately controlled.

KITTY'S GOING TO BE SICK

Cats vomit frequently, and owners hate to clean up after them. When cats live in the wild vomiting is not a big deal, but when they live in our homes it can create quite a mess. Sometimes vomiting is normal, but other times it is an indication of disease.

Some of the most common causes of feline vomiting are:

- Hairballs
- Sensitivity to a diet
- Eating too quickly
- Viral or bacterial infections
- Consumption of plants or other nonfood items
- Inflammatory conditions
- Metabolic imbalances
- Gastrointestinal parasites
- Foreign body ingestion
- Intestinal obstruction

Spitting Up Hairballs

If you have a cat who grooms himself regularly, you are probably familiar with hairballs. Some cats spit up hairballs regularly (that is, once or twice a week) and others may only produce a hairball a few times a year. The first time you see a hairball, you may not be sure which end of the cat it came out of, because hairballs can appear as long, tubular structures.

Many cats like the taste of lubricant hairball remedies and will readily lick them from your fingers. But hairball remedies do not cure hairballs; they merely help the hair to pass through the cat's GI tract (one way or the other) so that it does not cause an obstruction in the intestines. Commonly found hairball remedies include lubricant pastes, fiber supplements, special diets and treats. If your cat spits up hairballs regularly, one or more of these remedies may decrease the frequency. Mineral oil is not a safe or effective treatment for hairballs.

It is common to blame a cat's coughing and gagging on hairballs, but there are some serious conditions that can mimic the same signs (see Chapter 13). If your cat is not spitting up a hairball when he goes through those heaving motions, consult your veterinarian. Possible causes could be asthma, heart disease and other gastrointestinal problems.

Does Your Cat Have Food Issues?

Many cat owners know their cats do not always perform the second step of digestion—chewing the food. Cats who eat rapidly without chewing may regurgitate their meal within minutes and then simply go back to eating. Cats may eat rapidly because they feel competition at the food bowl or because they like to overeat. Cats who regurgitate tend to bring up piles of food that has not been chewed. These cats usually eat a dry (but sometimes canned) diet too quickly, which blows up and distends their stomachs, causing the regurgitation. Some suggestions for curbing this problem are:

- Feed a less palatable diet.
- Feed a diet with a larger kibble size so that the cat will have to chew.
- Add water to moisten the food before it is fed.
- Mix canned food with the dry to slow down eating and add moisture.

If you try these all of these suggestions and your cat continues to regurgitate, consult your veterinarian.

Does Your Cat Have the Flu?

Cats can contract viral or bacterial infections that cause vomiting. Because routine blood tests may show normal results, it is not easy to diagnose a gastrointestinal infection. If fever and discomfort are present, an infection should be suspected.

It is common for cats with infections to also have diarrhea. Infections can be contagious to other cats, but are rarely transmissible to humans or other species. When possible, an exact cause for vomiting should be determined.

Other Causes of Vomiting

A cat who is vomiting and is unable to hold down food and water can get dehydrated and feel quite poorly. If you have a cat with these symptoms, have him checked out as soon as possible. A veterinarian may want to treat the cat with fluids to improve hydration and also use other injectable medications. Injecting the medications will ensure that they get into the cat's system, rather than being vomited up.

Although blood tests are not very specific when it comes to diagnosing gastrointestinal disease, your veterinarian should perform them nonetheless. Other diagnostic tests that may be needed include:

- Fecal exam
- X rays
- Abdominal ultrasound
- Barium upper GI series
- Endoscopy
- Abdominal exploratory surgery
- Biopsy of the stomach and intestines
- Hypoallergenic food trial

Veterinary medicine is quite advanced with diagnostic options. Depending on where you live, some of these tests are readily available. Tests that use high-tech equipment tend to cost more money but are very effective at reaching a diagnosis.

What Is a Foreign Body?

A foreign body is an inanimate object a cat swallows and cannot digest. Any time a cat eats something other than his food, veterinarians call it dietary indiscretion. Cats may ingest plants, strings, cat toys, holiday decorations and even pieces of shoes and clothing.

We think of cats as being picky and extremely discriminating. So how is it that they willingly swallow inanimate objects that can lodge in their intestines? The answer to the question of dietary indiscretion is a mystery. It could be cats' hunting and stalking behavior gets the best

PUT AWAY THE TOYS

I have observed my own cats' attempts to swallow the string on their fishing pole toys. I now keep the toys in a closed closet whenever they are not in use. To protect your cat from potentially dangerous objects, such as toys with strings, sewing materials, ribbon and newspaper ties, store them in a secure place.

of them. They chase and pounce on a quick moving object and then ingest it as they would captured prey.

Another possible explanation is boredom. Cats like to indulge in attention-seeking behaviors. Some cats even seem to like being scolded and chased away from trouble. Playing with items they fish out of trash cans can be a game, as well. Unraveling balls of yarn or pulling apart a carpet or drape can be lots of fun. It is even more fun for the cat when you yell and run after him!

Early detection of foreign bodies means they can be successfully removed from the stomach and intestines of the cat. If not found promptly, foreign bodies can cause the intestines to become blocked or coiled, which can progress to intestinal rupture—a life-threatening situation. Some foreign objects can be easily found on an X ray, while others cannot and may not be found without exploratory surgery.

Although it may sound extreme, if you have a cat who is unable to hold down food or water, exploratory surgery can be the best way to find a foreign body that cannot be seen on an X ray. The risk of waiting for other diagnostic tests that may (or may not) show the problem can outweigh the risk of surgery.

GETTING TO THE BOX

Diarrhea is another common problem in cats. It can have many of the same causes as vomiting, and it requires the same diagnostic work-up. If your cat has diarrhea, a veterinarian will want to examine the cat and a fecal sample, because parasites are a frequent cause of diarrhea. If a fecal check is negative and the animal's physical exam is relatively normal, other diagnostic tests should be considered.

Diarrhea can be a sign of a mild problem, or it can indicate a serious condition. A cat can have one episode of diarrhea, which is not a big deal, or he can have chronic diarrhea and weight loss, which needs significant care.

Bland Is Better

A diet change or dietary sensitivity can cause diarrhea. Any time a cat eats something new, there is the possibility of gastrointestinal upset. Cats can also develop intolerance to foods that they have previously handled just fine.

Feeding your cat a bland diet and withholding treats and people food is always a good idea if he has diarrhea. A bland diet is one that is low in fat and easy to digest. Some cats will eat rice if it is mixed with canned food; the rice can help bind up their feces.

As contrary as it seems, feeding a cat who has diarrhea a high-fiber diet can firm the stool. Fiber helps stimulate normal GI contractions, reduce bacteria in the bowel and promote water reabsorption—all of which can lessen diarrhea.

Check Out the Litter Box

Although you probably do not want to talk about the size, shape and consistency of your cat's stool, these factors will help your veterinarian determine the cause of the problem. Helpful observations are:

- Is the stool formed (as opposed to watery)?
- Is there mucus present?
- Is there blood in the stool?
- Is there an abnormal odor?
- Can the cat make it to the litter box?
- When was the last normal stool?

Seeing blood in your cat's stool is scary, but it is unlikely to be a sign of grave illness. A cat with an irritated colon will pass bright red blood or clots. A cat with bleeding in the stomach will pass dark to black stools, because the blood is partially digested along the way. A one-time episode of blood in the stool may be insignificant, but if it continues, check with a veterinarian.

WHAT'S A BIOPSY?

Endoscopic biopsies are obtained by passing a fiber optic endoscope into the GI tract of an anesthetized cat. The scope enters the mouth, goes down the esophagus, enters the stomach and then passes into the intestines. Along the way all of the tissues can be examined and little bits of the tissue of the linings can be removed (called pinch biopsies). This diagnostic test is limited to the lining of the tubular GI tract, and it cannot tell you about the outer layers, lymph nodes, liver or pancreas.

There are risks and benefits to the different methods of obtaining biopsies. Needle biopsies do not require exploratory surgery, but they only provide a small number of cells for analysis. Surgical biopsies provide many cells and are more likely to confirm a diagnosis, but they are obtained in a more invasive manner. During exploratory surgery, though, tissues are visualized, palpated and more thoroughly assessed.

INFLAMMATORY BOWEL DISEASE (IBD)

Inflammatory bowel disease (IBD) is a condition in cats that can cause diarrhea and/or vomiting. A diagnosis can only be confirmed by a biopsy, which can reveal an abnormal infiltration of inflammatory cells into the lining of the stomach and/or intestines. Biopsies can be obtained through endoscopy or surgery.

When other causes of GI disease have been eliminated, IBD becomes a more likely diagnosis, although its specific cause is rarely found. Researchers think the bowel inflammation results from a sensitivity to proteins in the diet and an abnormal immune response. This same inflammatory response can affect the liver and pancreas of cats. When IBD, cholangiohepatitis and pancreatitis are all diagnosed in the same cat, it is called triad disease.

Cats affected with IBD vomit and/or have diarrhea. It is typically a disease of middle-aged to older cats, but it can affect young cats, too. It is always best to make a definitive diagnosis of IBD through biopsy but in some situations this may not be possible.

Treatment for IBD may include special diets, supplements, antibiotics, cortisone and other anti-inflammatory drugs. IBD is a condition that cannot be cured, but can be managed.

WHAT IS HELICOBACTER?

Helicobacter are spiral bacteria found in biopsies of some cats' stomachs. The significance of this organism in cats is unknown. One type found in humans, called *Helicobacter pylori,* has been linked to the development of stomach inflammation, peptic ulcers and even stomach cancer. Whether these specific bacteria can pass between cats and humans is unknown, but it has not been isolated in feline feces. *Helicobacter felis* is more commonly found in cats.

Helicobacter probably causes gastritis and vomiting in cats and may predispose them to food allergies and inflammatory bowel disease. Metronidazole alone or in combination with other drugs is used when clinical signs are present.

INTESTINAL CANCER

Cancer can only be definitively diagnosed by a biopsy. A type of intestinal cancer called intestinal lymphosarcoma (LSA) is common in cats. Intestinal lymphosarcoma can result from uncontrolled inflammatory bowel disease. The clinical signs associated with this disease are similar to IBD, but by the time it has progressed to cancer, the cat is usually in much worse physical condition. Cats with intestinal LSA can respond favorably to chemotherapy.

Intestinal adenocarcinoma is another type of cancer seen in cats. If this type of cancer has not metastasized, the treatment is surgical removal. The affected piece of intestine is surgically cut out, and the intestine is reconnected—similar to removing a bad piece of garden hose! Adenocarcinomas do recur, but surgery has the potential to extend the cat's life by several good years.

WHEN KITTY IS CONSTIPATED

Cats normally have one bowel movement a day. When stools become less frequent or straining is observed, it is important to determine:

- Is the cat able to pass stool?
- Is the cat eating?
- Is the cat dehydrated?
- Could the cat be straining to urinate instead?
- Is the cat defecating somewhere else in the house?

If your cat is constipated, there are a few things you can try at home. If you have any type of lubricant hairball remedy, these products also work as laxatives. Adding one teaspoon a day of psyllium, which is the ingredient in Metamucil and other fiber remedies, to cat food can also help the irregular cat. (Make sure the fiber remedy you choose contains only psyllium.) You may try feeding canned cat food and encouraging water consumption. Feeding canned pumpkin (pumpkin pie filling or plain cooked pumpkin) is another home remedy that can resolve constipation. Try one tablespoon, once or twice a day.

Don't let your kitty go more than two days without passing a stool. If you think an enema is needed, let your veterinarian administer it and then deal with cleaning up any mess. Never give a phosphate enema designed for a human to a cat—they are toxic to felines!

There are many reasons why a cat may become constipated, and it is a good idea to narrow down the possibilities so you can prevent recurrences. Causes of constipation include hairballs, dehydration, metabolic diseases, anatomical deformities, arthritis, megacolon and diet.

Megacolon is a chronic condition that causes constipation. The colon becomes dilated and stops having normal muscle contractions. Feces pack up and are not pushed through. Megacolon can be a progressive condition that needs long-term medical and dietary management. Cats who do not respond to treatment need a surgery, called a subtotal colectomy, to remove the inactive colon and restore the ability to defecate.

If your cat has more than one episode of constipation, work with your veterinarian to determine a diagnostic and treatment plan. Treatment can involve fluids, stool softeners, motility-enhancing drugs that promote intestinal contractions and even shaving a cat to reduce hair in the stool.

STRAINING FOR WHAT?

Cats have different postures for urinating and defecating, but if you are not sure and the animal is straining, you should take him to a veterinarian as soon as possible. Instead of being constipated, the cat may be unable to urinate. Urinary blockages can become life-threatening situations within a very short period of time—as little as 12 hours.

IS YOUR CAT TURNING YELLOW?

The liver is a vital organ with many functions, including digestion, vitamin and mineral storage, protein synthesis, general metabolism and toxin neutralization. A cat can become very sick when his liver is impaired.

Most of the signs of liver disease in cats are similar to those of other gastrointestinal problems, but one different sign seen in many cases is jaundice. Jaundice is a condition causing the eyes, skin and gums of an animal to take on a yellow tint. The color change is due to bile pigments in the blood that rise to abnormal levels in liver disease or gall bladder obstruction.

What Is a Fatty Liver?

Cats who do not eat begin to break down their body fat for energy. Even though many cats are overweight and have lots of energy stored, the liver becomes overwhelmed by the amount of fat it must convert, and a condition called hepatic lipidosis—fatty liver disease—can develop. Cats who start off with other problems, such as viral infections, can develop hepatic lipidosis if they stop eating. If the process continues, hepatic lipidosis can become life threatening.

A diagnosis of hepatic lipidosis can only be confirmed by a liver biopsy, but this disease should be suspected if a blood test shows elevated liver enzymes and a cat is not eating. Needle biopsies of the liver can be obtained with the aid of ultrasound, and wedge biopsies can be obtained through exploratory surgery.

If your cat is not eating for more than a day, it is crucial to get food into him as soon as possible. If you are unable to entice the cat with tuna, baby food or canned food, consult your veterinarian. Every day makes a difference when trying to prevent hepatic lipidosis.

Treatment for hepatic lipidosis may include force-feeding, treatment of an underlying medical condition, supplementation with essential amino acids such as taurine and carnitine, placement of a feeding tube, and extended supportive care for weeks to months.

A feeding tube can be a lifeline for a sick cat. Owners are able to easily feed their anorexic cats when tubes are in place. Tubes can be placed through the nose or esophagus into the stomach, or they can be placed directly into the stomach or intestine. Nasogastric tubes (nose to stomach) can be irritating. They are very narrow and so limit feeding that they are best used only in a short-term situation. Veterinarians currently favor esophagostomy tubes (a tube placed into the esophagus) because they can be easily placed in a sedated patient. Cats can still eat and if there are problems with the tube, there is no risk of peritonitis (infection of the abdominal cavity). Tubes placed directly into the stomach or intestine are more technically complicated, require general anesthesia, and leakage can cause peritonitis.

Other Causes of Liver Disease

Hepatic lipidosis is generally considered to be a secondary problem, occurring after another disease has caused loss of appetite. Some primary liver diseases are:

- Viral, bacterial, or parasitic hepatitis
- Cholangiohepatitis
- Exposure to toxins
- Congenital disease
- Liver shunts
- Hepatic neoplasia

A cat's liver is comprised of four lobes and may fill up to one-fourth of the animal's abdominal cavity. Seventy to 80 percent of a liver can be impaired before functional problems are apparent.

Blood tests can indicate that inflammation of the liver is occurring, and they can indicate that liver function is significantly impaired, but they are not specific when it comes to determining cause. A liver biopsy is needed to make a conclusive diagnosis.

Almost all cases of liver disease have similar clinical signs. Some types of liver disease are easier to treat than others, and the liver is an organ that can regenerate if it is not too severely damaged. Bleeding disorders can be a secondary problem in cats with liver disease, since the liver is responsible for creating the components needed for blood clotting.

Cholagiohepatitis

This disease is an inflammatory condition of the bile ducts and liver. Vomiting, anorexia and jaundice are common signs in affected cats. The cause of cholangiohepatitis is rarely found, and, as in other forms of liver disease, a biopsy is needed for diagnosis.

Antibiotics, cortisone, ursodeoxycholic acid, fluids, nausea control and nutrition are components of successful treatment. Long-term treatment to control inflammation may be needed.

Liver Shunts

Portal shunts are abnormal blood vessels that prevent the flow of blood from the stomach and intestines to the liver. Blood must pass through the liver for proper digestion and detoxification of materials absorbed from the digestive tract. Cats with shunts can have seizures, behavior changes and other neurological signs, especially after eating.

Congenital (present at birth) shunts are the most common type. Affected kittens tend to have retarded growth and development, in addition to neurological signs. It is very apparent that something is wrong in these kittens by the time they are six months old.

Acquired shunts are infrequently seen in older cats, and occur as a result of increased blood pressure around the liver due to other diseases.

Routine blood tests do not specifically diagnose a shunt, but a bile acids test suggests the problem. Ultrasound and hepatic scintigraphy (a special test using radiation) aid in the diagnosis. Contrast portography is another specialized test using dye and X rays to see the shunts.

Most congenital shunts involve one blood vessel that can be surgically closed to treat the problem and redirect blood flow. Medical management to control toxins in the blood and underlying liver disease are needed to treat acquired shunts. The prognosis depends on the age of the animal and the number of shunts present.

PANCREATITIS

The pancreas is an abdominal organ that aids digestion by creating and releasing enzymes and secreting insulin needed for glucose absorption. Bacterial infections, trauma and toxins can cause pancreatitis, an inflammatory condition of the pancreas, but the cause is unknown in 90 percent of cases. Clinical signs are nonspecific and can include lethargy, anorexia, vomiting, hypothermia, dehydration and abdominal pain.

Diagnosing pancreatitis in cats is a challenge. Abnormal levels of the pancreatic enzymes amylase and lipase in the blood are not diagnostic, the way they are in dogs. X rays, ultrasound and a special test for feline TLI (trypsin-like immunoreactivity) suggest the diagnosis, but it cannot be confirmed without a biopsy.

Treatment is focused on restoring hydration, maintaining the balance of electrolytes, controlling nausea, inflammation and pain, and providing nutrition. Most affected cats require hospitalization until they are able to handle oral medications and eat on their own.

THE END OF THE LINE—ANAL GLAND PROBLEMS

Cats, like dogs, have glands at the opening of their anus, located at five and seven o'clock. These scent glands are expressed (emptied) when an animal defecates or is very frightened. The material is normally brown and oily with a foul, musky scent. Most cats never have problems with theses glands, but occasionally they become impacted, infected or even abscessed.

Because of their physical conformation, overweight cats tend to have more problems emptying these glands. Some cats produce more waxy secretions that tend to build up in the glands. Veterinary staff and groomers can manually express them—most owners don't want the smelly and slightly uncomfortable (for the cat) job.

Signs of anal gland problems are scooting or dragging the rear end, excessive licking around the rectum and open sores under the tail. If your cat exhibits any of these signs, get him checked out.

Chapter 15

Skin and Dermatology

....

The skin is the largest organ of any animal's body; it comprises 12 to 24 percent of a cat's body weight. It protects the cat and is responsible for much of her external appearance. Changes in a cat's skin and haircoat can alert an owner to health and nutrition problems.

There are many dermatological conditions that can affect cats, and I'll discuss some of the most common in this chapter. Some feline skin conditions are contagious to humans and other animals, and others are not. Most skin diseases look the same regardless of the cause, so testing and observing how the cat responds to therapy are important to making a proper diagnosis.

ITCHY KITTY

We treat itchy cats just about every day at my clinic. Some cats are mildly itchy, and others are miserable and scratch themselves until they are raw. Historically, fleas have been the most common cause of itchy cats, but with improvements in the flea-control products available today, flea infestations can be easily controlled. (The specifics of flea control are discussed in Chapter 8.)

HELPFUL DEFINITIONS

Allergens are foreign substances that can cause an allergic response in some animals. *Antigens* are foreign substances that cause the body to produce an antibody that responds exclusively to that antigen.

When you bring your itchy cat to a veterinarian, the animal should first have a full physical exam. The doctor should check the cat for fleas and note the distribution of the lesions. (A *lesion* is a change or injury to a body tissue that impairs the tissue or causes a loss of function.) The vet should also review the cat's history with you. Many diagnoses can be made based on the animal's age and history and the location of the problem. If a diagnosis is not apparent based on this information, the next steps would be to perform some diagnostic tests, such as:

- Skin scraping
- Wood's lamp evaluation (a way to look for fungus)
- Fungal culture
- Microscopic evaluation of an imprint of the lesion
- Blood tests
- Allergy testing
- Hypoallergenic diet
- Skin biopsy

Allergies Can Cause Itchiness

An animal can be allergic to just about any substance in the world, so allergies are a difficult problem to diagnose. Most cats with allergies have itchy skin rather than respiratory signs. Allergies are suspected when infectious causes of itchy skin and miliary dermatitis are ruled out. (*Miliary dermatitis* is the term used by veterinarians to describe scabby, crusty skin. The infectious causes of miliary dermatitis are parasites, fungus and bacteria.)

Eosinophilic granulomas are inflammatory lesions frequently seen on cats that may be caused by allergies. The three types of lesions are rodent ulcer of the lip, linear granuloma of the back legs and eosinophilic plaque that can be found anywhere. Treatment for these lesions is similar to that of other allergies.

There are four types of allergies:

1. Inhaled allergies (atopy)
2. Food allergies
3. Flea allergies
4. Contact allergies

Inhaled Allergies

Inhaled allergies are generally managed rather than cured. If a specific allergen can be identified and eliminated from the cat's environment, the manifestations of that particular allergy will go away. To identify specific allergens, some type of allergy testing is needed.

Veterinary dermatologists believe intradermal skin testing is the most reliable way to test for allergies in cats. This test involves sedating the patient, clipping the hair on one side of the chest and then injecting tiny doses of antigens under the skin. The number of antigens injected can vary, but it would not be unusual for 60 different substances to be included in a test. The veterinarian then examines the cat's skin for wheals—red, raised skin reactions. Each site that forms a significant wheal is considered to be an allergen to that cat.

Other allergy tests involve checking the blood for high levels of specific antibodies to different allergens. There is usually a correlation between antibody levels in the blood and allergic reactions, and specific antibodies can pinpoint specific allergens.

If allergens are identified, a cat can receive allergy antigen injections that desensitize her to the substances she is allergic to. Most cats receive these "allergy shots" starting off weekly, and owners can learn to give the injections themselves. The injections contain small amounts of antigens that the cat is sensitive to, and this amount is slowly increased with each injection. This hyposensitization therapy is about 70 percent effective, but it can take 6 to 12 months to see results.

Treatment of atopy may include cortisone, given orally or by injection, antihistamines, fatty acids, antigen injections and antibiotics for secondary skin infections.

Food Allergies

Cats with food allergies are usually itchy around their heads and ears. Although intradermal skin tests and antibody blood tests can identify some food antigens, the best way to diagnose a food allergy is with a food trial. In a food trial, a cat is fed an entirely new protein source for four to six weeks. If the cat's condition improves, the animal can be challenged with different protein sources, offered individually, to find out which one was causing the reaction. That protein source is then eliminated from her diet.

Lamb used to be considered a hypoallergenic food and was used in food trials. Pet food companies all jumped on the bandwagon and started putting lamb in many commercially available products, so lamb is no longer a unique protein source. A lamb diet may help some food-allergic cats, but other less widely used protein sources are probably needed instead.

A successful food trial involves eliminating all treats and table scraps, serving distilled water and feeding the test diet exclusively. Some of the unique proteins currently being used are venison, duck and rabbit. Lamb or ham baby food may also be used for a hypoallergenic food trial.

Flea Allergies

The most common allergy in cats is flea allergy dermatitis. For a cat with this allergy, one flea bite can cause a reaction equal to 100 fleas. Cats with flea allergy dermatitis are very itchy and have hair loss and miliary dermatitis along their back, the base of their tail and behind their back legs. The hair loss is due to self-trauma—incessant chewing at the sites of flea bites.

To diagnose flea allergy dermatitis, look for fleas or flea dirt (which will look like tiny white and black specks—the white are flea eggs and the black are flea excrement) on the cat and hair loss in the typical pattern I've just described. The best way to look for fleas is by using a flea comb to hunt for evidence.

Some cats are so sensitive to fleas that they bite off every flea that jumps on them and leave no trace of infestation. If a veterinarian does not observe fleas but still suspects flea allergy dermatitis, he or she will treat it. Treatment involves flea control (the once-a-month topical adulticides work wonderfully) and, usually, cortisone to break the itch-scratch cycle.

Contact Allergies

These allergies are the least common in cats, but they can occur when a cat touches an allergen. The reaction is usually localized to the site of contact, but if the cat licks or rubs, the problem area can get bigger. Topical treatment with a cream, ointment or spray can be a first course of treatment, but oral or injectable medications will be needed if the cat insists on licking the irritated spot.

One potentially common contact allergy is with flea collars. Some cats develop a rash or hair loss on their necks when a flea collar is placed on them. The problem eventually goes away when the collar is removed, but it can take weeks. Since new flea control products have made flea collars obsolete, this problem is rarely seen anymore.

KITTY IS BALD!

Although grooming is a normal cat behavior, some cats get carried away and lick themselves until they are bald, red or create open sores. This condition is called psychogenic alopecia, and it is diagnosed by ruling out infectious and allergic causes of skin problems. I liken it to people who bite their fingernails too short as a nervous, unconscious habit. They don't know when to stop!

Treating this condition is a challenge, because it is difficult to break the behavior pattern. Since cats cannot tell us how they feel and what is bothering them, it is a hard to figure out why your cat developed this habit and what to do about it.

After any skin infection or irritation is treated, antihistamines or antianxiety medications may be used for their calming effects. Bad tasting sprays or gels will discourage licking, as will protective collars. If a source of stress or environmental change can be identified, steps should be taken to minimize their effect on the cat.

Sometimes the problem is caused by boredom, and environmental enrichment, combined with more play time, can help.

ZITTY KITTY

Feline acne is a fairly common problem that affects adult cats. Owners often look at me incredulously when I diagnose their pet with this condition. They say, "My cat is too old to have acne!" or "All he eats is cat food. Wouldn't he have to eat junk food?" Just as in most cases of human acne, more than one cause contributes to feline acne. Diet, hormones, allergies, bacteria and cleanliness can all play roles in the development of acne.

A diagnosis of feline acne is made during a physical exam. Sometimes the owner has noticed draining sores on the cat's chin, and sometimes a veterinarian will discover acne lesions while performing a routine examination. Blackheads and/or whiteheads are observed around the lower lips or on the chin. These clogged pores can become infected by bacteria and develop into a pustule. Pustules can burst and drain, or can enlarge and cause discomfort. Acne usually looks worse to the owner than it feels to the cat.

The onset of puberty does not trigger acne in cats, as it does in humans, and cats do not grow out of acne. Acne is actually more common in older cats, most likely due to decreased grooming activity—the chin is one of the areas a cat can have difficulty cleaning. Acne can occur as a one-time episode, or it can be chronic and recurrent. It is not contagious to other cats or to humans.

A topical reaction to plastic food and water bowls has been implicated as a cause of feline acne. Changing to glass, ceramic or stainless steel bowls helps in some cases. Food oil residues that build up on food and water bowl edges can also contribute to acne. If the animal's chin comes in continual contact with the dirty bowl, it makes sense that oily buildup could clog the pores. Properly washing and drying your cat's dishes every day will help in many cases.

Some cats immerse their chins in their food when they eat. I have had owners inform me that simply serving their cat's food on disposable paper plates has cured the acne.

In mild cases of acne, cleaning the animal's chin daily with hydrogen peroxide is helpful. It will open up the pores, remove the blackheads and clean out oils from the hair follicles. When more pronounced inflammation and infection are present, clipping the hair and a veterinary benzoyl peroxide scrub or cream is recommended. Oral antibiotics may be needed for 10 to 30 days.

Mucopurin (the brand name is Bactoderm) is a product that is useful in some cases of feline acne. It is not currently approved for use in cats, but it is an accepted treatment. Each patient responds differently to topical treatments. In some cases, the treatment can cause severe dryness and irritation, and should be discontinued.

Corticosteroids are useful in relieving inflammation and decreasing fatty secretions in the skin in some cases of acne, but if deep infection is present, corticosteroids can exacerbate the infection. In more advanced cases, vitamin A treatment may be necessary. Topical and oral preparations of vitamin A are available, but side effects are possible.

RINGWORM IS NOT A WORM

Ringworm is actually a fungal infection and has nothing to do with worms. The groups of fungi capable of causing ringworm are called dermatophytes. *Microsporum canis,* or *M. canis* for short, causes the most common type of feline ringworm. Fungal spores in the environment that land on and grow on the skin transmit the fungus. Typically, cats with ringworm are itchy and have red, scaly patches on their skin, along with areas of hair loss.

Diagnosing Ringworm

Ringworm is contagious to humans and other animals, but the good news is that just because you are exposed to it doesn't mean you will get it. If your cat has some sort of dermatitis, wash your hands after you touch her and don't allow the animal to sleep on your bed until a diagnosis has been made.

Ringworm is tentatively diagnosed by a positive Wood's lamp test. A Wood's lamp is a black light that causes shafts of hair infected with the fungus to glow an apple-green color.

To definitively diagnose ringworm, a dermatophtye test medium (DTM) culture should be performed. Ringworm fungus will grow a colony on the DTM, and the specific type of fungus can be isolated and identified.

Treating Ringworm

It can take four to eight weeks to cure a ringworm infection. To successfully treat ringworm, a multifaceted approach is needed. First, the cat should be treated with oral antifungal medication. Weekly shampooing and lime sulfur dips can make the skin more comfortable and decrease the number of contagious spores on the cat.

Giving ringworm-infected cats and nonaffected housemates the oral flea control product Program is a safe ancillary treatment. Program works to inhibit chitin, a protein in the skeleton of fleas and also in the fungal organism.

Ridding the environment of ringworm is almost impossible. Frequently washing the cat's bedding is helpful. Vacuuming can pick up spores, and it is difficult to clean and disinfect the brushes on the vacuum cleaner to prevent further spread. Using a cheap hand vacuum and then disposing of it is another option.

Human ringworm looks like red, circular patches on the skin. These areas are very itchy. Humans with isolated lesions respond well to topical antifungal creams. Creams are not particularly effective on cats because the cats often have multiple lesions, they lick off the cream, and it is hard for the medication to get through the hair onto all the affected skin.

Some cats have side effects from the medications used to treat ringworm, so a veterinarian should monitor the animal's response to treatment. After two weeks of treatment, the cat should be rechecked and a CBC and/or liver enzyme test run to be sure the cat is handling the medication without internal problems. Repeat DTM cultures should be performed, and the cat should continue to be treated for two weeks after the last negative culture.

If an animal is not treated completely, ringworm can quickly flare up again. In multipet households it is usually necessary to treat all the animals so that the infection is not passed back and forth between them.

Previous infection with ringworm does not confer immunity, so it is possible to have several episodes of infection within an animal's lifetime. It can be a frustrating condition to treat, but if you stick with it, the fungus can be controlled.

LOOKING MITEY MANGY

Mange is due to small bugs called mites. The two most common mites that can affect cats are *Otodectes cynotis* and *Notoedres cati*. A type of fur mite called Cheyletiella can also infect cats, and, rarely, a mite called Demodex will as well.

Mite infestations typically make a cat very itchy. These parasites can be diagnosed by finding their presence on an ear swab, skin scraping or tape impression examined microscopically.

Does Your Cat Have Ear Mites?

Otodectes cyanotis is the common ear mite. These mites can also infect dogs, but they are not transmissible to humans. Ear mites can live for short periods in the environment, but they must feed off a dog or cat. The classic signs of an ear mite infection are head shaking, brown crusty discharge from the ears and ear scratching.

If you have an indoor cat who does not come into contact with others, it is easy to cure an infection. If you have animals who go outside, they have the potential for re-exposure.

There are effective over-the-counter treatments for ear mites, but I recommend that if your cat has an ear infection, you have it properly diagnosed by your veterinarian. Although ear mites are frequently found in cats, they are not the only type of ear disease: Bacteria, yeast, allergies and polyps can also affect the ears of cats. If you treat for ear mites and there is another problem, your pet has to be uncomfortable for a longer period of time.

Some of the newer prescription medications used for ear mites are milbemycin oxime (MilbeMite Otic), ivermectin (Acarexx) and selamectin (Revolution). All are very effective.

A positive diagnosis of ear mites is made using an otoscope that looks deep into the ear and observing the mites crawling in the ear canal or by examining an ear swab under a microscope and observing live mites or mite eggs. There is a tendency to think of ear mites as not very serious, and some cat owners think cats with ear mites do not need to be treated. This is absolutely untrue. Ear mites are extremely uncomfortable for a cat—the itching and biting, plus the noise of the mites in the ear canals, are a real torment. In addition, cats with chronic ear mite infections can develop inflammatory polyps in their ear canals. They can also develop blood blisters on their earflaps (ear hematomas) secondary to constant rubbing. Ear mites must be taken seriously and treated promptly.

Can Your Cat Get Scabies?

Scabies is a type of mite infection caused by *Sarcoptes scabei.* This mite is rarely found in cats, but a similar mite, *Notoedres cati,* is common. Notoedres can jump on humans and cause temporary itchiness, but they cannot live on our skin. On cats the mites tend to live around the face and ears, and the cat develops a very crusty appearance. Affected animals are very itchy.

A veterinarian will perform a skin scraping to diagnose this type of mange and will be able to tell you within minutes if the parasite is observed. A skin scraping involves using a scalpel blade to scrape small amounts of hair and skin onto a slide with a drop of mineral oil. Mites or mite eggs are then observed on the slide.

Cats with mites are treated orally or injectably with the cattle dewormer ivermectin, or topically with the cat-approved product Revolution that contains selamectin. Bathing in pyrethrin shampoo will kill mites on contact and aid in treatment.

Cheyletiella

This fur mite is more difficult to isolate and identify than other types of mites. It is typically found on the trunk of a cat, and it causes hair loss, scaling and itchiness. When Cheyletiella is suspected, an impression of a lesion is made on a piece of transparent tape and then examined microscopically.

Treatment for this mite is similar to that of other types of mange, except that this mite can live in the environment for up to three weeks. Using some type of environmental premises treatments that are effective against fleas will also kill these mites.

Demodex

Demodex is a type of mange more frequently found on dogs, but it is occasionally found on cats. This mite does not cause the intense itching characteristic of other types of mange. It can cause patches of hair loss and redness. Your vet can diagnose the infection by observing the mite on a skin scraping.

INSECT AND SPIDER BITES

Cats have a fascination with bugs, and even if your cat lives indoors, she will likely find every creepy crawly in your house. Many of these creatures are harmless and your cat may eat them without a problem, but others will bite and sting when threatened. Some beetles and bugs taste bad and will cause drooling. Others will cause some minor gastrointestinal upset that passes within a few hours.

Cats usually receive bites and stings on their noses and paws, since they like to nose and bat at little creatures. If you notice swelling on these areas, it may be due to an insect bite.

Bee stings are painful and cause swelling on any animal. They are uncomfortable and look bad but are only dangerous if the animal has an anaphylactic reaction. In anaphylaxis, the allergic reaction that occurs causes fever, redness and difficulty breathing.

Antihistamines and/or cortisone can be used to decrease the swelling and itchiness associated with any sting or bite. The earlier these medications are used, the less swelling will develop.

I always know when there is a spider in my house because my cats go wild. They jump up the walls and cry in their desperate attempts to catch it. Most spider bites are not a big deal, but cats are not very discriminating and will hunt harmless and dangerous spiders alike. Depending on where you live, brown recluse and black widow spiders may exist, and these spiders can be quite dangerous.

With their bite, poisonous spiders inject venom that can seriously damage tissue. Initially, a bite wound may not be detected, but within a day or so you'll see an oozing wound with skin sloughing. These types of wounds can take weeks to heal and should be treated promptly by a veterinarian.

OTHER EAR PROBLEMS

Aside from mites, bacteria and yeast can infect the ear canals of cats. Just like some people have greasy hair, some cats have greasy ears and produce excessive amounts of wax. Chronic irritation in the ear canals from any cause can trigger the formation of benign inflammatory polyps. A veterinarian needs to examine the cat's ear canals with an otoscope and analyze ear swabs, because all of these conditions are treated differently.

Ear hematomas result when cats scratch at their ears too much, regardless of the underlying disease. This scratching breaks small blood vessels and causes a blood blister to form between the skin and the cartilage in the ear. This swells and makes the cat even more uncomfortable. Successful treatment must resolve the problem that caused the itching, and surgically drain and repair the damaged ear flap.

CATS CAN GET SKIN CANCER

There are a few different types of cancer that can affect the skin of cats, but squamous cell carcinoma is the most common. Squamous cell carcinoma (SCC) is a type of cancer that can be caused by excessive exposure to sunlight, but it can also occur for no known reason. Aside from the ears and face, SCC can occur in the mouth, on the body and on the feet.

Other types of feline skin cancer include malignant melanoma, mast cell tumors and cutaneous lymphosarcoma. Some can be cured by surgery, while others cannot.

In general, cats do not get many lumps and bumps on their skin, but benign growths called sebaceous cysts are sometimes found. Any time you notice a growth on the cat's skin, you should monitor it and have it checked out by a veterinarian. Increasing size, change in consistency, spread to other locations or pain associated with a growth are all reasons to have it examined.

When your veterinarian examines a growth on the skin, he will likely part the hair, assess the size and squeeze the tissue. Different types of growths have different characteristics.

To make a definitive diagnosis of any skin growth, some type of biopsy is needed. Some veterinarians will perform needle biopsies and cytology in their clinics. They will remove a few cells from the growth, place them on a slide and examine them microscopically. Inflammation, infection and fatty tissue are easily diagnosed this way. Other types of cells may be sent to a lab for a clinical pathologist to review.

Early detection and surgical removal can cure many cases of some types of skin cancer. Cryosurgery (freezing the tissue) and laser surgery are other methods for removing skin growths.

We have all heard about the damage the sun can do to our skin, but do we think about what it is doing to our pets? Fair-skinned people are more sensitive to the effects of sunlight, and the same is true for cats. Protruding areas with white hair and pink, unpigmented skin (such as the ear tips and the end of the nose) are the most affected parts on cats. Cats first become sunburned, then the skin is damaged and then squamous cell carcinoma can develop.

DEFINING SOME TERMS

Cytology is a term used to describe the evaluation of cells under a microscope. This is different than a full *biopsy* with *histopathology*, which involves microscopic evaluation of tissue. The larger the sample, the more cells there are available for making an accurate diagnosis.

If your veterinarian recommends a biopsy, the entire growth or just a piece may be removed. In general, it is a good idea to take as much tissue as possible the first time so that if a problem is found, the animal may not need another surgical procedure.

If you notice red, inflamed skin or scabs on your cat that seem to go away and then come back, you should have the area examined by a veterinarian. It is not common for a cat to injure herself repeatedly in the same area. Sores that don't seem to heal may be indicative of skin cancer.

Indoor cats are not at as much risk for SCC as outdoor cats, but many cats like to lie in shafts of sunlight that shine in through the windows. If the ultraviolet rays are not decreased by window shades or tinting, indoor sunlight is still harmful. Waterproof sunblock can be applied to white ear tips and pink noses to help protect skin against the sun. Keeping an at-risk cat inside between 10 A.M. and 2 P.M., when the sun is strongest, will decrease exposure to the most direct and damaging rays of sunlight.

INFECTIONS AND ABSCESSES

Pyoderma is a bacterial infection of the skin, but it usually occurs secondary to another condition such as a wound, allergies or excessive grooming. Pyoderma is a superficial infection that responds to antibiotics. Medicated baths can help cool the skin, remove crusts and dry out the infection.

Abscesses are deeper infections that start out as punctures or penetrating wounds, most often as a result of cat bites. The infection festers and pockets of pus form under the swollen skin. To effectively treat an abscess, the infected pocket must be surgically lanced and flushed, most often under sedation or anesthesia. A drain is placed to prevent swelling from again trapping infection under the skin, the surgical incision is closed with stitches, and the cat is started on antibiotics. The drain is removed in about three days, and the stitches in 10 to 14 days. A protective collar prevents a cat from chewing on her stitches or pulling out the drain during the healing process.

Chapter 16

The Cardiovascular System

The cardiovascular system in a cat is comprised of blood, blood vessels and the heart. All three components work in harmony to supply oxygen and nutrients throughout the body and remove carbon dioxide and metabolic waste products.

A heart is an amazing organ that will continuously pump throughout the entire lifetime of an animal. This adds up to more than 350 million beats for a 13-year-old cat! Yet this powerful organ weighs less than one-third of an ounce in an average cat.

Heart disease is a common problem in humans, but fortunately cats do not develop arteriosclerosis (hardening of the arteries), the leading cause of heart attack in humans. However, cats can develop hypertension and other cardiovascular diseases.

HOW THE HEART AND THE CIRCULATORY SYSTEM WORK

Blood leaves the heart through arteries and returns to the heart through veins. Arteries and veins channel into smaller and smaller blood vessels that meet at capillaries. Blood leaving the heart is full of oxygen that is sent out to nourish the body's cells. Blood returning to the heart is full of carbon dioxide that must be removed. Nutrients from digested food are absorbed by blood vessels in the intestines and liver and enter the bloodstream. Waste products are produced by all cells, and are filtered out of the blood by the kidneys and then made into urine.

The path the blood takes as it is pumped through the heart is complicated. The heart has four chambers with valves that regulate blood flow. The upper chambers are called atriums and the lower chambers are called ventricles. The major veins bringing blood to the heart are called the *vena cavas*. Blood first enters the right atrium of the heart. It flows into the right ventricle of the heart as it passes through the tricuspid valve. The right ventricle contracts and sends blood into the pulmonary artery through the pulmonary valve. Blood then goes to the lungs and becomes oxygenated.

Oxygenation is the process through which red blood cells become saturated with oxygen in the lungs. Oxygenated blood from the pulmonary vein enters the left atrium. It then passes into the left ventricle via the mitral valve. When the left ventricle contracts, blood is sent out of the heart through the aorta and circulates throughout the rest of the body. This entire cycle continues without pause, regulated by the pacemaker (also known as the sinoatrial node), which is tissue that sends out electrical impulses triggering the heart muscle to contract. Cats very rarely have problems with the pacemakers of their hearts.

The heart is covered by a sac called the *pericardium*. The pericardium is not essential for life, but serves the important role of protecting the heart against friction and inflammation. It stabilizes the heart's position in the chest cavity and maintains its shape.

BLOOD AND BLEEDING

Blood is the fluid that supports any animal's body. It is composed of three different types of cells:

1. Red blood cells, which carry oxygen
2. White blood cells, which fight infection
3. Platelets, which are needed for clotting

All of these cells must be present in sufficient numbers to keep an animal healthy.

Bleeding occurs when a blood vessel becomes damaged, and this can happen inside or outside the body. Under normal circumstances, platelets and clotting factors in the blood help to control bleeding, but if a large blood vessel is damaged, these components may not be able to form an adequate clot.

How to Stop Bleeding

Cats are just like humans when it comes to bleeding. And, just like humans, the first thing to do if a cat is bleeding is to apply pressure. Adhesive bandage strips are not very useful on cats because of all of their hair, so you'll need to apply a more secure bandage. Care must be taken when applying a bandage so that the right amount of pressure is applied to the wound—enough to slow or stop the bleeding, but not enough to stop the surrounding circulation.

Applying ice or cold water to a bleeding wound is also useful. Cold temperatures constrict the blood vessels so less blood is lost. Another helpful hint is to keep the cat calm and stay calm yourself. Cats are very attuned to their owner's body language, and they will be upset if you are. In turn, their blood pressure will rise and make the bleeding worse.

How Much Blood?

Cats have about 30 milliliters of blood per pound of their body weight. This means a 10-pound cat has about one and a quarter cups of blood in his body. It also means a little blood loss can be a serious thing.

If ice and a bandage do not stop bleeding, stitches are probably needed to close the blood vessel and surrounding skin. A veterinarian should do any suturing. Cautery (using chemicals or electricity to seal a blood vessel) can be used in some bleeding situations, such as a broken toenail. Cautery is safe and easy, but it is not appropriate for all types of wounds.

Generally, if you see a few drops of blood come from your cat in an isolated incident, there is no need for alarm. Often it is difficult to even determine where the bleeding is coming from. Common sources of bleeding are:

- Broken toenail
- Broken tooth
- Loss of a baby tooth in a young animal
- Rectal bleeding
- Any external wound
- Biting the tongue
- Bladder inflammation
- Ingesting rat poison (it contains a chemical that prevents blood clotting)

If you cannot isolate the source of the blood, or if there is more than one episode of bleeding, consult your veterinarian. Bleeding can be a sign of other diseases, and uncontrolled bleeding can lead to anemia.

Cats have veins in their toenails, so if a nail is cut too short or broken accidentally, bleeding can occur. You can apply ice, cornstarch, pet cautery powder or a styptic pencil (if you have one) at home, but if bleeding continues or recurs, seek help from your veterinarian.

Bruising is caused by bleeding under the skin. It can be difficult to find bruising on a cat because hair covers most of the skin. If you notice bruising and your cat has not sustained any known trauma, check with your veterinarian. It could be a sign of a clotting disorder.

IF YOUR CAT IS ANEMIC

Anemia is a low red blood cell count. This is not something you would likely be aware of, unless your cat had lost a significant amount of blood. The two major ways anemia is classified are lack of red blood cell production and loss of red blood cells through bleeding.

A veterinarian may suspect your cat is anemic if the animal's gums look pale. A relatively simple test called a packed cell volume (PCV) can be performed in a veterinary office in about five minutes, and will tell the doctor the percentage of red blood cells in a blood sample. A feline PCV should be around 37 percent. Once the value drops below 20 percent, the situation is serious.

A cat can die suddenly if his PCV drops below 15 percent. At this percentage, his body could become starved for oxygen and a blood transfusion must be considered.

Cats who are anemic will often breathe in rapid, shallow breaths. This is because their bodies are trying to get more oxygen, but there are not enough red blood cells with which to transport it. Anemic cats are generally weak and have poor appetites because it is too much work to eat.

Low Red Blood Cell Production

Red blood cells are made in the bone marrow. The marrow is the tissue at the center of bones where immature blood cells live and then become stimulated to mature. Diseases and nutritional deficiencies that affect the bone marrow will impair red blood cell production. Examples of these are cancer, lack of iron, toxins, hormonal imbalances, kidney disease, other metabolic diseases and drugs.

Red Blood Cell Loss

Bleeding due to trauma is an obvious cause of red blood cell loss, but red blood cells can be lost in other ways. One common and unfortunate cause of anemia is an overwhelming flea infestation. Fleas feed on the blood of cats, and if enough fleas are present, the animal can be drained of blood and severe anemia can result. While fleas can cause dangerous anemia in cats of all ages, they are especially dangerous to young kittens, who have very small blood volumes. Cats and kittens can die from flea anemia, but they can easily recover if flea control and supportive measures are done in time.

Another parasite that can cause anemia is called *Hemobartonella felis*, also known as *Mycoplasma haemofelis*. This parasite gets into a cat's blood and causes destruction of red blood cells within the animal's body. Hemobartonellosis is also called feline infectious anemia (FIA). This condition can be effectively treated with oral medications—if it is diagnosed in time.

Autoimmune hemolytic anemia is a disease in which the cat's body no longer recognizes its own red blood cells. The immune system actually destroys its own red blood cells. This type of anemia can be life-threatening if the process is not reversed. Jaundice is a clinical sign that is often observed in cats with hemolytic anemia.

Diagnosing Anemia

The different types of anemia are diagnosed based on the cat's history, exam, blood tests and testing the bone marrow. Once a specific cause or type of anemia is determined, steps are taken to correct the underlying problem and support the animal.

Severely anemic cats need blood transfusions or blood extenders to keep them alive. If the cause of anemia is not a problem with the bone marrow, the animal will usually eventually be able to generate new blood cells.

There are in-clinic test kits or samples can be sent to a reference laboratory to find out a cat's blood type. Most veterinary hospitals have a blood donor cat on the premises to use for transfusions. Modern technology has led to the production of a blood replacer that can be used when typed blood is not available, but it carries risks and must be used carefully in cats.

> **FELINE BLOOD TYPES**
>
> Cats have two main blood types: A and B. Almost all mixed-breed cats and most purebred cats in North America are type A. Abyssinian, Birman, British Shorthair, Cornish Rex, Devon Rex, Exotic Shorthair, Japanese Bobtail, Persian, Scottish Fold, Somali and Sphynx are examples of breeds that may have type B blood.

BORN WITH A BAD HEART

Congenital diseases of the heart do occur in cats but are not as common as they are in dogs. Any component of the heart can cause disease if it is defective. The important components of the heart are:

- The blood vessels leading into and out of the heart
- The four main chambers of the heart
- The valves between the chambers of the heart

Cats born with bad hearts may not show any signs of problems. Signs of heart disease are weakness, rapid or difficult breathing and exercise intolerance. A veterinarian may suspect heart disease in a cat after listening to the animal's chest with a stethoscope and evaluating the rate, rhythm and sound of the heartbeat.

LEAKY VALVES

The tricuspid and mitral valves are important in regulating blood flow through the heart. In cats, deformities of these valves are the most common congenital cardiac malformations. Problems with the valves can often be detected by cardiac auscultation. *Auscultation* means listening to the heart and lungs with a stethoscope. A murmur—a squishing noise that indicates there is blood leaking out of the valves when the heart contracts—can be detected during cardiac auscultation. Instead of forming a tight seal, blood escapes around the valve.

The intensity or loudness of a heart murmur does not say much about the severity of damage to the valves. Some kittens are born with murmurs that they outgrow, much like human children. Other cats have murmurs their entire lives that never get worse or cause heart disease. Unfortunately, some murmurs progress and lead to congestive heart failure.

Murmurs are also extremely common in older cats. Over time, the seal a valve forms may begin to leak. Leaky valves causing congestive heart failure are much less common in cats than they are in dogs, where this disorder is frequently observed.

HOW THE HEART IS EVALUATED

Hormones and other chemicals within the body affect heart output. Every cat owner has felt the pounding of their pet's heart when he becomes fearful. Adrenaline stimulates the heart to pump faster so the animal can react more quickly to fear. I meet many fearful animals at my veterinary clinic. Gentle stroking and calm words are often needed to relax the animal so that heart auscultation can be done properly. But I have to be careful not to relax the animal too much—if he really relaxes, I can't hear his heart over the purring!

The tests that are performed to check the heart are:

- Auscultation
- Chest X rays
- Electrocardiogram (ECG)
- Heart sonogram-echocardiogram

If an examination and auscultation cause a veterinarian to suspect heart disease, the next diagnostic step is chest X rays. X rays show the size, shape and location of the heart. They also show if there is fluid or other problems in the lungs or chest cavity.

An ECG may or may not be performed. This test measures the electrical activity of the heart and can localize some types of heart disease. The feline heart is relatively small, which makes diagnostic testing difficult, and electrocardiograph measurement in cats produces small tracings that can be a challenge to interpret.

Cardiac ultrasonography, or sonogram, is the most useful diagnostic tool available to assess the heart's function and appearance. X rays of the heart tell veterinarians about the size and shape of the heart, but not how the blood is being pushed through. Ultrasound enables the veterinarian to see and measure the individual heart chambers, valves and major blood vessels. It can also document cardiac output and blood-flow patterns. This information is crucial when diagnosing a problem with the heart muscle. It can also be used to measure a cat's response to drug therapy.

TREATING CONGENITAL HEART DISEASE

About 2 percent of cats are born with congenital heart defects. In addition to problems with the valves, which I have already discussed, there may be holes in different chambers of the heart or strictures in blood vessels leaving the heart. Some types of congenital heart diseases can be surgically corrected and the cat can live a normal life. Other types may be monitored throughout a cat's life but never cause any clinical signs, and still others may be life-threatening.

Heart surgery is tricky in any animal, but due to the small size of cats, it can be especially risky and expensive. Most congenital disease involves defects in the structures of the heart, and these problems generally do not respond to medication.

HEART MUSCLE DISEASE

The pumping action of the heart is achieved when the different chambers of the heart constrict in a specific sequence (see page 162). The heart itself is primarily composed of muscle tissue, and diseases can affect this tissue. The medical term for heart muscle disease is *cardiomyopathy*. There are three main types:

1. Dilated cardiomyopathy (DCM)
2. Hypertrophic cardiomyopathy (HCM)
3. Restrictive cardiomyopathy (RCM)

Cardiomyopathy should be suspected in the sudden death of an otherwise young, healthy animal. Often there are no obvious clinical signs of heart muscle disease, so the problem may not be detected or suspected before heart failure occurs.

Echocardiography is needed to definitively diagnose any type of cardiomyopathy. It is also used to monitor the progression of the disease and the cat's response to therapy. If your veterinarian does not have an ultrasound machine, a specialist with a mobile unit may be asked to come to the clinic or you may be referred to a specialty center that has this equipment.

Dilated Cardiomyopathy

In dilated cardiomyopathy (DCM), the heart muscle stretches out and becomes a thin, flaccid sack that is unable to contract properly. Blood is not effectively pumped between the chambers or out of the heart.

A few decades ago researchers discovered that dilated cardiomyopathy is most often caused by a dietary deficiency of the amino acid taurine. This discovery led pet food manufacturers to add more taurine to cat foods, which virtually eliminated this heart problem.

Hypertrophic Cardiomyopathy

Hypertrophic cardiomyopathy (HCM) is currently the most common type of heart muscle disease. The cause is unknown, but the disease may be the result of a congenital defect or may be acquired during a cat's lifetime. A cat with hypertrophic cardiomyopathy has thickened walls of the left ventricle. This can also lead to thickening of other heart chamber walls.

As the wall thickens, the size of the chamber decreases and less blood is pumped through the heart. Turbulence and pressure builds within the heart, aggravates the condition and makes the thickening worse.

There are some drugs that can be used to reduce the stresses to the heart and improve its function, but the disease cannot be cured. Cats with HCM have shorter life spans because at some point the heart fails.

A complication of HCM in cats is aortic thrombosis or saddle thrombus. This is a blood clot that forms in the heart and then becomes trapped at the splitting of the aorta, where this large blood vessel supplies blood to the rear legs. The prognosis for a cat with an aortic thrombus is not good. Treatment may dissolve the clot, but the underlying heart disease cannot be stopped and will progress.

Cats with aortic thrombosis will suddenly become weak or paralyzed in their back legs due to the interrupted blood supply. This loss of circulation is very painful to the animal. Less commonly, thrombi can lodge and obstruct circulation to the front legs. A cat with a thrombus will have cold, dark footpads and his toenails will not bleed where circulation is lost.

Restrictive Cardiomyopathy

There are cats with heart muscle disease that does not classically fall into either DCM or HCM. These animals are usually put in the category of restrictive cardiomyopathy. Medications can be used to help make the heart pump more effectively, but this disease will also progress.

HIGH BLOOD PRESSURE

For a long time, most veterinarians didn't know that feline high blood pressure, or hypertension, existed because they didn't know how to check for it. Measuring blood pressure in cats is now becoming more routine because veterinarians have fairly reliable equipment.

In humans both systolic and diastolic measurements are used to evaluate blood pressure. *Systole* is the highest blood pressure and occurs when the heart contracts and pumps blood. *Diastole* is the lowest pressure and occurs when the heart relaxes and fills with blood. Systolic values are considered the most sensitive indicator of feline hypertension, and values over 180 mm Hg are considered too high.

Hypertension is usually found in older cats who are also affected with kidney disease and/or hyperthyroidism, but it can also be a primary disease. If the heart sustains long periods of high blood pressure, it can weaken. Hyperthyroidism can lead to overstimulation of the heart muscle, which also wears the muscle out prematurely and leads to failure.

To control blood pressure in cats, the underlying disease must first be controlled. If no underlying disease is found, drugs are available to control blood pressure. Lower sodium diets are also useful.

FELINE HEARTWORM DISEASE

If you have a dog, you may be familiar with heartworm disease. The heartworm parasite *Dirofilaria immitis* is transmitted by mosquito bites, which inject the immature stage of the worm into an animal's blood. These larvae develop into adult worms that like to live in the heart or pulmonary blood vessels. Heartworm disease can cause breathing problems and damage to the heart.

Cats have natural resistance to heartworms, but they can still become infected. There is a higher risk of infection in areas where there are more mosquitoes carrying heartworm larvae. With no exposure to infected mosquitoes, cats cannot get heartworm.

Preventive medication is available to protect cats who are at risk for heartworms. Ask your veterinarian about the risk of heartworm in your area, and then decide if preventive care is needed.

Diagnosing Heartworms

Heartworms should be considered as a possible diagnosis for cats who have signs of heart disease, vomiting or asthma and live in a high-risk area where mosquitoes are present. Blood tests that look for antigens to the parasite and antibodies the cat produces against the parasite are useful in making a diagnosis. Heartworms can be observed on an ultrasound of the heart.

Dogs infected with heartworms have many adult worms in their bodies, whereas cats may only have one to three worms. Smaller worm loads in cats make diagnosis more difficult.

Treating Heartworms

Sudden death can occur in cats infected with heartworms due to embolization. This is because clots (emboli) caused by the worms can lodge in the heart, brain or lungs and block blood flow. There are potential complications regardless of the treatment used.

The toxicity and side effects of treatments that kill adult heartworms (adulticides) in cats are considered more of a risk than living with the parasites for cats who have mild clinical signs. Depending on their location in the heart, worms can sometimes be removed with special forceps or brushes. Adult worms usually only live for about two years in cats, so if the clinical signs they are creating can be controlled medically, adulticides are not used. Conservative medical treatment consists of using cortisone to control the inflammation caused by the worms in the airways.

Chapter 17

The Musculoskeletal System

A cat's body is shaped the way it is because of the cat's musculoskeletal system, which is comprised of the bones, the muscles and the tissues that connect them. The skeleton supports the structure of the cat's body and protects some internal organs. The muscles enable the body to move by controlling direction and range of motion. Cartilage, tendons and ligaments hold it all together.

Cats carry 60 percent of their weight on their front legs, so during normal activity less stress is placed on the back legs. Jumping up initially puts all the stress on the back legs, and jumping down puts all the stress on the front legs. These factors should be kept in mind when dealing with injuries.

House cats are fairly sedentary animals, but they have bodies that are designed for hunting and stalking. Cats are extremely flexible and quick (unless they are overweight), and they are able to perform some very athletic feats. It is not uncommon to find cats perched on top of dressers, on the high shelves of bookcases, or even climbing up on roofs of houses. This chapter will address some of the more common problems of the bones and muscles of cats.

IT'S HARD TO GET UP IN THE MORNING

"Fluffy doesn't jump up on my bed the way she used to. Could she have arthritis?" "Sly has a hard time walking after he's been asleep. What could this mean?" Questions such as these are commonly asked at my clinic. I tell owners that, just like humans, cats can develop arthritis.

Classic osteoarthritis (the medical term is *degenerative joint disease*, or DJD) can develop in cats. Arthritic animals have changes in the bones of their joints that cause discomfort and can decrease their range of motion. Your vet may suspect arthritis based on a physical examination and pain in the joints, but an X ray is needed to observe the characteristic changes and confirm the diagnosis.

The earliest clinical sign detected in cats with arthritis is lameness. As this gets worse, the cat becomes reluctant to perform certain movements or activities, and there is apparent stiffness or pain. Stiffness may become more pronounced after periods of rest, as the disease progresses. Affected joints may look and feel enlarged and swollen, and the range of motion becomes restricted.

There are some uncommon types of arthritis where inflammation of joints occurs but bony changes do not. This can occur with joint infection, trauma and immune–mediated conditions.

Can You Prevent Arthritis?

Once arthritis has developed it cannot be cured, and small changes do occur as a normal part of aging. Signs include:

- Stiffness after sleeping
- Inability to jump up on things
- Lameness
- Problems getting into and out of a litter box

HIP DYSPLASIA

Hip dysplasia is a type of degenerative joint disease most commonly seen in dogs, but it is also seen in cats. It is a disease of young animals who are born with poor conformation of their hip joints. Rubbing occurs between the bones in the hip joint and arthritis follows.

OTHER POSSIBILITIES

If a veterinarian suspects arthritis but X rays don't support the diagnosis, it is likely that nerve pain rather than bone or muscle pain is the problem. You may need a referral to a veterinary neurologist and additional diagnostic tests, such as a special X ray of the spine, called a myelogram, or an MRI.

Joints are made up of bones that have cartilage on their ends. The cartilage cushions the bones and decreases friction. Each joint has a small amount of fluid in it called synovial fluid that lubricates the cartilage and adds more cushioning. In an arthritic joint, the cartilage becomes rough, the joint fluid becomes thick and abnormal calcium deposits are formed at the ends of the bones.

You can decrease the risk of arthritis for your cat by feeding her a good diet that ensures proper bone growth and development. Controlling a cat's weight is very important because the heavier a cat is, the more stress is placed on her joints. Keeping a cat indoors will lower the risk of trauma to bones and joints, and trauma can lead to arthritis. Cold temperatures make joints ache more, so allowing an older animal with arthritis to sleep on a padded, warm surface can help make the cat more comfortable.

Don't Take Two Aspirin . . .

Cats are very stoic animals, so it is difficult to assess how much pain an arthritic cat is in. The worst thing you can do is try to treat pain without consulting a veterinarian. Over-the-counter anti-inflammatory and pain medications for human should *never* be given to a cat. If you think that your cat has arthritis and discomfort, consult your veterinarian to find out what safe medical treatments exist.

Medications used to treat arthritis may include children's aspirin or other nonsteroidal anti-inflammatory drugs (NSAIDs), cortisone and nutritional supplements. One 83-mg children's aspirin can be safely given once every three days—but only under the supervision of a veterinarian. Any other NSAIDs, such as carprofen and ketoprofen are much more toxic and are prescribed much less frequently.

Cortisone is often used in cats to reduce pain and inflammation. Owners are sometimes reluctant to use corticosteroids because, they have heard of the problems these drugs cause in humans. Cats are much less sensitive to the effects of these drugs and most show no side effects. Corticosteroids can be given orally or by injection. Whenever this class of drugs is used, the lowest dose that controls the symptoms is best.

Glycosaminoglycans (GAGs) have also been used in the management of arthritis. They are available as injectable drugs or as oral supplements. Various manufacturers make glucosamine nutritional supplements that contain slightly different forms of the chemical. GAGs do not provide immediate relief from pain or inflammation; rather, GAGs improve the consistency of the cartilage and joint fluid so that joint friction is reduced. This process takes from three to six weeks, because that's how long it takes to remodel the tissue. In many cases cats can be managed with these products alone.

Other nutritional supplements helpful to some cats are fish oils, antioxidants (vitamins E and C and zinc) and MSM (methylsulfonymethane). Make sure you give your cat the right dose, because supplements can create problems when a cat gets too much.

Helping a cat with arthritis to get up and down to familiar spots is beneficial. This can be done by physically placing the cat or by using a step or stool to help the cat reach her destination. It is also helpful to be sure food and water bowls are easily accessible, and that the animal is able to get in and out of her litter box.

GLUCOSAMINE AND ARTHRITIS

Glucosamine and chondroitin sulfate are nutritional supplements that may help humans and animals with arthritis. These products can improve cartilage and joint fluid but are not anti-inflammatories. There are hundreds of products available that contain these ingredients, but a study performed at the University of Maryland Pharmacy School and published in the *Journal of American Nutraceutical Association* in Spring 2000 showed that 84 percent of products tested did not meet their label claims. The same study looked at absorption of chondroitin sulfate and found much variability.

The bottom line is use a product that guarantees its analysis and has research data to back up its claims. This is true for any supplements, since, unfortunately their manufacture and marketing is not well regulated.

IT'S BROKEN

Any bone in the body can break if enough force is applied to it. Cats break bones when they are hit by a car, fall from a height, get shaken by a dog or larger animal, get caught in a garage door or even get stepped on by their owner. The bad news is that fractures are painful injuries, but the good news is that cats generally heal well.

There is significant pain and swelling associated with a fracture. A veterinarian may be able to feel the ends of the broken bone or hear abnormal cracking sounds, but an X ray is always needed. At least two views of the bone are necessary to properly evaluate the fracture and assess options for setting and immobilizing it. Aside from diagnosing the fracture, it is necessary to evaluate the surrounding tissues to see if there is other damage.

Some fractures heal adequately without surgery or a cast, such as pelvic fractures that don't involve the hip joints. If there is no damage to the nerves, hip joints or other organs, cats with pelvic fractures can be confined and treated with supportive care, and may be up walking and functioning on their own within two weeks. This is quite a feat, considering that humans with the same injury can be bedridden for months.

Putting the Pieces Together

The location of the fracture and the number of pieces of bone involved will determine how easy or difficult the repair will be. Many veterinarians do basic orthopedic procedures in their hospitals, but complicated injuries may need to be referred to a board-certified veterinary surgeon. Surgeons usually have more experience and equipment available for good repair of fractures. The equipment used to repair bones includes:

- Surgical wires
- Stainless steel pins
- Bone plates
- Bone screws
- External fixation apparatus
- Casts
- Splints

Is Amputation an Option?

There is an art to fixing leg fractures, but sometimes the damage is so severe or expensive that amputation may have to be considered. It is an idea that may be hard to accept, but cats with three legs can do extremely well and lead normal lives. It may take cats a few weeks to figure out how to make the remaining limbs work together, but after awhile you both may forget that the animal is handicapped.

Amputation may also be necessary when tumors affect bones or tissues of the limbs. This is done to prevent the spread of disease and create surgical borders that are free from cancerous tissue.

The Healing Process

The younger the animal, the quicker the bones will heal. Complete healing can take 6 to 12 weeks, depending on the severity of the fracture. During this period the cat should be kept indoors and her activity restricted. It's hard to restrict a cat, but lifting her up and down and carrying her up steps is helpful. It may be necessary to confine her to one room if you are unable to get the cat to rest.

Follow-up X rays will show how the bone has healed. Even if healing is not perfect, pet cats will do well since they don't have to hunt to feed themselves and they can stay indoors and be protected. Sometimes when orthopedic hardware is used to immobilize the bones, it needs to be removed once the bone has healed. This may involve tranquilization or sedation.

SPRAINS AND STRAINS

Sometimes cats have soft-tissue injuries, including sprains and strains. Sprains are twisting or pulling of ligaments, which are the tissues that connect bones. Strains are twisting or pulling of tendons, which are the tissues that connect muscles to bones.

Soft-tissue injuries can be just as painful and swollen as fractures. To diagnose a sprain or strain, a veterinarian will first examine the cat and manipulate the affected limb, joint by joint, to find out the exact location of the injury. If pain and/or swelling can be isolated and a joint is involved, the stability of the joint will next be evaluated.

An X ray of a sprain or strain may show swelling, but it won't show the specific tissues involved or the amount of damage. This is because

X rays don't show much contrast between different soft-tissue structures. If a significant number of ligaments around a joint are seriously damaged, however, the bones may not line up as expected and this will show on an X ray.

Cats don't know when they need to rest, so it can be difficult to keep an animal confined so that healing can occur. Pain relievers can be used, but there may be a trade-off between pain control and activity: Cats may need to feel some discomfort so that they will take it easy.

You can place a limb in a sling or put a support wrap on a soft-tissue injury, but often the cat is more bothered by the wrap than by the injury. Cats are free spirits who hate having their movement restricted in any way, so it may be better to do nothing.

It usually takes from two to six weeks for a sprain or strain to heal, and once a joint has been damaged, it is never the same again. It is easy for injuries to recur after a sprain or strain, because the scar tissue that forms during healing is not as strong as the original tissue.

DO CATS GET CRUCIATE INJURIES?

Sports fans may be familiar with the anterior cruciate ligament (ACL), which is one of the main ligaments that hold an animal's (or a person's) knee together. Tearing it is a common injury of football players.

Even though most house cats are agile athletes, they can get their leg stuck or land on it in an awkward position and sprain or tear their anterior cruciate ligament. Depending on the severity of the injury, the cat may or may not be able to walk on a leg with cruciate damage.

A veterinarian can determine if the ACL has been injured by performing an anterior drawer test. This involves measuring the amount of laxity present when the knee is moved forward and back. The more lax the movement, the more damage the ligament has sustained.

Most ACL injuries in cats will heal if the animal is put on injured reserve for two to four weeks. If, during this time, adequate healing does not occur, surgery may be needed to stabilize the knee.

BORN WITH UNIQUE BONES

Kittens can be born with a variety of skeletal problems. Some give them an unusual appearance, and others affect the way they function. If functioning is a problem, surgical correction is necessary.

Some breeds of cats developed because they were selectively bred to emphasize conformational differences of certain bones. The most popular of these is the Persian, with its round skull and flattened, brachycephalic face. Burmese and Himalayans are other breeds that share the "pushed-in nose" look. (You may think of the skull as one unique bone, but this is not the case. Cats have 29 different bones that make up the skulls.)

Different numbers of tailbones characterize some breeds. Most cats have between 18 and 20 caudal vertebrae that make up their tails. Manx cats have far fewer, and are considered "rumpys" or "stumpys," based on how much of a tail they have. Their lack of tail is due to an inherited dominant trait. Japanese Bobtails and Pixie Bobs are other breeds with shorter-than-average tails.

Another tail defect is a congenital kink. Many cats are born with kinks in their tails, and this is considered a recessive trait. The kink can come from trauma at birth (or immediately following), or it can just be the way the kitten turned out. Most owners think the kinky tail gives their cat character.

A polydactyl cat is one who has extra toes, and this trait results from an autosomal dominant gene. Domestic cats have 19 pairs of chromosomes. Eighteen pairs are autosomal, meaning nonsex-determining chromosomes, while the last pair are the sex-determining sex chromosomes.

Some cats have extra toes on their front feet and some have extras on all four feet. Polydactyl cats need more help keeping their nails short because the extra nails usually do not get worn down during normal activity. Unclipped nails that continue to grow will actually penetrate into the footpads, causing pain and infection.

Humans can also be born polydactyl. Throughout history, people with extra fingers were considered to be witches. Anne Boleyn, one of Henry VIII's wives, had six fingers on one hand. She was decapitated following accusations of adultery, before a strong witchcraft case could be made against her.

Polydactyl cats can be awfully cute.

SURGERY FOR BONE DEFORMITIES

Hip dysplasia can occur in cats, but because most cats, unlike dogs, don't do a lot of running, they live fairly comfortably with this condition. If pain or problems progress, a surgical procedure called a femoral head osteotomy can help keep the hip bones from rubbing and worsening the condition. This surgery is also used when a cat dislocates her hip as the result of an injury and it will not stay back in place.

Pectus excavatum is a congenital deformity of the rib cage. Kittens with pectus have a flattened chest cavity and their breathing can be impaired. Some cats grow out of this condition, but for others, breathing worsens and a surgical procedure that pulls out the ribs is needed to correct the defect. This defect may be seen in any cat, but certain lines of Bengal cats seem to have a higher incidence.

Some cats are born with a luxating patella, which is a kneecap that pops out of joint. This condition is usually due to an abnormally shallow groove in the femur (the long bone the kneecap sits on) but can also result from trauma. Cats with luxating patellas may have an intermittently collapsing rear leg. They may hop temporarily until the kneecap pops back into place. A surgical procedure that deepens the groove and tightens the knee joint can successfully correct this problem.

Chapter 18

The Endocrine System

The system of glands that secrete hormones is the endocrine system. Hormones are chemicals that produce an effect on another part of the body. Some hormones have very specific functions, while others affect many other body systems in a subtle manner.

There are many different hormones produced throughout a cat's body, but there are only a few that cause common imbalances or problems. Hormones are usually transported through the blood to their target tissues. The main endocrine glands that produce hormones are the pituitary, thyroid, parathyroid, pancreas, adrenals and ovaries or testes.

IF YOUR CAT HAS A HYPER THYROID

Cats have two thyroid glands located on their lower neck. A normal thyroid gland is difficult to palpate during a physical exam but may be detected if it is enlarged. Hyperthyroidism is the most common endocrine abnormality seen in cats. This condition is usually caused by a benign growth, known as a thyroid adenoma, that overproduces thyroid hormone.

Cats nine years old and up are most affected by hyperthyroidism. While it is common for cats to be hyperthyroid, it is common for dogs to be hypothyroid, which means they have underactive thyroid glands. Humans can have thyroid imbalances either way.

Signs of Hyperthyroidism

The thyroid gland produces hormones that have many different functions. Their main purpose is to regulate metabolism. Thyroid hormone affects every part of the body to some degree, but its major effects are on the heart, skin and gastrointestinal tract.

The common clinical signs associated with hyperthyroidism are:

- Weight loss
- Increased appetite
- Increased thirst
- Increased urination
- Increased heart rate and possibly irregular heartbeat

Owners might notice these changes in their cat, but often they are discovered during a routine physical examination and discussion with a veterinarian. If a veterinarian suspects your cat is hyperthyroid, she will want to perform some blood tests.

Blood tests are good for pinpointing hyperthyroidism and for differentiating the disease from other metabolic imbalances. If the thyroid hormone level is not out of the normal range on a basic test, but clinical signs suggest a problem, the veterinarian may want to perform either a T3 suppression test or free T4 by equilibrium dialysis. A T3 suppression test is a blood test that looks at whether the thyroid gland reacts normally to the administration of supplemental thyroid hormone. A normal cat's T4 values will go down in this situation, but a hyperthyroid cat's will not. Free T4 by equilibrium dialysis is a blood test that is felt to more accurately evaluate T4 levels. These tests are straightforward but not without some false positives.

Finally, another test called a technicium scan may be required. This test highlights the thyroid gland through special imaging and shows if there is overactive tissue.

Treating Hyperthyroidism

Uncontrolled thyroid disease will lead to many problems. Aside from poor general condition and a slow wasting process, a hyperthyroid cat can develop serious heart disease. Heart disease occurs because the heart is under too much continual stimulation and the muscle begins to weaken. High blood pressure can also result from hyperthyroidism.

There are three accepted treatments for hyperthyroidism:

1. Drug therapy
2. Surgery
3. Radioisotope treatment

Each treatment has its pros and cons. A veterinarian should discuss all the options and help you decide on the most appropriate course, based on your individual situation. Once a cat becomes hyperthyroid, it will always be hyperthyroid unless the overactive tissue is removed.

Drug Therapy

This is the least expensive option for treating hyperthyroidism, and usually means giving the cat methimazole twice a day. Most cats tolerate this drug extremely well, but others can have side effects such as vomiting, bone marrow suppression and dermatitis.

To monitor for side effects and the effectiveness of the treatment, a cat is started on a low dose of medication and then evaluated two weeks later. At that time it is advisable to do a red blood cell count to look for bone marrow suppression. Based on the results, the cat may stay on the same dose or the dose could be modified. Cats are generally checked every two weeks until the thyroid level is in the normal range.

Medical treatment will continue the rest of the cat's lifetime. It is not the end of the world if an owner misses giving a dose every now and then, but to be properly regulated, the cat must receive medication regularly. Long-term medication costs and repeated follow up testing will add up over years, so don't disregard other treatment options.

Take Them Out

Surgical removal of the thyroid glands can be a successful treatment. Both glands are usually removed because it is difficult to tell if one or both glands are affected without looking at the tissue microscopically. The surgery involves the tissues of the neck and no body cavities are opened. Once the thyroid is removed, it will not grow back. Some glands have malignant tumors called thyroid carcinomas, which are discovered when a biopsy is performed.

One risk of surgery is that the parathyroid glands, which are located close to the thyroid glands, can be accidentally removed at the same time. The parathyroid glands are responsible for calcium balance in the body. Other risks of surgery are that a cat's thyroid level can become too low if both glands are removed, and if overactive thyroid tissue is located outside the gland itself, it will remain in the body and continue to cause problems.

If an owner does not want to medicate his cat, surgery is a reasonable option. There is not a long recovery period, but hormone and calcium levels should be checked postoperatively, and supplementation may be needed for the cat's lifetime.

Nuke Them Out

Radioisotope therapy involves treating the cat with radioactive iodine. The thyroid gland naturally takes up iodine from the blood and concentrates it, so the radioactive iodine gets to its target tissue easily. The radioactive isotope destroys the abnormal tissue.

Radioisotope therapy is considered superior to surgical removal and medical treatment because:

- It's a one-time treatment
- The overactive tissue is selectively destroyed, rather than removing the entire gland
- There is no risk of anesthesia
- The parathyroid glands are untouched

The disadvantages are:

- Significant expense
- Hospitalization for approximately 3 to 14 days (depending on local environmental regulations) while the radiation is eliminated from the cat's body
- Some cats develop kidney disease when their thyroid level drops too low too quickly

Radioactive iodine treatment is only available at special veterinary hospitals with the proper facilities. Depending on where you live, this mode of treatment may not be easily available. If you have a hyperthyroid cat, discuss all of the options with your veterinarian.

IODINE

Iodine is an essential mineral for animals, including humans. There was a time when iodine deficiency was common in humans, and people developed goiters (swollen thyroid glands) because they did not get enough in their diets. Today, good old table salt is iodized and provides iodine to the body.

FELINE DIABETES

Diabetes mellitus is a disease in which glucose in the blood cannot be properly taken up and used by the cells of the body. This is usually due to a lack of insulin, a hormone responsible for transporting glucose into cells. The pancreas is the organ that produces insulin.

Diabetic cats eat but are essentially starving because the glucose in their blood cannot be used for energy. As this process continues, the animal's body condition declines. Muscle and fat are broken down for energy—in essence, the body is eating itself—because the body is not obtaining glucose from food.

Signs of Diabetes

The classic signs of diabetes are increased thirst, increased urination and weight loss. Other signs that can be associated with the disease are bladder infection (caused by too much glucose in the urine), abnormal posture (cats get a nerve disorder that makes them walk on their heels), loss of muscle tone and shock.

There are some drugs that can cause diabetes mellitus as a side effect. Megestrol acetate is the most common culprit, but some cats are sensitive to even routinely used corticosteroids. (Megestrol acetate, a synthetic progestin, is currently not used often in feline medicine. It can be used for behavior problems, to suppress estrus and for some dermatological conditions, although it is not a first-choice treatment.) Drug-induced diabetes is usually a temporary condition, but it may need treatment for months.

Overweight, older cats are at greater risk for developing diabetes. The disease is diagnosed by finding high levels of glucose in the blood and urine of the affected animal. If the disease has been present but undetected for awhile, other metabolic imbalances may also be present.

TWO TYPES OF DIABETES

There are actually two major types of diabetes in animals. Diabetes mellitus is the disease with which most people are familiar. Diabetes insipidus is a less common disease involving water balance in the body.

Hyperglycemia is the medical term used to describe higher-than-normal levels of glucose in the blood. Although this situation is usually attributed to diabetes, cats who are stressed will have high blood glucose levels. Truly diabetic cats will have significantly higher blood glucose levels than stressed cats. If there is any question, a blood test that measures serum fructosamine can differentiate between the two.

Treating Diabetes

If left uncontrolled, diabetic cats will starve to death, but the progression may take years. Each veterinarian has her own way of treating diabetic cats. The choices for treatment are insulin given by injection or oral hypoglycemic agents (drugs that lower blood glucose by making cells more sensitive to insulin), along with a change in diet. The problem with the disease in cats is that cats metabolize some drugs very rapidly, and insulin's effects are variable.

Most cats need insulin injections twice a day, ideally 12 hours apart, to begin good blood glucose regulation. Insulin is given by subcutaneous injection, and giving insulin injections is relatively easy if you are willing to learn.

Although most diabetic cats will require insulin for their entire lives, some are transient or temporary diabetics, and their need for insulin will come and go. Even when regulated, diabetic cats should be examined and have their blood glucose monitored at least every six months. If there is ever any doubt as to how a diabetic cat is doing, or if the animal is not eating, it is always better to skip an injection rather than to keep giving insulin. Too much insulin, or insulin given without food, can cause hypoglycemia, which can be a life-threatening condition.

My personal experience using oral hypoglycemic agents has been variable, with effective results obtained after first starting treatment with insulin. I have had poor success with initial glucose regulation on oral medication alone. If a cat is doing well on insulin, the treatment is continued. If good regulation is not achieved with insulin, then I add in an oral agent. The combination typically lowers the amount of insulin needed. If a cat seems to need less insulin, I will try to maintain the patient on oral treatment alone. Managing this disease requires a balancing act.

Diet can play a role in managing diabetes, but it can also be a cause. Since cats are naturally carnivores and metabolize protein for glucose, it is thought that dry cat foods that contain a high percentage of carbohydrates may predispose certain cats to developing diabetes. Although older research indicated that fiber added to a diet helped control blood glucose, newer studies show that higher protein and lower carbohydrate diets may be more ideal for diabetic cats. Fiber is actually a type of carbohydrate.

Canned foods tend to contain higher protein levels than dry. There is a specially formulated high-protein diabetes diet that comes in both canned and dry forms, but most canned kitten food contains similar protein levels. Whichever diet is chosen, weight management is another important aspect to controlling diabetes.

UTERINE INFECTIONS

One of the reasons spaying is recommended for cats is that intact female cats are at risk for pyometra, a uterine infection. Pyometra is a serious condition in which the uterus becomes distended and filled with pus. If the infected organ ruptures, pus can spread all over the abdominal cavity and cause peritonitis—a potentially fatal infection of the abdomen.

Fortunately, most pet owners spay their cats at an early age and do not have to worry about this problem. Experienced cat breeders are aware of the condition and monitor their queens for the telltale sign of creamy-colored vaginal discharge.

Cats with pyometra can have fever, lethargy and poor appetite. If a veterinarian suspects pyometra, she may confirm the diagnosis by palpating the abdominal cavity and finding an enlarged, fluid-filled uterus. If this is not found, she may do a blood test to look for a high white blood cell count. Other useful tests are vaginal smears to look for white blood cells (the components of pus) and bacteria, and X rays or ultrasound, which can be more sensitive for identifying uterine enlargement.

Unless there is an exceptional reason to keep a female cat intact, the best treatment for a cat with pyometra is spaying her. The surgical procedure is more complicated than a routine spay surgery because the infected uterus is fragile and must be handled carefully to prevent problems. A cat with pyometra is usually not in prime health, because she has been fighting an internal infection. Under these circumstances, close monitoring and strong supportive care is needed.

If an owner does not want to have the cat's uterus and ovaries removed, medical treatment is an option. Antibiotics and drugs called prostaglandins are used to treat the infection and shrink the uterus. Prostaglandins stimulate uterine contraction, but they can also cause general cramping and discomfort.

Cats who have had pyometra have a high chance of recurrence.

CATS CAN GET BREAST CANCER

We're all quite aware of breast cancer, and most women do their best to routinely screen themselves for problems. Cats can get breast cancer too, and the type they get is usually malignant. Cats most at risk for developing breast cancer are unspayed older females, cats who had litters earlier in their lives, and cats who were spayed after they had several heat cycles.

The risk of breast cancer in a cat who has never had a heat cycle is close to zero, so again, this is another reason to spay a young animal. There are no other specific actions you can take to prevent breast cancer, but monitoring the mammary glands for lumps so that any problem can be detected early is a good idea.

There are astute owners who feel the lumps on their cats. Initially, a malignant growth will feel like a hard BB near one or more of the nipples. The smaller the growth and the earlier it is removed, the better the cat's chances for survival.

During a routine annual physical exam, a veterinarian should palpate all eight mammary glands on a cat and search for lumps. Occasionally cats will develop cysts or benign growths, but a biopsy is the only way to know the exact status of a lump.

Most often a veterinarian will remove the entire growth, rather than take a small biopsy. Mammary cancer tends to run down the mammary chain first on one side, then the other, so a radical mastectomy may be recommended. All of the glands on one or both sides are removed in a radical mastectomy.

Mammary cancer is not strictly a disease of female cats; male cats can be affected, too. Even though they have not been in heat or had female hormonal stimulation, male cats have nipples. If you have a male cat with a growth near a nipple, have it examined by a veterinarian.

As with most cancers, it's important to begin treatment right away. Surgical removal of the affected tissue and even unilateral or bilateral radical mastectomy may be needed. The tissue should definitely be sent for biopsy.

Your veterinarian may recommend additional chemotherapy, or you may want to consult with a veterinary oncologist. Chemotherapy is an aggressive approach, but it is well tolerated by most cats and may help to preserve a good quality of life.

The conservative approach is to monitor the cat for recurrences, and surgically remove any new lumps that develop. Taking chest X rays every six months or so will monitor for metastasis of cancer to the lungs. If a cat who has been previously diagnosed with breast cancer starts to have problems coughing or breathing, there is a good chance the cancer has spread to the lungs.

ADRENAL GLAND DISEASE

Adrenal gland disease is not common in cats, so only the basics will be mentioned here. These glands are located near the kidneys and are responsible for producing mineralocorticoids and glucocorticoids. Mineralocorticoids are hormones responsible for regulating sodium and potassium balance in the body. Glucocorticoids regulate glucose, protein and fat metabolism within the body and have effects on inflammation and immune response. Small amounts of sex hormones are also produced in the adrenal glands.

Cushing's disease is the term for hyperadrenocorticism, which is overactive adrenal hormone production. Signs of this disease are increased thirst, urination and appetite, hair loss, muscle weakness and thin skin. It is diagnosed with special blood tests and ultrasound. Treatment involves suppressing hormone production or surgically removing an adrenal tumor, if present.

Addison's disease is the term for hypoadrenocorticism, which is underactive adrenal hormone production. Signs of this disease are vomiting, diarrhea, general malaise and poor body condition. It is diagnosed with special blood tests. Treatment involves hormone supplementation and supportive care for shock if the condition is advanced.

Chapter 19

The Nervous System and the Senses

••

What makes a cat want to hunt birds? Why does a cat recognize the sound of the can opener? How does a cat think? How do reflexes work? These and many other questions are answered by the intricate feline nervous system. It is the control panel for every sense and body system.

The central nervous system is composed of the brain and spinal cord. The brain is the computer that commands the other parts of the body. Cerebral spinal fluid surrounds the brain and spinal cord and acts as a shock absorber. It helps prevent concussions when the head is traumatized.

There are five primary senses: vision, hearing, touch, smell and taste. There are additional body-monitoring sensors for balance, temperature, muscle tension and blood oxygen level.

There are millions of stimuli bombarding the nervous system every second. The able central nervous system makes sense of it all and preserves and protects each animal, so it is important that it functions properly. Damage or disease affecting the nervous system can have far-reaching implications.

THE EYES SEE YOU

The eye can be compared to a computerized camera. The pupil is the camera's aperture, or opening, and can change from wide open to barely open. The iris works as the shutter, regulating the amount of light entering the eye. The lens is the focusing mechanism. The retina is the film; it is where photoreceptors convert the image into electrochemical signals. Nerves to the brain are the computer lines that transmit the signal. The brain is where the finished photo is assembled. There are 193,000 optic nerve fibers that transmit information to the cat's visual cortex in the brain.

Diseases such as cataracts, dry eye, eyelid deformities and glaucoma are not frequently found in cats. Most veterinarians can treat common diseases of the eyes, but will refer you to a specialist if needed. Board-certified veterinary ophthalmologists have specialized equipment and can perform advanced diagnostic and surgical procedures on the eyes.

A Scratch on the Eye

A common cause of a squinting and red eye in a cat is a corneal ulcer. Corneal ulcers are irregularities on the surface of the eye. They are detected by placing a drop of a fluorescent dye on the eye surface and then rinsing it off. A normal cornea is smooth, and the dye will flush off. If any abrasion, scratch or other lesion is present that has affected the integrity of the cornea, the dye will stick to it.

Ulcerated corneas are quite uncomfortable to an animal, so you may see a decreased activity level in a cat with an ulcer.

In the springtime when plants and weeds are growing, it is common for cats to accidentally get foxtails in their eyes. Foxtails are pointy grass awns that are quite sharp and can get stuck under the eyelids when a cat goes outdoors. If you live in an area where these annoying plant seeds are present, be on the lookout for them. They can also get stuck between toes and in ear canals, and be found throughout a cat's coat. They can penetrate into the skin and cause more serious problems, as well.

An antibiotic drop or ointment is usually prescribed to treat a corneal ulcer. A protective Elizabethan collar may be recommended as well. An Elizabethan collar is the protective "lampshade" animals wear to prevent them from rubbing their eyes or faces or to stop licking an area.

Lesions can clear up in about a week if they are properly treated. If the eye is very painful and the cat squints it shut, another drop called atropine may be added to decrease eyelid spasms and discomfort.

Many prescription eye drops and ointments contain a combination of antibiotics and cortisone. Drops that contain cortisone should never be used on cats with corneal ulcers, because cortisone retards corneal healing.

Persian and Himalayan cats have very prominent eyes that are easily injured. These cats can develop a condition called corneal sequestrum, in which part of the cornea actually dies and turns black. A veterinary ophthalmologist can perform a procedure called a keratectomy to remove this damaged corneal tissue. A corneal sequestrum is not painful, but it will block vision through that part of the cornea.

Kitty Pinkeye

The most common problem directly affecting the eyes of cats is conjunctivitis. This inflammation of the tissue around the eye can result from viral or bacterial infection, allergies, trauma or immune-related diseases. Conjunctivitis does not directly affect vision, but it can do so indirectly if a cat is squinting due to discomfort or if the cornea is also affected.

A red, puffy eye or an eye that is tearing are typical signs of conjunctivitis. Cultures and conjunctival scrapings are not routinely reliable diagnostic tools, so it can be difficult for a veterinarian to determine the exact cause of a case of conjunctivitis.

It is not uncommon for kittens to be infected with feline herpesvirus or chlamydia, which can cause conjunctivitis. Both can be difficult to treat, and herpes can cause recurrent draining of the eye and conjunctivitis throughout the cat's life. Feline chlamydia can be transmitted to humans and cause conjunctivitis. To prevent the spread of infection, wash your hands before touching your own eyes after handling a cat with conjunctivitis.

Can't Stop Crying

Many cats have eyes that tear regularly. The most common cause of chronic tearing is a flare-up of a feline herpesvirus infection, or scarring of the nasolacrimal drainage duct that resulted from a previous herpesvirus infection. The nasolacrimal duct provides drainage from the eye out through the nose.

Chronic tearing can also be the result of facial conformation and breed predisposition. This is something owners of Persians and other breeds with shortened faces already know. The normal drainage system for the tears does not function in these cats due to the size and shape of the eyes and nose. They may also lack drainage ducts.

Allergies can trigger conjunctivitis or mild chronic tearing. Intermittent use of an eye treatment that contains cortisone can help cats with eye problems due to allergies.

Just as many people have "sleep" in their eyes each morning, so do many cats. Wiping with a moist tissue or cotton ball should be enough to clean most cats' eyes. Short-nosed cats, such as Persians, may need their eyes cleaned two to three times a day to prevent buildup. If the discharge is allowed to accumulate, it can cause hair loss and dermatitis in the skin folds around the eyes.

Regarding ocular discharge, the general rule is that clear is good and yellow or green is bad. A dark, crusty material in the corners of the eyes can also be normal. Tears contain pigments that turn dark when exposed to light. This coloration is not due to blood or infection.

Anterior Uveitis

Inflammation of the uveal tract (vascular and pigmented parts of the eye) is called uveitis. Anterior uveitis involves the iris (the colored portion of the eye surrounding the pupil) and the fluid-filled chamber in front of it. Signs of anterior uveitis can include squinting, redness of the eye, a cloudy appearance when looking into the eye, change of iris color, abnormal pupil shape, tearing and a visible third eyelid.

There are various causes of this condition, but most often a specific cause cannot be identified. Possibilities include trauma, viral infections (including feline herpes, FeLV, FIV and FIP), fungal infections (such as cryptococcus), parasitic infections (such as toxoplasmosis) and even cancer. Blood tests are useful for identifying some of the infectious causes.

Treatment for uveitis involves using topical and sometimes oral anti-inflammatory drugs, along with treating any underlying disease. Monitoring for secondary glaucoma is recommended, because inflammation in the eye can lead to a buildup of fluid pressure in the eye chamber.

Should You Worry About Blindness?

It is normal for the lenses in a cat's eyes to thicken with age and for clarity of vision to diminish. Very few felines go blind from cataracts; blindness is usually the result of another condition or trauma. If a cat loses vision in one eye, an owner may not even realize it because the animal will still be able to function fairly normally. Even when both eyes are blind, a cat can get around quite well in familiar surroundings, and will use her other senses to compensate for her lack of sight.

The most common cause of blindness in cats is acute retinal detachment, which occurs as a result of high blood pressure. If blood pressure is controlled and the retina does not become torn or scarred by bleeding, it will reattach and vision will be restored.

THE EARS HEAR YOU

The anatomy of the cat's ear is complicated, and the way it functions is amazing. The precise interactions involved occur in milliseconds. Balance and equilibrium are reflexes that involve the ears. The brain processes the information it receives from the ears and reacts without any conscious thought.

Deafness

Assessing the hearing abilities of a cat is difficult. The only definitive diagnostic tool is the electroencephalograph, which measures brain waves in response to sound stimuli. This test is performed under anesthesia and is only available through certain veterinary specialists. It is specifically called brain stem auditory evoked response (BAER) testing. Most veterinarians rely on less scientific testing, such as the animal's response to a loud noise.

Loss of hearing in cats can be the result of a variety of problems. Trauma to the head or ear canals can impair hearing or cause complete deafness. Aging changes can decrease hearing, but complete deafness is not common in old cats.

Deafness in cats can be a congenital abnormality. Developmental problems during gestation could lead to improper formation of ear structures. White cats, especially those with blue eyes, have a higher incidence of deafness. This is because of genetic defects that cause numerous abnormalities in the bones of the ear.

Tumors in the ear or brain could affect hearing abilities. Prolonged administration of certain antibiotics can cause hearing loss by damaging the hairs in the organ of Corti. Ear infections can cause permanent damage to the tympanic membrane (eardrum), middle or inner ear.

At this time, hearing aids are not available for cats. If you have a deaf cat, you need to protect her from outdoor dangers. Hearing is more important to a cat who spends unsupervised time outside. Good hearing will help alert a cat to cars and other animals that can pose a threat. Deaf cats are at risk when they are outside unsupervised.

Deaf cats are easily startled, and in my experience can be more aggressive. This may arise from the cat feeling more defensive due to an inability to hear anyone approaching. Still, deaf cats can make good pets and live normal life spans. If you are unsure about your cat's ability to hear, consult your veterinarian.

Head Tilt

A head tilt is a sign of diseases of the external, middle or inner ear as well as diseases of the brain. Diseases that affect the ear include trauma, bacterial or mite infections, polyps, tumors, foreign bodies, punctured eardrums and ototoxic drugs. In addition to a head tilt, other possible clinical signs of ear disease are circling, loss of equilibrium, vomiting and listlessness. A head tilt could be a symptom of serious disease, so a thorough workup by your veterinarian is warranted.

The workup for a head tilt is similar to that of other neurological diseases, and may include an exam of the ear canals and tympanums (eardrums), blood and urine tests, skull X rays, CAT or MRI scans, cerebral spinal fluid tap and a BAER test. Treatment and prognosis depend on the cause, but cats with head tilts often need help in getting around, jumping up or down, using stairs, eating and getting in and out of the litter box.

KITTIES AND CONVULSIONS

A seizure is an uncontrolled release of electrical activity from the neurons of the brain. When you observe a seizure, it may seem as though it lasts for a long time, but in reality seizures rarely last more than 30 to 60 seconds. Seizures are scary, because your normally responsive pet will not recognize you and may even bite you if you try to hold her down.

There is nothing you can do to stop a seizure in progress. The best thing to do is to be sure the animal cannot fall off something and hurt herself, and then leave her alone. Why do cats have seizures? There are many possible causes.

Epilepsy, a disorder that triggers recurrent seizures but has no underlying disease process occurring in the brain, is not as common in cats as it is in dogs or humans. Most feline seizures are triggered by specific causes. Idiopathic epilepsy is a seizure condition with no known cause.

Diagnosing Seizures

A diagnostic work-up for seizures and other diseases of the brain will initially include a history, physical and neurological exam, a complete blood count and chemistry panel and urinalysis. If the veterinarian is unable to make a specific diagnosis based on this information, and the cat is continuing to have seizures, further diagnostic testing should be pursued. Such tests might include:

- Blood pressure measurement
- Skull X rays
- Cerebral spinal fluid tap and analysis
- Electroencephalogram (EEG), a kind of brain scan
- Computerized tomography (CT) scan
- Magnetic resonance imaging (MRI)
- Radioisotope brain scan

As you might imagine, it can be expensive to pursue a definitive diagnosis, and referral to a veterinary neurologist may be needed to provide access to diagnostic equipment and to properly interpret the test results.

There are many possible causes for seizures, including:

- Congenital disease
- Metabolic disease
- Neoplasia
- Nutritional imbalances
- Infections with viruses, bacteria, protozoa or fungi
- Trauma
- Toxins
- Parasites
- Vascular disorders

Treating Seizures

If a specific trigger for the seizures is identified, treatment for the underlying problem may be successful in controlling future seizures. Some of these conditions are more responsive to treatment than others.

If a seizure is an isolated incident, no treatment may be recommended. If seizures occur at least once a month, oral anticonvulsant

IT'S JUST GOOD, CLEAN FUN

Some cats almost appear to be having seizures when exposed to catnip. Catnip, *Nepata cataria,* is a member of the mint family. But really, they are just enjoying themselves. The active chemical in catnip is called nepetalactone, which is a hallucinogenic compound that induces a pleasure response in cats. A cat's genetic makeup is a factor affecting the animal's responsiveness to catnip. Apparently catnip is an acquired taste, as young kittens usually do not respond to it.

therapy is usually started. The most commonly used drug to treat seizures is phenobarbital, but diazepam is sometimes used. Potassium bromide, although effective for controlling seizures in dogs, has been implicated as a cause of lung disease in cats.

BORN WITH NEUROLOGIC PROBLEMS

Three congenital abnormalities are occasionally seen in cats. The first is hydrocephalus, otherwise known as water on the brain. In a hydrocephalic animal, cerebral spinal fluid (not water) abnormally pools in certain parts of the brain. The classic appearance of a cat with hydrocephalus is a dome-shaped skull. Siamese are the most commonly affected breed. This condition is noticed in young kittens. Abnormal physical appearance, behaviors and seizures may be seen, and there is no treatment.

The second congenital abnormality can be found in some Manx cats. Manx cats do not have normal tails, and some are born with malformations of nerves and spinal cord segments. One condition is called spina bifida, which is a defect in the closure of the vertebrae. This condition leads to a protrusion of the spinal cord and nerves. The clinical signs observed are loss of urinary and fecal control, otherwise known as incontinence.

Even if a Manx cat does not have spina bifida, she may have minor spinal cord defects. Possible clinical signs associated with these defects are difficulties with urination and/or defecation, and rectal prolapse (where the rectum protrudes from the anus). Most Manx cats "bunny hop" when they run, a significantly different movement from that of other cats. This change of gait is related to their short tails and possible vertebral malformations. Bunny hopping, without incontinence, does not create any management problems for Manx owners.

The last congenital abnormality is cerebellar hypoplasia. This is another condition seen in young kittens. The signs are tremors, imbalance and an exaggerated gait. There is no treatment for this condition. Owners need to decide if they can live with a pet who does not function normally. Cats with cerebellar hypoplasia need help eating, eliminating and getting around, although their external physical appearance is normal.

CATS WITH BAD BACKS

Compared with dogs, cats have quite flexible backs. Thick, spongy cushions between their vertebrae enable cats to extend and contract their spines like an accordion. As a result, they don't often sustain back injuries. If injury or disease affects a cat's spine, clinical signs might include:

- Limb weakness or paralysis
- Instability
- Stiff or painful muscles
- Loss of normal reflexes
- Urinary or fecal incontinence

The diagnostic work-up options for cats with suspected spinal problems are similar to those for brain disease. Additional tests that might be performed are a myelogram (an X ray taken after dye is injected around the spinal cord), an electromyelogram (which measures the electrical activity of muscles) or an MRI (magnetic resonance imaging). Some diseases of muscles have clinical signs similar to those caused by nerves.

Traumatic Experiences

Examples of trauma that can damage the spine are when a cat is hit by a car or becomes stuck under a garage door. The back end of the animal is most often affected in these situations. The tail can be damaged, back end nerves can be torn and the spinal cord can be injured. Cats are amazing creatures with an unbelievable capacity to heal. Many cats with severe damage will regain normal function with treatment, tender loving care and time.

Generally with spinal disease, the more severe the signs, the less optimistic the prognosis. Once a nerve is cut, it will not reconnect, but it can regenerate at a very slow rate. It is not particularly difficult to control pain and inflammation in cats who have sustained trauma, but managing the inability to eliminate is difficult. If control of these processes has not returned within a couple of weeks, it most likely will not return. Owners can be faced with making a decision about euthanasia if the animal is unable to regulate her bodily functions.

Cats with broken, limp tails can do very well, if there are no other problems, by amputating their tails. When the tail loses feeling and motor control, it is not doing the cat any good anyway, so it is best to surgically remove it.

Kitties With Slipped Disks

Intervertebral disk disease is occasionally seen in cats. A veterinarian might suspect a disk problem in a cat as he pinches down the spine from the neck to the tail and finds a sensitive spot, and the cat presents with pain, instability, weakness or paralysis. Disks in the neck are more commonly affected than those farther down the spine. Disks can degenerate with aging, be pushed out of place by trauma or tumors, become infected or be pinched by arthritic changes.

If intervertebral disk disease is diagnosed, the cat should be confined so that she can rest, and anti-inflammatory doses of cortisone used to help with pain and swelling. If the condition progresses to paralysis, surgical decompression of the spinal cord is needed immediately.

Cauda Equina Syndrome

This condition has clinical signs that are very similar to intervertebral disk disease, although it affects only the nerves at the end of the spinal cord. Cauda equina syndrome occurs most frequently in senior cats. Signs observed in cats with cauda equina syndrome include:

- Difficulty in rising
- Rear-limb lameness that progresses with use
- Dragging the rear toes
- Rear-limb and tail weakness
- Urinary or fecal incontinence
- Pain at the lumbosacral junction of the spine, the area of the spine where the lumbar and sacral veterbrae come together in the lower back

If treatment with rest and corticosteroids does not give the cat significant pain relief or return of function, discuss decompression surgery with your veterinarian.

If your cat requires surgery on any part of her spinal cord, consider consulting with a board-certified veterinary surgeon. Spinal surgery is a delicate and risky procedure that is best left to the experts.

FELINE HYPERESTHESIA SYNDROME

Staring off into space and chasing objects we can't see are normal feline behaviors, but these behaviors can become more extreme in cases of hyperesthesia. No one knows what actually causes this syndrome, but it is typically seen in young adult cats.

The most common sign of hyperesthesia is frantic licking and biting at the air, especially when the cat is touched around the end of her spine. Other possible signs are mood swings, vocalizations, seizures, excessive grooming, skin rippling, dilated pupils, tail swishing and hyperactive behavior.

I have seen mild forms of this condition most often in overweight cats with matted coats and fleas. They cannot reach around and scratch themselves, so they go crazy when scratched or combed along the end of their spines. I think the stimulation is so overwhelming because the cat has been dying to do the same herself but cannot. Regular grooming, flea control and use of anti-inflammatory drugs often control the condition.

There are more extreme manifestations of hyperesthesia with prolonged unpredictable behavior. There are many theories about what triggers this bizarre behavior, including an underlying seizure disorder, obsessive-compulsive behavior, an inherited reaction to stress, and muscle inflammation and abnormalities.

If the problem does not respond to skin care, treatment should focus on relieving stress, engaging the cat in play activities and medicating with either anti-anxiety drugs or the anticonvulsant Phenobarbital.

Chapter 20

The Urinary Tract

··

The popularity of cats has flourished over the last decade because of their ability to thrive with less human care than a dog requires. Their willingness to use a litter box is a big part of this, since owners do not need to rush home to take their cats out for a walk. Cats are born with the instinct to bury their urine in dirt or sand, and proper litter box use makes things comfortable for both cat and owner.

When a cat stops using his litter box, the very first thing to suspect is a medical problem. Previous chapters have mentioned diseases, such as diabetes, where frequent or inappropriate urination is one of the signs. There are also health problems that can affect the urinary tract directly.

The urinary tract is composed of the kidneys, which are responsible for filtering blood and producing urine; the ureters, which transport urine from the kidneys to the bladder; the bladder, which stores urine; and the urethra, which is the passageway from the bladder to the penis or vulva. All parts of the urinary tract play a role in eliminating fluid waste products from the body.

LOWER URINARY TRACT DISEASE

Lower Urinary Tract Disease (LUTD) is a broad term encompassing many different syndromes. The lower urinary tract of cats involves the bladder and urethra.

Theories about what causes bladder problems in cats have changed over the past 20 years. In the past, owners were concerned about the "ash" content (and later the magnesium content) of their cat's food, but LUTD involves a complex interaction between genetics, diet, water intake and stress.

Recommendations about canned food or dry for cats with bladder problems have gone back and forth, and recently the pendulum has swung back to recommending more canned food. Canned food increases a cat's water intake. If cats will not eat canned food, moistening dry food or installing a circulating water drinking fountain are two other ways to increase water intake. When a cat drinks more water, his urine is more dilute and crystals, which are among the main culprits in LUTD, are less likely to form in the urinary tract.

The feline urinary tract is a part of the cat that is constantly being researched in academia and the pet food industry, so expect new information to be available each year. Litter box use and diet are important issues to discuss with your veterinarian at each annual visit, since they both have an impact on the urinary tract.

Blood in the Urine

Bloody urine is a frequent finding in cats with LUTD. Owners notice blood in the litter box or on other objects the cat has decided to eliminate on. Blood is a sign of inflammation of the bladder (cystitis), but it does not necessarily mean a bacterial infection is present.

DIFFERENT NAMES, SAME PROBLEM

You may hear your veterinarian use the acronym FUS when referring to urinary tract problems. FUS stands for Feline Urologic Syndrome. Medical personnel may use the terms LUTD and FUS interchangeably, but the former is the more accurate terminology used today.

A veterinarian must examine cats with blood in their urine. The veterinarian will want to perform a urinalysis to help reach a diagnosis. A proper urinalysis will:

- Check the cat's ability to concentrate urine
- Show if red and/or white blood cells are present
- Show the pH of the urine
- Show if glucose is present
- Evaluate protein levels in the urine
- Check for the presence of other metabolic chemicals, crystals, or cells

Urine can be cultured for bacteria, and antibiotic sensitivities can then be determined. For advice on how to collect a urine sample, see Chapter 22.

There are a host of reasons for blood in a cat's urine, including:

- Bacterial infections
- Viral infections
- Trauma to the kidneys or bladder
- Stress
- Bladder stones
- Crystal buildup
- Tumors
- Blood clotting disorders
- Idiopathic (no known cause) interstitial cystitis

Interstitial cystitis is a benign inflammatory condition that can affect the bladders of cats. It is one of the LUTD syndromes. Although there are no treatments that have been conclusively proven effective for every cat, veterinarians can prescribe a mild human anti-anxiety drug called amitriptyline. It is often effective in cases of human interstitial cystitis.

How to Make Your Cat More Comfortable

Cats with LUTD may strain to urinate and pass only a few drops of urine at a time. You will observe them making frequent trips to the

---

SENDING A MESSAGE

Cats who urinate outside of their litter box may be trying to get your attention and let you know they are not well. Don't automatically blame the problem on bad behavior. Have the cat examined by a veterinarian so that if there is an underlying medical problem, such as LUTD, it can be treated.

---

litter box. The most important factor is that they are able to pass some urine, differentiating them from cats with urinary blockages.

The results of a physical exam and urinalysis will give a veterinarian a good idea about what is causing LUTD. Controlling bacterial infections is fairly easy with antibiotics, but decreasing the straining and increased frequency of urination can be more difficult. A host of medications can be tried, and time can also heal. It usually takes three to five days for a case of LUTD to improve.

When cats have recurrent bouts of LUTD, further diagnostic testing is needed. Tests that are helpful include:

- X rays
- Contrast X rays (where the bladder is first injected with a contrasting dye—this enables better evaluation of the lining and certain stone types)
- Ultrasound
- Urine culture
- Bladder biopsy

KITTY CAN'T PEE!

If an owner calls my clinic and tells my receptionist that his cat can't urinate, she becomes alarmed, especially if a male cat is involved. Due to the length and shape of their urethra, male cats are more susceptible to developing life-threatening urethral obstructions. This narrow exit passageway from the bladder can become clogged with mucus, crystals and even small stones.

A cat who cannot urinate should be examined *immediately*, because if he is truly obstructed, he could die within hours from to toxins building up in the blood and pressure on the kidneys.

It's Going to Cost *How Much*?

It is good to know ahead of time that effectively treating a urinary blockage is expensive. Expenses will be even higher if you must visit an emergency veterinary clinic, but you really have no choice. Factors that affect the amount of treatment a cat will need are:

- Duration of the obstruction
- Whether there is kidney damage
- The degree of difficulty in unblocking the urethra
- The cause of the obstruction
- Whether the cat blocks up again

Each veterinarian will probably treat a blocked cat a little differently, but the basic steps are:

1. Pass a urinary catheter into the bladder.
2. Drain out the retained urine.
3. Determine what other metabolic imbalances exist.
4. Treat for infection and shock (if necessary).
5. Maintain the cat's hydration.
6. Flush debris out of the bladder.
7. Evaluate the cat's ability to urinate once the catheter has been removed.

A blocked cat may require one to five days of hospitalization and nursing care. Home care will likely involve treatment with antibiotics and possibly a diet change. Some cats need medication to relax their bladders and urethras to ease elimination.

Three Strikes and You're Out

For some reason, some cats that will become re-obstructed. Medication and diet are just not enough to keep things flowing smoothly. Again, each veterinarian will have their own approach to the problem, but my rule is that if a cat obstructs three times, he needs a procedure called a perineal urethrotomy.

We call perineal urethrotomy surgery our "kitty sex-change operation" because afterward, the urinary tract and genitalia look more like those of a female than a male. Males are more prone to obstruct because of their narrow, twisting urethra that ends at their penis. Females have a short, wide urethra that ends in the vulva. Cats who have perineal urethrotomies lose their penis, and are given a new opening from which to urinate.

This surgery successfully opens up the urethra, but it is not without risk. If it is not performed carefully, or if there is trauma or excessive scarring, a cat may not be able to control his urination and dribbling will occur. Scarring can also cause another obstruction. The shortened urethra may increase the likelihood of bacteria entering the urinary tract.

STONES IN THE SYSTEM

Stones can form throughout the urinary tract, but are most often seen in the bladder. The medical term for stones of the urinary tract is *uroliths*. Kidney stones are the second-most frequent type of urolith, but unless they block the ureter, they are usually left alone.

When dissolved minerals are present in high concentrations in the urine, they can reach a saturation point and begin to precipitate out of the urine as crystals. Bladder stones are formed this way—which is similar to the way rock candy is formed. Some crystals stick together to form a small center, then other crystals join on and make a stone.

Struvite is the name used to describe magnesium ammonium phosphate crystals or stones. High levels of magnesium, combined with a high urine pH, create an environment that enables struvite to precipitate in the urine.

Calcium oxalate, ammonium and urate stones can also develop in cats when certain metabolic conditions exist. Each type of stone requires different conditions to form. Some can be controlled by diet, but others can be difficult to prevent.

Struvite stones are the only type that can be dissolved by feeding a special prescription diet, which is only available through veterinarians. After a stone-dissolving diet is fed for about two months, a preventive diet is fed to prevent recurrence. To monitor the response to diet, follow up X rays of the bladder are needed.

How Stones Are Diagnosed

It is not common to feel stones in a cat's bladder on palpation, because the stones are relatively small. Stones should be suspected any time a cat has more than one episode of LUTD or develops a urinary blockage. Most feline uroliths are visible on regular X rays, if they are large enough.

To make stones more visible, a special X ray called a pneumocystogram is performed. The procedure involves putting a catheter in the bladder and injecting air as a contrast agent. Ultrasound is also able to detect small stones and piles of crystalline sand on the bladder floor.

Urine pH, appearance on X ray and blood work can give clues as to the type of stone present. A definitive identification of the stone is performed at a lab, where its chemical components are analyzed.

Treating Stones

If the veterinarian is unsure whether the stones will dissolve with a change in diet, or if you want to get them out and make your cat

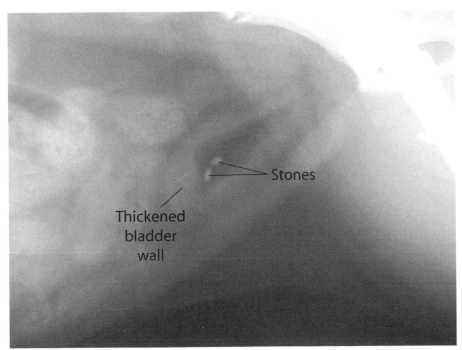

Two large bladder stones and a very thickened bladder wall are revealed in this special X ray, called a pneumocystogram.

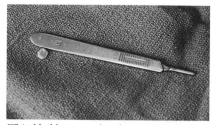

This bladder stone has been surgically removed. It is almost one centimeter across.

comfortable as soon as possible, surgical removal is recommended. The procedure is called a cystotomy and involves abdominal surgery and an incision into the bladder. Stones are removed, and the bladder and urethra are flushed out.

The bladder is an organ that heals incredibly well, so although it seems traumatic at the time, cats have excellent recoveries from cystotomies. The key to success with the surgery is thorough removal of all stones and follow-up with an X ray.

In certain situations, urohydropropulsion can be used to remove stones. Urohydropropulsion is a technique that forces small uroliths out of the body, and is an option for female cats with small stones.

If your cat is found to have stones that cannot be prevented with diet, there is a good chance they will recur. There are usually some steps that can be taken to decrease risk, but the cat should be monitored with urinalyses and X rays about every six months.

WHAT ABOUT DIET?

It is normal for cats to have some crystals in their urine. To determine whether crystals are a problem or not, the number of crystals, the presence of other cells and the pH of the urine should all be taken into consideration. Your veterinarian may recommend a special diet if she feels crystals in the urine are a problem.

Most cat foods are now low in magnesium and are formulated to mildly acidify the urine (remember, *higher* acid is the same as *lower* pH). This is because research has shown these dietary changes can help reduce the likelihood that a cat will form struvite crystals. A carnivore like the cat would naturally have slightly acidic urine, so this makes sense.

The incidence of struvite formation in cats has declined since cat food makers began reformulating their food. However, only about 15 to 25 percent of all cases of LUTD are caused by struvite stones. And a mildly acidifying diet has increased in incidence of cats with calcium oxalate stones, which form more easily in acid urine.

There are prescription brands and grocery store cat foods that are formulated to improve urinary tract health. The grocery store brands usually are made to help with struvite formation, while your cat will need a prescription brand food that helps with calcium oxalate stones. If your cat has a history of urinary tract problems, the urine should be monitored after his diet is changed to be sure the correct balance is being achieved.

I would not recommend feeding a special urinary tract diet without first consulting your veterinarian. Special diets may be harmful to young, growing kittens or older cats with other medical conditions.

As I've mentioned, feeding more canned food and increasing water intake is recommended for cats with urinary tract problems. Special diets are usually available in canned and dry forms. Ultimately, your cat may be the decision-maker and choose what he is willing to eat.

KITTY'S KIDNEYS

The kidneys are responsible for filtering out waste products from the blood, conserving water in the body and producing urine. A cat's body is a wonderful machine, and even though it works best with two kidneys, it can do well with one kidney or 50 percent kidney function.

Your veterinarian (or your physician) might use the term *renal* to describe things having to do with the kidneys. For example, renal insufficiency means loss of kidney function.

There are many diseases that can affect the kidneys, but regardless of the cause, most renal diseases are treated similarly. The prognosis for cats with kidney disease depends on whether the disease is acute or chronic. Long-standing problems tend to have a less favorable outcome. Unlike other vital organs, such as the liver, the kidneys are not capable of regenerating themselves.

Signs of Dysfunctional Kidneys

Clinical signs associated with kidney disease are similar to those of other diseases, and can include:

- Increased thirst
- Increased urination
- Weight loss
- Dehydration
- Dental disease
- Vomiting

DEADLY ANTIFREEZE

Antifreeze is a potent toxin when ingested by cats. A chemical in antifreeze, ethylene glycol, irreversibly destroys kidney cells. If you have any reason to suspect your cat has licked even the tiniest bit of antifreeze, get him to a veterinarian immediately. If treatment is not started within four hours of ingestion, the prognosis is very poor.

Blood tests and urinalysis results will not indicate that kidney function is compromised until more than 50 percent function is lost. In fact, they may not show abnormal results until more than two-thirds of kidney function has been affected.

The most common parameters for assessing kidney function are blood levels of BUN and creatinine, and urine-specific gravity. BUN stands for blood urea nitrogen, a breakdown product of protein metabolism. Creatinine is another type of nitrogenous waste product. Both build up to abnormal levels when the kidneys aren't working. Urine-specific gravity relates to the concentrating ability of the kidneys. Cats typically have very concentrated urine, meaning it has low water content. In cats with kidney disease, the urine-specific gravity drops because the urine becomes dilute and too much water leaves the body.

Cats with kidney disease tend to become dehydrated. A skin turgor test is a simple procedure that cat owners can do at home to check on their cat's hydration. If neck skin is pinched up and does not fall back into place within a second or two, the cat is significantly dehydrated. In this situation, injectable fluid supplementation is probably needed.

Kidney Infection

Pyelonephritis and glomerulonephritis are terms used to describe infection and inflammation involving different cells within the kidneys. Because the kidneys filter all of the body's blood, any infectious agent in the blood is transported to the kidneys.

The clinical signs of pyelonephritis are the same as other types of kidney disease, but fever and pain on palpation of the kidneys may be present. White blood cells can also be present in the urine.

Young adult cats are most often affected with glomerulonephritis, although it is not a common disease. It can present itself in two ways: nephrotic syndrome and renal failure. In nephrotic syndrome cats develop swelling, fluid in their abdominal cavity, high levels of protein in their urine, increased blood cholesterol levels, decreased blood albumin levels, mild weight loss and loss of appetite.

Kidney infections are very serious, and are usually treated by giving intravenous antibiotics. After initial treatment, oral antibiotics can be used, but three to six weeks of medication may be needed. When pyelonephritis is suspected, a urine culture and antibiotic sensitivity should be started before treatment begins, and done again afterward as follow-ups to treatment.

Breed-Specific Kidney Disease

Particular kidney diseases are seen in certain lines of purebred cats. The two most common types are renal amyloidosis in Abyssinians and Somalis, and polycystic kidney disease in Persians and Himalayans. Genetic kidney diseases cannot be cured and are progressive. Treatment focuses on keeping the cat comfortable and maintaining fluid and electrolyte balance.

There is no screening test for renal amyloidosis, but it is suspected in young to middle-aged purebred cats who develop kidney disease of no other known cause. A kidney biopsy can be performed that may show the particular protein deposits that are the characteristic lesions of this disease.

Polycystic kidney disease (PKD) is found in purebred cats and in related longhaired cats. This disease can be diagnosed by feeling lumpy, bumpy kidneys on palpation and by seeing the cysts on ultrasound. The presence of cysts will not necessarily cause significant kidney disease, and some affected animals live normal lives. Others develop kidney dysfunction at a young age as the cysts grow and destroy the normal kidney tissue.

Old Cat Kidneys

The kidneys tend to wear out faster in cats than other organs. Chronic tubulointerstitial nephritis is the medical term for the slowly progressive loss of kidney function found in older cats. It is the most common disease of cats over the age of 10 years.

As a cat ages, the kidneys scar and become smaller and less efficient at filtering the blood and preserving water balance in the body. The progression of chronic tubulointerstitial nephritis can vary depending on the individual animal and the amount of nursing care an owner is willing to do. The goals of treatment are:

- Maintain hydration and electrolyte balance
- Keep blood waste product levels down
- Prevent anemia
- Control secondary infections

Although veterinary diets with lower protein levels have been developed for cats with kidney disease, the amount of protein in these diets is controversial. Cats are carnivores, so when their physical condition is diminished, adequate protein is needed more than ever. On the other hand, the breakdown products of protein metabolism become a problem in cats with kidney disease. The dietary needs of cats with kidney disease are significantly different from those with bladder disease, so pick a diet with the help of your veterinarian.

Specific Treatments

Fluid therapy is the cornerstone of helping cats with kidney disease. The fluids given to affected cats are balanced electrolyte solutions. Cats who have high levels of waste products in their blood should initially be treated with intravenous fluids (diuresis). They also may be given diuretics to help flush waste products.

Diuresis is easily performed in most veterinary hospitals over several days of treatment. (This differs from hemodialysis, a common human treatment. In hemodialysis, a machine removes the blood from the body and cleans it when the kidneys are unable to do the job. This kind of dialysis for animals is only available at a few specialty referral hospitals and is most useful in cases of acute renal failure, where the kidneys are likely to heal if given time.)

In cases of chronic kidney disease, owners can learn how to inject fluids under the skin of their pets. This procedure, called subcutaneous administration, can be done at home long term. In my clinic, we have owners who have happily given their cats subcutaneous fluid injections for years.

Maintaining proper levels of minerals in the blood is important in controlling kidney disease. The two minerals that need to be closely watched are potassium and phosphorus. Cats with kidney dysfunction tend to have insufficient levels of potassium but an overabundance of phosphorus. Potassium supplements and phosphate binding agents can be used to create the right balance. Some veterinarians treat cats with kidney disease with a drug called calcitriol, to control phosphate and calcium levels.

Cats suffering from chronic kidney disease can become anemic because their kidneys stop producing enough erythropoietin, a hormone that stimulates the bone marrow to produce red blood cells. Erythropoietin can be supplemented by injection if the red blood cell count gets too low, and this is another treatment owners can learn to perform.

Some cats with kidney disease become anorexic and can be helped with appetite stimulants, anabolic steroids and by hand-feeding. If there is concern of nausea or upset stomach, oral antacids can be used. Antibiotic treatment may be required if infection is a secondary problem.

Kidney transplants are available for cats. The surgery is performed at a few specialty clinics and universities around the country. It is an expensive procedure with risks of organ rejection, but a successful transplant may buy a cat a few more years of life.

Is the Clock Ticking?

Even if a cat is being well maintained on fluid therapy and other treatments, kidney disease will invariably progress past a treatable stage. Cats with kidney disease should be monitored at least every six months.

Cats in end-stage renal disease continue to lose weight, are unable to maintain hydration even with fluid supplementation and even develop sores in their mouths. It is difficult to know how painful this is to a cat, but there is no doubt that they are nauseous, weak and very uncomfortable. Euthanasia needs to be considered at this point.

Chapter 21

The Dreaded Viruses

••

Viruses are microorganisms that are composed of protein chains (DNA or RNA). They are considered living organisms, although they cannot reproduce unless they attach themselves to other living cells. They cause infection but they do not respond to antibiotics, because antibiotics only fight bacterial infections. Most viruses are species-specific, which means cat viruses affect cats and human viruses affect humans.

Viruses mutate and change, which is why people are subject to so many flu "bugs." There are numerous viruses that affect cats, but some are more dangerous than others. Viruses are destroyed in the body by the host animal's immune system, but some viruses hide out and cannot be totally removed. Some viruses can be fought through vaccination, which stimulates an animal's immune system to fight the infection.

FELINE LEUKEMIA VIRUS

Feline Leukemia Virus (FeLV) is a serious virus in cats because at this time it has no cure. Unlike some of the other deadly viruses that affect cats, there are reliable screening tests for FeLV. This makes it possible to identify sick cats and healthy cats who are carrying the virus.

FeLV is contagious and is passed by direct, cat-to-cat contact, such as fighting and biting, mutual grooming and from a queen to her kittens. Not all cats who contract FeLV die from the disease, but any cat who tests positive should be monitored closely.

How Reliable Is the FeLV Test?

Most veterinary clinics have the capacity to test for Feline Leukemia in the office, with results in 5 to 10 minutes. The most reliable tests use small amounts of blood, but saliva and tears can be used in some test kits. Most of the tests used in clinics are very reliable. However, when a test comes up positive, it should be verified, because there are sometimes false positive results for the FeLV test.

The regular test used in most clinics checks for FeLV antigens in the blood (or body secretions). If this type of test is positive, a secondary, verifying test should be performed. The secondary test, called an IFA (immunofluorescent antibody), checks for FeLV antigens within blood cells, and is available through a reference laboratory. There also is a test for FeLV that looks for viral DNA in the blood (FeLV PCR). The results of different FeLV tests can be confusing if they are not all positive or all negative. If this happens, a veterinarian should follow the American Association of Feline Practitioner's FeLV testing guidelines and consider retesting before making a final diagnosis.

Another problem with testing for FeLV is that if an animal was exposed to the virus within a few weeks of being tested, the test could be negative because measurable viral antigens would not yet be present in the blood. If there is any question as to the status of a cat, he should be retested one to three months later.

What Is FeLV?

Feline leukemia virus can suppress a cat's immune system so that other diseases make the animal extremely sick. It can also cause lymphatic cancer and suppress a cat's bone marrow and blood cell production. Once a cat has developed clinical signs and tests positively for FeLV, the animal usually only lives a few months, at best.

A small number of cats contract FeLV, never get sick and live normal life spans. This is because their immune systems are able to fight off active infection. Some animals carry FeLV and are healthy for years before any signs of illness develop.

Protection Against the Virus

There are steps that can be taken to prevent your cat from contracting FeLV. These include:

- Test all cats for FeLV before introducing them into your household.
- Keep your cats indoors.
- If your cats go outdoors, vaccinate them against FeLV.
- Spay and neuter your cats so that they are less likely to fight and come in contact with cats who carry FeLV.
- Lock any pet doors to prevent unknown cats from entering your home.

Kittens are most at risk for infection with FeLV because of their immature immune systems. Even if you don't plan on letting your kitten go outside, it is a good idea to test him and initially vaccinate him against FeLV. If your kitten's lifestyle changes and he starts going outdoors, you would want him protected. If, after a year, the cat never goes outside, vaccination for FeLV can be discontinued.

Coping With FeLV

If all tests and clinical signs point to a diagnosis of FeLV and the animal is sick, the prognosis is poor. At this time there are no effective treatments or cures for FeLV. There has been experimentation with some drugs that stimulate the immune system, and although none has been conclusively shown to have any effect, they are worth a try.

Treatment of FeLV-positive cats is aimed at making the cat as comfortable as possible and controlling secondary problems. If clinical signs respond to treatment, FeLV cats can live for years. If clinical signs are not well controlled, an owner is usually faced with deciding whether to continue to support the cat as his condition declines, or to humanely euthanize him.

Humans cannot transmit FeLV from one cat to another. FeLV does not live outside of infected cats, but it is always a good idea to wash your hands and clean thoroughly if an infected cat has been around.

FELINE IMMUNODEFICIENCY VIRUS

Feline immunodeficiency virus (FIV) is in the same family as human immunodeficiency virus (HIV), but it is not transmissible to humans.

Although drug cocktails are currently helping humans with HIV from developing full-blown AIDS (acquired immunodeficiency syndrome), we have not yet made the same strides in veterinary medicine. The good news is that FIV in cats usually does not progress to a debilitating, life-threatening condition.

How Cats Get Infected

FIV is another virus that is passed by direct cat-to-cat contact. It is most commonly transmitted during cat fights when cats bite one another. Not surprisingly, the highest incidence of FIV is found in stray, intact male cats. It is rare for kittens to be infected with FIV, but it has been documented. Most veterinarians are not worried about FIV in kittens under the age of six months.

Diagnosing FIV

Good tests are available for detecting FIV in cats. Tests done in a veterinary clinic can be completed in about 10 minutes, and the incidence of false positives is lower than that for FeLV. If a cat fits the demographic profile—outdoor and male—then a positive test is most likely truly positive. One of the most popular in-clinic tests checks for FeLV and FIV at the same time. To confirm a positive test, a test called a western blot can be sent out to a lab.

Whereas FeLV makes cats very sick, FIV is comparatively subtle. This is because cats have a relatively short life span, and it usually takes many years for the virus to create life-threatening immune suppression. Cats are diagnosed with FIV when they are tested as new additions to a home or if a general blood panel is run that includes viral tests. FIV is not typically suspected as a primary disease.

The Impact of FIV

FIV does not cause cancer the way FeLV can, but it does suppress a cat's immune system. It usually is not a fatal disease, and there are few external clinical signs. I have often been surprised when doing full blood panels on cats as old as 18 years and to find a positive FIV test.

Cats infected with FIV will have a harder time fighting other infections. They need more supportive care and a longer course of antibiotics when they have bacterial infections. They can handle anesthesia if needed, and they can tolerate other routine health care. It is important to extend treatments beyond normal durations when dealing with FIV-positive cats.

One clinical sign commonly seen with FIV-positive cats is gum disease. They can have red, inflamed, malodorous gums that do not respond to brushing. If your cat has bad gums, his FIV status should be checked because it will affect how well the cat will respond to treatment.

Care for FIV-Positive Cats

A vaccine for FIV became available in late 2002. Unfortunately, this vaccine is far from ideal and should only be administered if your veterinarian recommends it. The first problem with the vaccine is its effectiveness. In trials it protected against only two of the four common strains of FIV, and did not confer 100 percent protection against those two. The biggest problem is that vaccinated cats will test positive on standard FIV screening tests, making it impossible to differentiate between cats who have been vaccinated and cats who are infected.

If you choose to vaccinate against FIV, I recommend first testing the cat to ensure his negative pre-vaccine status. Be sure the cat has a microchip if he is then vaccinated, so that if he is picked up as a stray, he will not be destroyed because he tests positive and fits the "at-risk" description.

There is a controversy in veterinary medicine over what should be done with stray cats who test positively for FIV. These animals can live relatively normal lives, but they are a potential source of viral spread. It is not recommended to bring an FIV-positive cat into a household with FIV-negative cats, but the animal could be a great pet in a single-cat home or in a home with other FIV-positive cats. If no one wants the cat and he will be returned to an outdoor life, euthanasia may be considered to prevent the spread of the disease.

The most important thing an owner of an FIV-positive cat can do is to keep the cat indoors. Indoor living fulfills two purposes: it decreases the cat's exposure to infectious agents, and it prevents the cat from spreading the disease to other cats.

FELINE INFECTIOUS PERITONITIS

Feline infectious peritonitis (FIP) is one of the most frustrating and scary diseases in veterinary medicine. It is frustrating because of the difficulty in making a definitive diagnosis, and it is scary because there is no cure. I hate to mention FIP to owners of a sick cat.

What Is FIP?

FIP is a coronavirus, and feline coronaviruses are common and usually don't cause many problems in affected cats. The current theory is that

FIP is a mutation of a common virus called feline enteric corona virus (FECV). Why this virus mutates to become deadly FIP in some cats is not known. It is possible that stress, genetics, a poor immune system and concurrent diseases may predispose a cat to developing FIP.

The clinical signs associated with FIP can include:

- Fever
- Failure to gain weight or weight loss
- Lethargy
- Poor appetite
- Vomiting
- Diarrhea
- Fluid buildup in the abdominal or chest cavities
- Neurological disorders

There are two forms of FIP: wet and dry. The wet form is the "classic" disease, in which fluid builds up in a cat's abdominal and/or chest cavity, making the animal uncomfortable and giving him a potbellied appearance. In the dry form, the virus is present but does not create fluid.

Cats with FIP have a waxing-to-waning illness. This means they have good days and bad days, so an owner may not be able to tell how sick the cat really is. The progression of signs is slow, and cats with FIP can have undiagnosed illness for months.

A kitten can be exposed to FECV by his mother, start off fairly normally, and then develop full-blown FIP as late as two years of age. Fortunately, the viral mutation to FIP usually occurs in only a small percentage of cats, and in a litter of four kittens, one could become infected and die and the others could grow up normal and healthy.

Building a Diagnosis of FIP

Diagnosing FIP is like putting together a puzzle. The only test that conclusively diagnoses the disease is a tissue biopsy. Performing exploratory surgery to obtain a biopsy is not what most owners with a gravely sick cat and a poor prognosis want to do.

Instead, the diagnosis is presumed, based on other tests and typical clinical signs. The tests that can be performed are:

- Complete blood count (CBC)
- Blood chemistries

- Corona virus titer (FECV titer)
- 7B ELISA for FIP (an antibody titer to a specific viral protein (7B); a positive result supports a diagnosis of FIP, but the test is not definitive)
- X rays
- Ultrasound
- Fluid analysis
- FIP PCR (this test uses polymerase chain reaction technology to look for specific viral proteins; the test can be run on blood, but it is most useful on body fluids)

A lack of response to supportive therapy and not being able to pinpoint any other disease, along with suspicious test results, can lead to a presumption of FIP. In a multicat household it is not necessary to isolate an FIP suspect because all of the cats will have had same exposure to coronavirus, and odds are that no one else will get sick.

Dealing With FIP

Owners of cats suspected of having FIP are faced with the tragic decision of ending their cat's life as body condition and quality of life diminishes. Veterinarians can help support the sick animals with fluids, antibiotics, anti-inflammatories and immunostimulants, but the ultimate outcome will be the same. Veterinarians are researching ways to effectively treat FIP, so there is hope for the future.

What About the FIP Vaccine?

A vaccine is available that claims to protect cats against FIP, but the veterinary community questions its effectiveness. Independent clinical studies on this vaccine have not proven that it confers significant protection under normal conditions.

TITER TESTS

Although it may be called an FIP titer, the commonly run corona virus titer present on many blood panels is not diagnostic for FIP. Cats truly infected with FIP can have positive or negative tests, and normal cats who have been exposed to FECV can actually have positive tests. An FIP titer alone means nothing.

The vaccine is considered to be safe and is likely most useful for cats who have not had any previous exposure to FECV. Figuring out who those cats are is the problem.

Decreasing Risk

FIP occurs most frequently in purebred cats who come from catteries, and in cats who have come from shelters. This is because exposure to FECV is higher in environments with many cats, and larger multicat facilities have more environmental stresses and less ability to isolate sick cats.

Purebred cats may also be more at risk due to genetics and weaker immune systems. The more closely related cats are, the fewer different genes there are to make their systems stronger.

If a purebred cat breeder tells you he has never had a case of FIP in his cattery, don't believe him. Odds are that if a breeder has been in business for a few years and has bred multiple litters, FIP has occurred at one time or another.

To try to decrease the risk of FIP, take these steps:

1. If you go to a cattery or shelter, pick a big, healthy-looking kitten and have him examined by a veterinarian.
2. Isolate the new kitten from other cats for at least a week to monitor his health.
3. Allow the kitten to adjust to his new environment before performing any elective medical procedures.
4. Decrease environmental stresses on the animal.
5. Keep litter boxes and food bowls clean.
6. Feed the kitten a good-quality diet and be sure he is eating.

Even if you follow these suggestions, there is no guarantee you will prevent FIP. FIP occurs in only a small percentage of the cat population, but it is devastating if it affects your cat.

Filling the Loss

If you have had the sad and tragic experience of losing a cat to FIP, you may wonder when and if you should get a new cat. There is no definitive answer to this question. Research shows that FIP can live in the environment for months, but in reality, if you throw away disposable items that the sick cat used and clean any other inanimate objects with a solution of 1 part bleach to 10 parts water, the risks of transmission are slim.

I think the best new animal is an unrelated kitten or cat who is at least 16 weeks old and appears hearty and healthy. But unfortunately, there are no guarantees with FIP.

COULD YOUR CAT BE RABID?

Rabies is a virus that can affect any warm-blooded animal. In certain parts of the country, rabies is present in a large number of wild animals, so the risk of exposure to outdoor cats is high. Skunks, bats and many other animals can carry rabies but not develop outward signs of disease. Depending on where you live, laws may mandate that your cat be vaccinated against rabies.

Animals infected with rabies usually die within weeks of infection, because the virus attacks cells in their brains.

Vaccinating Against Rabies

The recommended protocol for immunizing a cat against rabies is to give the first vaccine at three to four months of age, repeat the vaccine one year later, and then revaccinate every three years. Some states require a different schedule, and your veterinarian will know the law in your area. If a rabies vaccine is not legally required in your state and your cat does not go outdoors, it can be an optional vaccine. But if your cat does go outdoors, you should consider vaccination whether or not it's legally required in your state.

You might also consider vaccinating your cat against rabies if the cat is aggressive and ever bites humans. If a bite wound requires medical attention, the doctor performing the treatment is required to report the bite to local animal control authorities. Any animal who bites a human is placed under some type of quarantine, but unvaccinated animals are placed under stricter rules.

Signs of Rabies

People occasionally joke about "looking like a rabid dog"—this expression is used to describe somebody or something with wide-open eyes and drool on their lips. In fact, these are actual clinical signs seen in cases of rabies. Because rabies affects the brain, seizures, blindness, clumsiness, drooling and behavioral changes are seen in afflicted animals. I hope none of you ever come in contact with a rabid animal, because if there is any risk that exposure has occurred, humans have to go through a battery of multiple, painful injections.

As gruesome as it sounds, the suspicious animal must be dead to definitively diagnose rabies. The diagnosis is made by observing characteristic microscopic changes in the animal's brain.

FELINE PANLEUKOPENIA

Feline panleukopenia is actually feline parvovirus. The incidence of this disease is extremely low because of the effectiveness of the currently available vaccines. Today the infrequent cases that are seen occur in stray cats or cats in animal shelters who have never been vaccinated. Panleukopenia is a component of kitten vaccines and the basic booster shot that most adult cats receive.

Signs of Panleukopenia

Cats infected with this virus can have fevers and diarrhea that do not respond to treatment. Anorexia, vomiting and lethargy are other possible signs. It takes a few weeks after an animal is vaccinated for protective immunity to be conferred, so a kitten who was recently vaccinated could still be at risk.

Testing for Panleukopenia

The definitive diagnostic test for panleukopenia is an extremely low white blood cell count. The term *panleukopenia* actually breaks down as *pan* (all), *leuko* (white cells), *penia* (low count). Another way this virus can be diagnosed is by doing a canine parvovirus test on an affected cat's stool or blood. The viruses are so similar that the test can diagnose both.

What's the Prognosis?

Most cats with panleukopenia die from the virus, but if the disease is diagnosed early and the animal receives enough supportive care, there is a chance of recovery. The virus attacks the rapidly growing cells in the body, so the stomach, intestines, heart and brain are the organs most affected. Supportive care is aimed at maintaining hydration and electrolyte balance, controlling vomiting and diarrhea, treating secondary bacterial infections and keeping up the blood cell count.

Chapter 22

Understanding Diagnostic Testing

In this chapter I will explain common and not-so-common diagnostic testing. A thorough history and physical exam are crucial to a diagnosis, but more evidence is often needed to reach a conclusive answer (which veterinarians call a definitive diagnosis). Diagnostic testing provides this evidence. There are a host of different tests that may be needed, depending on the clinical signs a cat is exhibiting. It is important to have a basic understanding of the costs, risks and benefits of performing certain tests, so that you can make good decisions about your cat's care.

FECAL ANALYSIS

There are two basic ways in which feces is examined in a veterinary clinic: fecal flotation and direct smear. To rule out intestinal parasites, it is recommended that up to three separate fecal analyses be performed. Fecal examination should be performed on all kittens and on any cat with vomiting and/or diarrhea. A fecal exam should also be run at least once a year on all cats who go outdoors.

In a flotation test, stool is mixed with a fluid that causes eggs and protozoa to rise to the top of the mixture. The material is transferred to a slide or coverslip, which is examined under a microscope. In a direct smear, a swab transfers a small amount of stool to a slide, where it is mixed with a drop of saline solution and smeared. The slide is then examined under a microscope. A smear reveals certain protozoa, such as giardia, and bacteria.

URINALYSIS

Unfortunately, we cannot hand cats a cup and ask them to provide us with a urine sample. Urine is obtained in several ways: collecting from a litter box, expressing the bladder, passing a urinary catheter, and cystocentesis (inserting a needle through the body wall into the bladder). Although cystocentesis sounds like an aggressive way to get a sample, it is the preferred method and the only way to get a sterile sample if a culture is needed. If your cat's bladder is empty when a urine sample is needed, you may be asked to leave your cat for several hours until enough urine builds up for collection, or to come back for another try.

I never have cat owners get urine samples, because there's too much risk of contamination and improper storage of the sample. At the clinic we prefer to obtain urine through cystocentesis, and a sterile sample obtained through cystocentesis is needed for culture. Most male cats can be catheterized through their urethra if we cannot get a needle into the bladder. Sometimes I manually express a bladder and get a "free catch" sample. If you are trying to get a sample at home, sometimes cats will urinate into an empty plastic litter box. A commercial litter of plastic beads can replace normal litter at home to get a sample you can pour off.

Most veterinarians perform urinalyses in their clinic, but they may also send samples out to a laboratory. One component of a urinalysis tests the concentration of the urine. Cats normally have very concentrated urine, with specific gravity above 1.040. Concentration is determined by kidney function and water intake.

A dipstick is used to check urine for pH, chemistry values such as glucose, and blood. The urine is spun in a centrifuge and the sediment is examined under a microscope to look for crystals, cells and bacteria. If infection is suspected, the urine is cultured for specific bacteria.

BLOOD TESTS

The blood carries information about numerous body systems and organ function. Values can change quickly, depending on what is being measured, so a blood panel is a snapshot of what is going on inside a cat's body at a particular time. Blood tests are not directly useful for evaluating the central nervous system, intestinal function or bladder disease.

Many veterinary clinics have machines capable of doing some blood tests, but all clinics send at least some samples out to a reference lab. When results are conclusive, blood tests are wonderful for supporting a diagnosis. Unfortunately, cats don't always do what they are supposed to, and results may not fit with the suspected disease.

Reference ranges are the values that have been established as normal for a particular test on a particular machine. Often healthy cats have values outside of these ranges. The significance of a test result above or below the reference range depends on the particular test. Minor elevations are significant in some situations, while in others a value might need to be at least two times above normal to be important. Results always need to be interpreted based on a cat's condition and clinical signs.

Blood samples are obtained from the blood vessels. The amount of blood needed to perform tests depends on the number of tests run and the equipment used. Many in-house blood chemistry tests can be performed with a few drops of blood obtained through a leg vein. A full panel sent to a lab requires several milliliters of blood, usually obtained through the jugular vein.

CBC

CBC stands for complete blood count, and this includes white blood cells, red blood cells and platelets. White blood cells respond to infection and inflammation. There are five types of white blood cells: neutrophils, monocytes, lymphocytes, eosinophils and basophils. Red blood cells carry nutrients and oxygen to other cells in the body. Platelets are important for blood clotting.

All of the blood cells are produced in the bone marrow and released based on the body's need and normal aging of the cells. The different blood cells respond to injury and other disease states within the body in ways that are reflected in their counts.

Not every cat with an infection will have an elevated white blood cell count. In fact, viral infections often cause low white blood cell counts. Allergic reactions and parasites can cause elevations in feline eosinophil (a specific type of white blood cell) levels. Cats with cancer can have high neutrophil cell (another type of white blood cell) counts. These are a few examples of information a CBC can provide.

Blood Chemistries

There are numerous blood chemistry tests available, and those used most frequently are typically packaged together as a panel to evaluate a patient. Although each test has individual significance, it is important to look at the whole panel, since some tests are best understood in relation to others. I will touch on the most common tests.

Tests that relate to the liver are ALT (alanine aminotransferase) also known as SGPT (serum glutamic-pyruvic transaminase), AST (aspartate aminotransferase), alkaline phosphatase, and total bilirubin. ALT and AST are "leakage enzymes," released when the liver is infected, inflamed or diseased. The values do not necessarily correlate to the amount of liver damage. Alkaline phosphatase becomes elevated when there is liver disease, especially when bile flow is impaired. Bilirubin becomes elevated with liver disease and when red blood cells break apart within the body (hemolysis). Increased circulating bilirubin is responsible for jaundice. GGT (gamma-glutamyl transferase) is another enzyme linked to bile flow obstruction or administration of cortisone in some cats. These tests all tell a vet that the problem is the liver, but do not show the specific cause of liver disease.

Proteins are synthesized within the body and are present in the blood. When blood protein levels are low, this indicates lack of protein production or a loss through the GI or urinary tracts. Protein is separated into two components: albumin and globulin. Albumin is necessary to keep fluid within the blood vessels and to carry other compounds within the blood. Globulins are antibodies produced by white blood cells. High globulin levels are seen in dehydrated patients and those with infections.

Kidney function is assessed through BUN (blood urea nitrogen) and creatinine values. These values rise when more than two-thirds of kidney function is compromised. BUN and creatinine are also affected by the hydration status of the patient, blood flow through the kidneys and urinary tract blockages. Osmolality is a value based on electrolyte values in the blood and also relates to the kidneys' ability to concentrate urine.

Blood glucose is important in assessing starvation, stress and diabetes mellitus. In healthy cats the value varies but remains within the reference ranges, depending on what and when the animal eats.

Electrolytes are minerals present within the blood. They are necessary for some body functions. Calcium is needed to relax and contract the heart muscle. Potassium is also needed for heart muscle relaxation and general muscle contraction. Sodium and chloride are essential for fluid balance within the body. Phosphorus is needed for energy reactions and regulating the metabolism of bone. Phosphorus levels are elevated in cats with chronic kidney disease. Magnesium is a mineral that can be elevated in neuromuscular or heart disease, but rarely shows up as an imbalance in a cat's blood. Disease states such as dehydration, vomiting and diarrhea can all affect the body's electrolyte balance.

CPK (creatine phosphokinase) is an enzyme that is released during muscle exertion and trauma. It can elevate in anorexic cats when they break down muscle proteins for energy.

Thyroid Tests

T4 is the active thyroid hormone routinely measured in cats to test for hyperthyroidism. Low thyroid levels are only rarely found in cats, but high levels are common in cats nine years and older. T4 levels can be suppressed when other diseases are present, and hyperthyroidism is then masked. Currently, a test called T4 by equilibrium dialysis is used to confirm a diagnosis of hyperthyroidism when regular T4 results are inconclusive but clinical signs suggest the thyroid is the problem.

Fats

Cholesterol and triglyceride levels are often reported on blood panels. They relate to fat metabolism, but high cholesterol is not a danger and does not cause arteriosclerosis in cats. These values are often elevated in cats with liver disease or diabetes mellitus.

Pancreatic Enzymes

Amylase and lipase are two enzymes produced by the pancreas. In dogs they are fairly reliable indicators of pancreatitis, but this is not true in cats. Currently it is believed that these values do not relate to any disease or problems in cats.

Viral Tests

There are reliable diagnostic tests for the feline leukemia (FeLV) and feline immunodeficiency viruses (FIV). There is also a test for feline corona virus (FCV) that is used to support a diagnosis of feline infectious peritonitis (FIP), but alone is not diagnostic. Any positive test should be confirmed by other means.

FeLV is initially screened through an ELISA (enzyme-linked immunosorbant assay) test for viral antigens in the blood. The confirming test is an IFA (immunofluorescent antibody) that detects viral antigens associated with cells. When both tests are positive, the cat is likely to be persistently infected with FeLV. When there is a discrepancy in the results (one positive, one negative), the tests should be repeated in 60 days and then annually until they concur. Discordant results may reflect the stage of infection.

FIV is initially screened through an ELISA test that detects antibodies against the virus in the blood. Most cats develop antibodies within 60 days of infection. A western blot test confirms the diagnosis of FIV by showing that the antibodies are specific to FIV structural proteins. There are PCR (polymerase chain reaction) tests for FeLV and FIV viral RNA or DNA, but currently these tests have not been standardized or validated.

FIP cannot be definitely diagnosed by any blood test. The tests used that may support a diagnosis are an antibody titer test to FCV, FIP 7B ELISA and FIP PCR, but none of these are conclusive blood tests.

X RAYS

X rays are diagnostic images, also called radiographs. They are produced on film, and now also digitally, when a beam of electromagnetic energy is transmitted through part of the body and the image it creates is captured. The density of various tissues affects the way the energy beam relays the image. X rays are very good for evaluating bony structures and of variable usefulness for soft tissue structures. They are excellent for detecting metal and rubber objects inside a cat's body.

X rays provide a two-dimensional image of a three-dimensional animal, so at least two views are needed to properly assess a body part. X rays are a relatively inexpensive test and are readily available in veterinary hospitals.

When patients are fairly cooperative, animal technicians wearing protective aprons and gloves position and hold the animal during exposure. Fractious animals, or those in pain, require sedation or anesthesia for proper images to be recorded.

Contrast materials make visualization of certain body parts clearer on X rays. In a barium upper GI series, a cat is made to drink a chalky liquid that outlines his esophagus, stomach and intestines as it passes through. Some abnormalities in the lining of the tubular GI tract and obstructions are found this way.

Another type of contrast X ray is a pneumocystogram. In this type of X ray, a catheter is placed through the urethra into the bladder. Urine is drained out and air is instilled. The air provides contrast to the bladder wall and helps in visualizing the bladder lining and stones.

ULTRASOUND

Sound waves transmitted through body tissues produce ultrasonic images. Ultrasound is an imaging technique that is better for evaluating many of the soft tissue structures that are not well defined by X rays. The most common uses for ultrasound are to evaluate the heart (echocardiogram) and the abdominal cavity.

An echocardiogram is necessary to evaluate heart disease in cats. This test can to measure the size and shape of the heart chambers, evaluate blood flow through the heart and the functioning of the valves, and see through any abnormal fluid buildup in the chest cavity.

Abdominal ultrasound evaluates the liver, gall bladder, bile ducts, stomach, kidneys, spleen, bladder, intestines and lymph nodes. It can provide guidance for needle biopsies of organs. Most cats will tolerate ultrasound without sedation. Shaving the body part to be evaluated is necessary to obtain the best image.

Many private practitioners offer ultrasound in their hospitals. Specialists and referral centers also provide the service.

ENDOSCOPY

Fiber optic scopes provide images of body parts that may not be easily reached without invasive surgery. The scope is a flexible camera that can enter into areas inside an animal. A scope can give your veterinarian a direct look at internal tissue and guide a pinch biopsy or retrieve small objects from the nose, main airways, esophagus, stomach, intestine or colon, depending on its size.

Proper endoscopic evaluation requires general anesthesia and good technique. The test is typically performed without a hospital stay. Endoscopy is less invasive than surgery, but limited in the areas where it can be used and the size of biopsies obtained.

BIOPSIES

A biopsy is a piece of tissue that is evaluated microscopically. There are three common types of biopsies: needle, pinch and full thickness.

There are two kinds of needle biopsies. Fine needle aspirates obtained through palpation or guided by ultrasound, and tru-cut guided by ultrasound. The number of cells obtained by a fine needle aspirate is small and may not be diagnostic. Tru-cut needles are fairly large and take a small core of tissue. The larger the needle, the more risk of bleeding and tissue damage, but also the higher likelihood of obtaining a diagnostic sample.

Pinch biopsies are obtained when a small sample is grasped and pulled manually with a hemostat or through a special tool used in conjunction with an endoscope. Pinch biopsies are usually larger than needle biopsies.

Surgery is used to obtain full thickness biopsies. A wedge of tissue is taken in most situations. A thin slice is taken for intestinal biopsies. Full thickness biopsies are the most diagnostic, since they contain the largest amount of tissue.

When tissue biopsies are submitted to a lab, they are preserved in formalin, embedded in wax, cut into microscopic sections, affixed to a slide, stained and read by a pathologist. The process takes two to five days. Certain conditions may require special stains be applied to tissues in order to make a diagnosis. Interpreting biopsy results should be based on the clinical signs of the patient, because the pathologist's assessment is subjective.

CYTOLOGY

Cytology is another way to microscopically examine cells that is less invasive for the patient than a biopsy. With cytology, cells are placed on a slide and read in a veterinary hospital or sent to a lab for pathologist review. The cells come from a needle aspirate of a mass or tissue, a swab of tissue or an organ (such as a vaginal smear to evaluate a heat cycle), or from an impression smear (placing a slide directly on material you want to examine).

Results are immediate or can take a day, depending on whether the sample is sent out to a lab. Unfortunately, cytology samples are not always diagnostic, and sampling needs to be repeated or a biopsy taken when results are inconclusive.

ELECTROCARDIOGRAM

This test is commonly called an ECG or EKG, and is a record of the electrical activity of the heart. Electrical activity relates to heart function and is tested by attaching clips to certain parts of the body and measuring the electrical impulses. Most cats will not tolerate clips

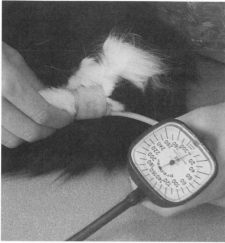

A small cuff around the leg is inflated as part of a blood pressure measurement.

if they are not sedated. Some newer technology replaces clips with a contact plate, but these machines currently are not routinely reliable for measuring cats. The electrical impulses produced by cats are weak and difficult for devices to pick up.

BLOOD PRESSURE

Getting a diagnostic blood pressure reading in cats requires practice and a relatively calm patient. It is easy to practice but not always easy to relax a cat in a veterinary clinic. There are various ways for measuring blood pressure, but the most widely used technique uses a Doppler device. Dopplers use sound waves to measure blood flow.

In cats only systolic readings are used to evaluate blood pressure. Systolic measurements correlate with heart muscle contraction. At this time, reliable diastolic measurements cannot be routinely obtained non-invasively.

CEREBRAL SPINAL FLUID TAP

A cerebral spinal fluid tap is used to obtain a sample of the fluid that bathes the brain and spinal cord. Anesthesia and skill are needed to get a diagnostic sample. Cerebral spinal fluid analysis aids in the diagnosis of many neurological conditions. Most veterinarians refer this procedure to veterinary neurologists or internists, who perform it frequently, in order to achieve good results. A needle is placed between two vertebrae at the base of the skull or in the lumbar region, and about 1.5 milliliters of fluid is removed for analysis.

MAGNETIC RESONANCE IMAGING

A magnetic resonance imaging (MRI) machine uses a computer to interpret how electromagnetic currents pass through tissue. Specifically, it measures the differences in hydrogen protons in diseased versus healthy cells. MRI is far superior to X rays in evaluating soft tissue structures, especially the brain, nasal passages and intervertebral disks.

MRI technology is expensive but is becoming more widely available in veterinary medicine. Patients must be restrained with anesthesia to obtain a diagnostic scan, but they are not exposed to significant radiation as with a CT scan (see next section).

COMPUTED TOMOGRAPHY

A CAT or CT scan uses rotating X-ray beams captured on a detector to "slice" through the body and examine internal structures. CT scanning is much more sensitive than conventional X rays for evaluating soft tissue structures, but patients are exposed to more radiation. CT scans provide more information about bony structures and acute bleeding than do MRI scans.

The most advanced CT scanners are able to produce three-dimensional images of the body. CT scans are expensive but, like MRIs, they are becoming more widely available in veterinary medicine.

NUCLEAR IMAGING

Radioactive compounds can be administered internally and used as a diagnostic tool. Scintigraphy creates an image of the way certain structures within the body take up radioactive compounds. This information can demonstrate the size, shape and location of certain conditions. In veterinary medicine, scintigraphy is performed at some specialty centers and veterinary colleges.

The most common uses of scintigraphy with cats are to evaluate problems with the bones (chronic lameness or bone tumors that are not visible on X rays), portal shunts (abnormal blood flow through the liver), blood flow through the kidneys and thyroid disease.

TECHNOLOGICAL ADVANCES ARE AMAZING!

Our cats are able to benefit from human medical advances to aid in diagnosing their diseases. Today, reaching a definitive diagnosis is possible in almost all instances, but the costs involved and the availability of testing are significant limitations. Unfortunately, even if getting the answer is possible, treatment may not be. Each cat and situation is unique, so work with your veterinarian to provide the best practical health care.

Chapter 23

What Can You Catch From Your Cat?

Humans have successfully lived with cats for thousands of years, so it always surprises me when a pregnant woman comes into my office and tells me she needs to find a new home for her cat. In these situations, I wonder if her gynecologist has read any medical literature in the last 20 years, because cat ownership is probably one of the smallest risks a pregnant woman faces.

Overall, cats are extremely safe pets to own, and they rarely transmit diseases to humans. You are much more likely to contract a disease from your friends and family members than you are from a cat. Diseases that can pass from animals to humans are called zoonoses.

There certainly are diseases cats can transmit to humans, and I've described some of these, such as giardia, rabies and ringworm, in other parts of the book. I will shed light on some other transmissible diseases here, along with the problem facing many people—cat allergies.

GESUNDHEIT!

It is estimated that 15 to 20 percent of the human population may be allergic to pets. Humans who are allergic to cats can experience a range of signs, from sniffling and sneezing to life-threatening asthma. Many cat owners know they are allergic to their pet, but they believe the benefits of cat ownership far outweigh the discomfort of the allergy.

An allergy is a reaction to a substance that is not inherently harmful. In an allergic reaction, this means the immune system makes antibodies and triggers histamine release. This combination produces an inflammatory reaction.

How Do You Know It's the Cat?

If you experience watery eyes, sneezing, sore throat or congestion every time you are around a cat, chances are you are allergic to cats. However, if you have cats and are having an allergic reaction whenever you're home, it doesn't necessarily mean the cat is the culprit. You may be allergic to dust or mold or the houseplant on your windowsill. Some allergists assume that if you have a cat and are experiencing allergic symptoms, you must be allergic to the cat. But the only way to know for sure is with allergy testing.

Some people's allergies worsen over time. Others are only sensitive when exposed to a large dose of an allergen. For example, you might be able to tolerate living with one cat but have a terrible time when you go over to a friend's home where there are four cats.

Unfortunately, there are no cures for allergies. Avoiding the allergen is the best way to prevent problems. However, allergies to things like dust and trees and grass—which can never be removed from your environment—can usually be easily managed. Allergies to cats can often be managed as well.

Less-Allergenic Cats

Fel-d-1 is the cat allergen that causes most human allergies to cats. This allergen is found in the skin, oil glands and saliva of cats. Dander is dried skin that is shed, so Fel-d-1 is spread through dander. All cats lick and groom themselves, so this allergen can cover their entire body. Since all cats have skin and saliva, all breeds are potentially allergenic.

Some people believe allergic people better tolerate the breeds with little or no hair. Breeds with little hair include Cornish and Devon Rexes, while the Sphynx is a breed with no hair at all. Longhaired cats may shed hairs with more dander attached, but their hair is no different from that of shorthaired cats.

Each cat's chemistry is slightly different, so an allergic person would have to spend time with any prospective pet to see what their reaction might be.

Making Life More Bearable

There are some ways to make life easier for an allergic person. If you are allergic, you should:

- Wash your hands every time you touch a cat. If you touch your face before you wash, you're asking for trouble.
- Change clothes after playing with a cat, or have a robe or smock that you wear when you're interacting with a cat.
- Consider wearing a face mask and protective glasses when playing with your cat.
- Avoid touching cats in the areas where they have the most oil glands, such as the chin, cheeks, between the shoulder blades and the base of the tail.
- Never allow cats in your bedroom. There is nothing worse for an allergic person than to place their face into a pillow full of dander.
- Consider using a HEPA filter unit or air purifier to knock allergens out of the air. There are also special vacuum cleaners with HEPA filters.
- Wipe the cat down with a damp rag or use a commercial anti-allergy pet solution daily or weekly, so that loose allergens are removed.
- Have the cat professionally groomed and well brushed out regularly. This will limit allergens on top of shedding hairs.
- If possible, have just one cat. More cats mean more allergens.
- Carpet, decorative pillows and draperies can trap allergens, so consider replacing them with tile, washable materials, and blinds or shutters.

People can work with their allergists to find treatments that help relieve the symptoms of cat allergies. Allergy shots and antihistamines are commonly used. There are several antihistamines that can be taken regularly without side effects or drowsiness. Research is being conducted today that is looking at other ways the production of antibodies and release of histamine can be stopped in allergic individuals. In the future, there may be better options for controlling allergies to cats. Scientists are even trying to genetically engineer cats without fel-d-1!

HONEY, IT'S YOUR TURN TO SCOOP

Toxoplasma gondii is a protozoan parasite (protozoa are one-celled organisms). Toxoplasmosis, the disease caused by Toxoplasma organisms, can occur in any human or four-legged animal who ingests one of the infective stages of the protozoa. This organism has a complicated life cycle, which requires that it spend some of its development inside a host.

Humans are frequently exposed to Toxoplasma and don't even know it. That's because the protozoa lives in raw meat, and we can become infected when we handle the meat. The biggest threat to humans is when a pregnant woman, during her first trimester, becomes infected with the organism. An infection at this time can cause congenital malformations or mental retardation of the unborn child. Studies have shown that the vast majority of pregnant women infected with Toxoplasma got it by handling raw meat.

How Cats Become Infected

Cats become infected with Toxoplasma after they eat raw meat, birds or mice carrying an infective stage of the organism. Cats shed Toxoplasma oocysts (the egg stage) in their feces 3 to 10 days after eating infected tissues. They will shed the oocysts for up to 14 days, and afterward it is unlikely that they will ever shed them again—even after repeated exposure. Within one to four days of being passed in the feces, the oocysts become infectious to other animals and humans. Infective oocysts can live for months in the environment (the litter box or yard, wherever the cat has defecated).

If feces are scooped daily and/or if rubber gloves are worn while scooping, there is little risk of exposure to Toxoplasma from your cat. Keeping your cat indoors and only feeding commercially prepared cat food will eliminate the risk of exposure.

Cats who are infected with Toxoplasma usually do not show any clinical signs and are healthy, although a cat who is also infected with FeLV or FIV is more likely to become sick. If a cat develops Toxoplasmosis, the signs of illness can be:

- Lethargy
- Anorexia
- Fever
- Diarrhea
- Pneumonia
- Hepatitis
- Uveitis (inflammation of the eye)
- Neurological disease

A blood test that measures antibodies to Toxoplasma is used to diagnose the disease in cats. Testing for two different antibodies (Ig G and Ig M) a few weeks apart and finding rising titers is the best way to make an accurate diagnosis.

How Humans Are Infected

Humans can become infected if they touch an oocyst, don't wash their hands and then touch their mouths. Handling or eating raw meat or drinking unpasteurized dairy products can also expose people to the parasite. Healthy humans who are exposed to Toxoplasma may suffer a brief illness with fever, muscle pain, enlarged lymph nodes, anorexia and sore throat. People who have compromised immune systems—such as organ transplant recipients and AIDS patients—need to be as careful as pregnant women to prevent infection.

There are many precautions that can be taken to prevent infection:

- Wear rubber gloves and wash hands thoroughly after outdoor gardening.
- Cover up children's sandboxes when not in use to prevent cats from using them as litter boxes and depositing oocysts.
- Empty litter boxes daily so that oocysts will not have the opportunity to develop to the infective stage. Wear rubber gloves for this job or have another family member do it.

- Eat only thoroughly cooked meat and wash your hands vigorously if you handle raw meat or vegetables.
- Consume only pasteurized dairy products.
- Have yourself tested for antibodies to *Toxoplasma gondii*. If you are already positive, there is little risk that you will become ill unless your immune system is compromised.
- Wash your hands after coming in contact with your cat.

For a pregnant woman to become infected through her cat, an unlikely series of events must occur. The cat must first have recent exposure to Toxoplasma. Then, the cat's feces must sit, unscooped, for 3 to 10 days, while the oocytes become active. Then the woman must actually touch the feces, and then touch her mouth or nose before washing her hands. In actuality, it would be extremely rare for a pregnant woman to be directly infected by a cat.

If you have an indoor cat who never eats raw meat or goes outside to hunt and eat birds and rodents, you are essentially at no risk. In fact, 30 to 50 percent of women in the world have been previously exposed to Toxoplasma. These women develop immunity, and in these situations there is no risk to a later pregnancy.

Treatment for Toxoplasmosis

There are medications that are effective for treating cats and healthy humans with Toxoplasmosis. Unfortunately, even if an infected pregnant woman receives treatment in her first trimester, birth defects cannot be prevented.

We have reached the 21st century, but many physicians are ill-informed about pregnant women and cats. Any woman considering pregnancy should know about Toxoplasmosis. But to hear some doctors talk, if you want to get pregnant, you should get rid of your cat, and this is ridiculous. Millions if not billions of women have lived with cats over time and have somehow managed to produce healthy children.

INFECTED MEAT

It is estimated that in some parts of the world, 10 percent of the lamb and 25 percent of the pork are infected with Toxoplasma cysts. Cows and goats can also be infected, so consuming unpasteurized dairy products is not recommended.

CAT SCRATCH FEVER

You may not realize it, but cat scratch fever is more than just a song. It is caused by *Bartonella henselae,* a common bacteria found worldwide. Infection typically occurs when a kitten breaks the surface of a person's skin through a bite or scratch. Eighty percent of the cases occur in people under the age of 21. People who have compromised immune systems are also at risk for cat scratch disease.

It is possible that at some time in their lives about half of all cats will have an infection with *Bartonella henselae,* and although they appear healthy, they can carry the bacteria for months. Cat scratches are common, but fortunately, cat scratch disease in humans is uncommon.

Signs of Cat Scratch Fever

Humans become infected when a kitten or cat scratches or bites them and injects *Bartonella henselae* bacteria into their body. It may take two to three weeks, but a lymph node near the initial injury site will then swell, and the surrounding tissues will become red and tender. Other clinical signs that can be seen in humans are:

- Fever
- Fatigue
- Loss of appetite
- Headache
- Sore throat
- Blurred vision
- Joint pain

Diagnosis and Treatment

When clinical signs in humans suggest that cat scratch disease is a possibility, a positive diagnosis is made by:

- History of exposure to a cat or kitten
- Tests to rule out other causes of swollen lymph nodes
- A positive cat scratch disease blood test

In almost all cases, the swollen lymph nodes usually resolve within a few weeks to months, even without treatment. If you have had a previous exposure to cat scratch disease, it is unlikely the bacteria will ever bother you again. People can take anti-inflammatory medications to help reduce the pain of the swollen lymph nodes.

In some individuals, the lymph nodes become abscessed and need to be surgically drained. In these cases, or when individuals with compromised immune systems are infected, antibiotics are used. People with cat scratch disease are not contagious to others.

If you are concerned about cat scratch disease because of your personal health problems, there is a test that can check your cat's blood for the agent. Because they show no signs of the disease, cats are not routinely treated with antibiotics. To help prevent cat scratch disease, be cautious when handling unfamiliar cats, keep your cat's nails trimmed, and do not allow your cat to bite or scratch you during interactive play.

OTHER ZOONOSES

Although zoonotic agents have the potential to infect any human, immunocompromised patients are most at risk for developing severe disease. Healthy adult, parasite-free, indoor cats are unlikely to pose any threat to humans.

Cryptosporidia

Cryptosporidia is a protozoal parasite that can potentially pass between cats and humans. Contaminated water is thought to be the most common source of human infection, but humans could become infected through contact with infected cat feces. Eating infected rodents most likely infects cats. Cryptosporidial infections cause severe diarrhea that can require hospitalization and intravenous fluid therapy for both two- and four-legged victims. Examining and testing feces can detect the parasite.

Roundworms and Hookworms

Roundworms and hookworms can potentially infect humans. Children can accidentally ingest roundworm eggs if they play in sandboxes or dirt contaminated by dog or cat feces. Eggs hatch in their intestines, and larvae can then penetrate the intestinal wall and invade other tissues. The condition is called visceral larva migrans.

Hookworms are transmitted to humans if their skin comes in direct contact with moist soil or sand contaminated with larvae. The parasite migrates through the skin and leaves a trail of inflammation. This condition is called cutaneous larva migrans.

Salmonella

Cats can carry *Salmonella*, a bacterium capable of causing severe gastrointestinal disease. Cats who eat infected birds or raw meat are at risk for infection. Fortunately, very few cats become infected with *Salmonella*; a recent study in Colorado found only about 1 percent of cats were infected. Human exposure is prevented with good hygiene and sanitation around feces.

WATCH OUT FOR PLAGUE

If you know history, you may know that epidemics of bubonic plague have occurred around the world. But did you know that plague occurs in random cases in the United States each year? Infrequent cases have occurred in New Mexico, Arizona, Colorado and California. The last epidemic in the United States was in Los Angeles in 1924 and 1925. Fortunately, there have only been 8 to 20 human cases annually in the United States over the past 10 years.

Bubonic plague gets its name from *bubo* which is a swollen, hot lymph node. Plague is caused by the bacteria *Yersinia pestis*, and is transmitted from rodent to rodent by fleas. Rock squirrels, ground squirrels, prairie dogs, wood rats and chipmunks are other commonly infected species.

Cats can become infected with plague by infected fleas or by ingesting an infected rodent, and infected cats are possible sources of infection to humans.

Aside from direct flea bites, plague can be transmitted through a skin wound and contact with fluids of an infected animal. Inhaling droplets in the air that are produced when an infected animal coughs can also transmit plague.

The most characteristic clinical sign of plague is the presence of bubos. Fever, headache, general illness and exhaustion accompany these painful, swollen, hot lymph nodes. The progression of disease is very rapid, and occurs within two to six days of exposure. Bacteria can invade the bloodstream and produce potentially fatal plague septicemia.

Once bacteria enters the blood, it can go to the lungs and cause pneumonia. If antibiotic treatment is not initiated in time, death can result. Half of all of humans who develop plague pneumonia die.

People most at risk are Native Americans, campers, hikers and hunters who may travel in plague areas, as well as veterinarians and pet owners. Use caution if you live in a plague state and your cat exhibits bubos or pneumonia, and contact your veterinarian immediately.

THE JOYS OF CAT OWNERSHIP

I included this last chapter as an information resource to help dispel myths surrounding diseases that cats may transmit. Unfortunately, some people are allergic to cats, but aside from this problem, the likelihood of any other health problems arising from cat ownership is extremely low.

Owning a cat will enrich your life and offer far more benefits than risks. Cats are wonderful additions to the family who really do want and need us. Studies show that on average, pet owners live longer than people without pets. I know that after a long day at the office, there is nothing I like better than to cuddle with one of my cats and have him purr in my ear! Cats are super stress relievers. They are curious, mischievous and very entertaining to watch. They also do a good job of ridding your house of bugs.

Most cats require little care and live long lives. They can easily fit into our busy lives or be constant companions. If you've made it to this part of the book, you have the tools you need to keep your cat healthy and enjoy a long life together.

Appendix A

Glossary of Veterinary and Cat Terms

abscess   A hole filled with pus and surrounded by infected tissue.

acute   A disease that begins quickly.

adulticide   A product that kills adult insects.

allergen   A foreign substance that causes an allergic response in some animals.

alopecia   Hair loss.

anaphylaxis   A severe and potentially fatal allergic reaction that causes fever, redness and difficulty breathing.

anemia   Low red blood cell count.

anorexia   Lack of appetite for food.

anterior drawer sign   Laxity present in the knee when the anterior cruciate ligament is damaged.

antibody   A protein produced in the body as a response to contact with another foreign protein.

antigen   A foreign substance that causes the body to produce an antibody.

arrhythmia   Irregular heartbeat.

atopy   Inhaled allergy.

auscultation   Listening to the heart and lungs with a stethoscope.

benign   Harmless.

bilateral   On two sides.

biopsy   Removing tissue for microscopic examination and diagnosis.

brachycephalic   Flattened facial structure, characteristic of
   Persian cats.

bubo   A swollen, hot lymph node.

cancer   Cells whose growth is uncontrolled.

cardiomyopathy   Heart muscle disease.

carnivore   A meat-eating animal.

castration   Removing the testicles.

catnip   A plant in the mint family that has hallucinogenic effects
   on cats.

cattery   A facility where cats are bred.

chitin   A protein found in insect skeletons.

cholagiohepatitis   Inflammation of the bile ducts and liver.

chronic   A disease that develops slowly or persists for a long time.

coccidia   A type of protozoal parasite of the gastrointestinal system.

colostrum   The antibody-rich first milk an animal produces.

congenital   A condition a cat is born with.

conjunctivitis   Inflammation of the tissue around the eyeball.

corneal ulcer   An abrasion or scratch on the surface of the eye.

cryotherapy   A medical procedure that freezes tissues.

cryptococcus   A type of fungus.

cryptorchid   A cat with one or both testicles retained.

cystitis   Inflammation of the bladder.

cytology   Microscopic evaluation of cell structure.

dermatophytes   A group of fungi capable of causing ringworm.

dialysis   A process where a body fluid is removed from the body
   and cleaned.

diaphragm   The muscular band that separates the chest and
   abdominal cavities.

diastole   Blood pressure when the heart relaxes.

dietary indiscretion   Eating something other than food.

diuresis   A process that causes the body to produce and eliminate
   more urine.

dystocia   Difficulty during the birthing process.

ECG   An electrocardiogram, which measures the electrical activity of the heart.

echocardiogram   A test that evaluates the heart using sound waves.

EEG   An electroencephalogram, which measures the electrical activity of the brain.

estrous cycle   The normal four-stage fertility cycle in a female cat.

foreign body   A substance that is not supposed to be located where it is found.

giardia   A type of protozoal parasite of the gastrointestinal system.

gingivitis   Inflamed gums.

hepatic lipidosis   A disease of the liver caused by too much fat breakdown.

hernia   A protrusion of an organ through a tear in a muscle.

hip dysplasia   Poor conformation of the hip joints.

holistic   A system of total patient care that considers physical, emotional, social, economic and spiritual needs.

housesoiling   When a cat eliminates inappropriately outside of a litter box on a horizontal surface.

hypertension   High blood pressure.

hyperthyroid   Having an overactive thyroid gland.

hypoglycemia   Low blood sugar.

hyposensitize   Decrease an allergic response by injecting antigens.

idiopathic   Occurring for no known cause.

incontinence   Loss of control of a body function.

inguinal   Near the groin.

intact   A cat who has not been spayed or neutered.

interstitial cystitis   A benign inflammatory condition of the bladder.

jaundice   A yellowish discoloration of tissues due to bile pigments in the blood.

lesion   A change or injury to a body tissue that impairs the tissue or causes a loss of function.

lethargy   Feeling indifferent or sluggish.

luxating patella   A kneecap that pops out of joint.

malignant   A tumor that can invade other tissues and/or spread through the bloodstream.

mastectomy   Surgically removing an entire mammary gland.

maternal immunity   Protective antibodies received from the animal's mother through nursing.

megacolon   Abnormal widening of the large intestine that causes constipation in cats.

metastasize   When a cancer spreads from its original site to another part of the body.

miliary dermatitis   A crusty, scaly skin condition.

mutation   A change that occurs within a gene.

nebulization   A process that creates an aerosol mist.

neoplasia   An abnormal growth of new tissue.

neuter   Removing an animal's sex organs.

nocturnal   Something that functions or is active at night.

oncologist   A doctor who specializes in treating cancer.

ovariohysterectomy   Surgical removal of the uterus and ovaries.

palpation   Using the fingers and hands to examine parts of the body.

pectus excavatum   A congenital bone abnormality causing a flattened ribcage.

pericardium   The sac that surrounds the heart.

peritonitis   Inflammation within the abdominal cavity.

pheromone   Chemical signals that are present in different animal secretions.

pleural effusion   A build-up of fluid in the chest cavity.

polydactyl   Having more than the normal number of toes.

polyestrus   Able to have multiple estrus cycles throughout the year.

prostaglandins   Special fatty acids that can act like hormones.

protozoa   A type of single-celled organism.

pulmonary edema   A build-up of fluid in the lungs.

pyometra   An infected, pus-filled uterus.

queen   A mother cat.

radioisotope   An element that gives off radiation.

renal   Having to do with the kidneys.

rhinoscopy   Examination of the back of the nasal passages with a fiber optic scope.

seasonally polyestrus   During certain seasons of the year, cats can go through their heat cycles multiple times.

spay   Surgically removing the uterus and ovaries.

spray   Depositing urine on a vertical surface.

squamous cell carcinoma   A type of skin cancer.

subcutaneous   Having to do with the tissue under the skin.

systole   Blood pressure when the heart contracts.

tomcat   An intact male cat.

trichobezoar   A hairball.

turgor   The normal strength and tension of the skin created by fluid.

unilateral   On one side.

urohydropropulsion   A technique for forcing small stones out of the bladder.

urolith   A stone in the urinary tract.

uveitis   Inflammation of the iris, choroid and ciliary body of an eye.

vascular   Having to do with blood vessels.

zoonosis   A disease that can pass from animals to humans.

Appendix B

Where to Learn More

INFORMATION ON POISONS

ASPCA Animal Poison Control Center
(888) 426-4435
$45 per case, credit cards only
www.aspca.org/site/PageServer?pagename=apcc

Poisonous plant guides

www.ansci.cornell.edu/plants/index.html
vet.purdue.edu/depts/addl/toxic/cover1.htm
gateway.library.uiuc.edu/vex/vetdocs/toxic.htm

GENERAL INFORMATION ABOUT CATS

American Animal Hospital Association (AAHA)
12575 West Bayaud Avenue
Denver, CO 80215
(303) 986-2800
www.healthypet.com

American Association of Feline Practitioners (AAFP)
618 Church Street, Suite 220
Nashville, TN 37219
(615) 259-7788
www.aafponline.org

American Veterinary Medical Association (AVMA)
1931 North Meachum Road Suite 100
Schaumburg, IL 60173
(847) 925-8070
www.avma.org/care4pets/default.htm

Cornell Feline Health Center
College of Veterinary Medicine
Cornell University
Ithaca, NY 14853
(607) 253-3414
web.vet.cornell.edu/Public/FHC

Appendix C

Pet Loss Grief Counseling Hot Lines

....

Chicago Veterinary Medical Association Pet Loss Hotline
(630) 603-3994
Leave voice mail message; calls will be returned 6 P.M. to 8 P.M. (CT)
Long distance calls will be returned collect

Colorado State University's Argus Institute Family Support Services
(970) 491-1242
Offers individual and group counseling

Companion Animal Association of Arizona's Pet Grief Support Hotline
(602) 995-5885
24 hours a day
www.caaainc.org

Cornell University College of Veterinary Medicine Pet Loss Support Hotline
(800) 253-3932
Tuesday to Thursday, 6 P.M. to 9 P.M. (ET)
Messages will be returned
web.vet.cornell.edu/public/petloss/

Iams Pet Loss Support Center and Hotline
(888) 332-7738
Monday to Saturday, 8 A.M. to 8 P.M.

Iowa State University Veterinary Teaching Hospital Pet Loss Support Hotline
(888) 478-7574
Operational seven days a week, 5 P.M. to 8 P.M. (CT)
www.vm.iastate.edu/animals/petloss/about.html

Michigan State University's College of Veterinary Medicine Pet Loss Support
(517) 432-2692
Tuesday to Thursday, 6:30 P.M. to 9:30 P.M. (ET)
Long distance calls will be returned collect

The Ohio State University's Pet Loss Hotline
(614) 292-1823
Monday, Wednesday and Friday, 6:30 P.M. 9:30 P.M. (ET)
Voice mail messages will be returned collect during operating hours

Tufts University Pet Loss Support Hotline
(508) 839-7966
Weekdays 6 P.M. to 9 P.M. (ET)
Voice mail messages will be returned daily, collect outside of Massachusetts
www.tufts.edu/vet/petinfo/petloss.html

University of California–Davis Pet Loss Support Hotline
(800) 565-1526
Weekdays, 6:30 P.M. to 9:30 P.M. (PT)
www.vetmed.ucdavis.edu/petloss/C-Caring.html

University of Florida Pet Grief Support Hotline
(352) 392-4700, ext. 4080
7 P.M. to 9 P.M. (ET)
neuro.vetmed.ufl.edu/alt_med/petgrief/petloss.htm

University of Illinois' College of Veterinary Medicine's CARE Pet Loss
Helpline
(877) 394-2273
Leave voice mail message; calls will be returned 6 P.M. to 8 P.M. (CT)
Sunday, Tuesday and Thursday
Long distance calls will be returned collect
www.cvm.uiuc.edu/CARE

University of Pennsylvania's School of Veterinary Medicine's Pet Loss
Support Hotline
(215) 898-4529
Weekdays, 9 A.M. to 5 P.M.

Virginia-Maryland Regional College of Veterinary Medicine Pet Loss
Support Hotline
(540) 231-8038
Tuesday and Thursday, 6 P.M. to 9 P.M. (ET)
www.vetmed.vt.edu/Organization/Clinical/petloss/petloss.html

Washington State University's Pet Loss Support Hotline
(509) 335-5704
24-hour voice mail and staffed Monday, Tuesday and Thursday, 4 p.m.
to 6:30 p.m. (PT), and Saturday 10:30 A.M. to 12 P.M.
www.vetmed.wsu.edu/PLHL/index.htm

About Elaine Wexler-Mitchell, D.V.M, ABVP

Dr. Wexler-Mitchell obtained a bachelor of science degree from Cornell University and then went on to the Virginia-Maryland Regional College of Veterinary Medicine to earn her doctorate in veterinary medicine. After working in general small animal practice for five years, she opened The Cat Care Clinic in Orange, California, in 1991. She became board certified in feline practice through the American Board of Veterinary Practitioners in 1995, one of the 24 charter diplomates. She is a member of many veterinary organizations, including the American Association of Feline Practitioners, AVMA, AAHA, SCVMA, CVMA, and she is a former past president of the Academy of Feline Medicine.

Dr. Wexler-Mitchell is a feature writer, columnist, and contributing editor to *Cat Fancy* magazine. In addition to lecturing about cat care, she has appeared numerous times on television and radio. She has served as an appointed member of the Orange County Animal Control Advisory Board.

In her free time, Dr. Wexler-Mitchell enjoys tennis, golf, yoga, skiing, and traveling. She lives with her husband, Howard, and her two Somali cats, Keiki and Shaka.

More information about Dr. Wexler-Mitchell and her clinic can be found at www.catcare.com.

Index